LAST STAND!

LAST STAND!
Famous Battles Against the Odds
Bryan Perrett

'The fame of this death of theirs has spread far and wide. They reap the benefit of it, for their story is immortal and will be told hundreds of years hence when it matters no more to them whether they died by shot and steel, or in age and sickness. Surely, it is no small thing to have gained such a death.'

– H. Rider Haggard on the fate of the Shangani Patrol, Matabele War, 1893.

'Forget Queen and Country. Forget Maggie. Forget all that. You fight for yourself and your mates. Without your mates you're nothing.'

– Falklands War veteran, ex-3rd Battalion The Parachute Regiment, 1990.

ARMS AND
ARMOUR

Arms and Armour Press
A Cassell Imprint
Villiers House, 41–47 Strand, London WC2N 5JE.

Reprinted 1991 (twice), 1992 (three times), 1993
First printed in paperback in 1992
Reprinted 1993

Distributed in the USA by Sterling Publishing Co. Inc.,
387 Park Avenue South, New York, NY 10016-8810.

Distributed in Australia by Capricorn Link (Australia) Pty. Ltd.,
P.O. Box 665, Lane Cove, New South Wales 2066.

British Library Cataloguing in Publication Data
Perrett, Bryan *1934–*
Last stand!: famous battles against the odds
1. Battles, history
I. Title
355.409
ISBN 0-85368-997-0
ISBN 1-85409-188-3 (PBK)

Maps by Sampleskill Ltd, West Hampstead.

Designed and edited by DAG Publications Ltd.
Designed by David Gibbons; edited by Michael Boxall; typeset by
Typesetters (Birmingham) Ltd, Warley, West Midlands;
camerawork by M&E Reproductions, North Fambridge, Essex;
printed and bound in Great Britain by
Mackays of Chatham PLC, Chatham, Kent

Contents

Acknowledgements

I should like to express my sincere appreciation and thanks to the following for their generous assistance: Major R. D. Cassidy, MBE, Curator of the Royal Green Jackets Museum; Lieutenant-Colonel W. H. R. Charley, JP, DL, Regimental Association Secretary, The Royal Irish Rangers; Mr Danny J. Crawford, Head, Reference Section, History and Museums Division, US Marine Corps; Brigadier J. M. Cubiss, CBE, MC, Regimental Secretary, The Prince of Wales's Own Regiment of Yorkshire; the Daughters of the Republic of Texas and the staff of The Alamo; Mr T. L. Hewitson, Hon Curator of the Royal Northumberland Fusiliers Museum; Lieutenant-Colonel D. C. MacDonald Milner, The Royal Hampshire Regiment; Lieutenant-Colonel H. L. T. Radice, Hon Archivist, and Major C. P. T. Rebbeck, Regimental Secretary, The Gloucestershire Regiment; Mr John J. Slonaker, Chief, Historical Reference Branch, US Army Military History Institute; and Brigadier K. A. Timbers of The Royal Artillery Historical Trust.

Bryan Perrett

Introduction
THE LAST STAND

The concept of men selling their lives as dearly as possible forms an honoured part of most national histories and also the basis of much military tradition. This in itself serves to underline the fact that while all armies talk of fighting to the last man and the last round, such events are the exception rather than the rule.

Disregarding the results of pursuit following a set-piece battle, and also those of a protracted formal siege, the phenomenon of the last stand can be seen to arise only within a highly motivated environment, and then only in time of total war or when feelings on both sides are running extremely high. The phenomenon appears from time to time in the Classical period, the most notable example being the defence of the Pass of Thermopylae by the Greeks against the Persians in 480 BC, where King Leonidas and his bodyguard of 300 Spartans refused to surrender and died to a man. At Hastings in 1066, when the rest of the Saxon army had fled, King Harold's Huscarls fought to the bitter end and almost killed William, Duke of Normandy, later known as the Conqueror, when he unwisely pressed their retreat. In general, however, this aspect of war was largely absent during the medieval wars of western Europe. It was true that the peasant levies which formed the bulk of the infantry had to take their chances, but for their heavily armoured masters the concept of fighting was rather different; unless the issue to be resolved was extremely personal, capturing an opponent was preferable to killing him, for a live enemy noble or knight was valuable for the ransom he would bring, but a dead one was worthless. The constable of a fortress under siege was permitted a statutory period during which he could seek his master's instructions as to whether to submit or fight on, a truce being granted for the purpose. If his orders were to hold out, he would then be subjected to contrary internal pressure, for the garrison was aware that at the end of the period the enemy was free to sack and massacre without restraint. All in all, it was a useful means of neutralizing a strong position without recourse to bloodshed. In Palestine, where Cruaders fought Saracens for possession of the Holy Places, the rules were different. The Knights Templar, for example, let it be known that they neither gave nor accepted quarter, and their foes reacted accordingly; after the Battle of Hattin in 1187 some 200 captured Templars and Hospitallers were beheaded on the spot.

During the fifteenth and sixteenth centuries bands of professional mercenaries became a feature of European warfare, notably the Italian Condottiere. Some, including the Swiss, were honest enough to fight for their pay, but others had no intention of putting themselves at risk; often, to the annoyance of their paymasters, deals were struck between opposing mercenary captains on the eve of a battle, and no one was hurt. The seventeenth century, however, was a period of political and religious turmoil during which men fought bitterly to protect vested interests or deeply held convictions. Massacres were commonplace, one atrocity begetting another. At Marston Moor and again at Naseby there were Royalist regiments who went down fighting rather than surrender to an enemy they loathed and despised. The wars of eighteenth century, on the other hand, were mostly fought without rancour by small professional armies. There was no disgrace in surrender by a commander and troops who had done their best, and often their opponents would accord them the Honours of War. It is only in the nineteenth and twentieth centuries, in the age of total war begun by Napoleon and the era of Western expansion across the globe, that last stands became a regular feature of warfare.

Much, of course, depends on the character of the commander concerned, but this in itself is not enough unless he has the complete support of his men. From what, then, does this fierce motivation stem? Anger? Fear? *Esprit de corps*? Tradition? Discipline? Loyalty? Belief in a cause? Hope of relief? Or self-sacrifice on behalf of others? Some of these elements are present in most last stands, but rarely all.

Here a further factor for consideration arises. Armies do not fight to the last man and the last round; nor do large formations such as corps and divisions. Those units that do so are invariably small, ranging in size from a platoon to a battalion, and sometimes in the British Army to a brigade, which is the equivalent of a regiment in other armies. Recent studies by military psychologists conclude that a soldier's primary loyalties lie to the men in his own platoon, then to his company, and finally to his battalion and regiment; to higher formations the soldier accords a general but impersonal loyalty, since they lie beyond his immediate family and are peopled by strangers. There is nothing new or surprising in this, and indeed the average senior NCO would comment tersely that this had always been the case and was likely to remain so. Robert Fox, the BBC reporter who witnessed the epic battle against odds by 2nd Battalion The Parachute Regiment to secure Goose Green, subsequently commented that despite their fearsome reputation the paratroopers cared deeply what happened to their comrades and that this was one of the reasons why they were so very formidable. As if to emphasise the point, the two Victoria Crosses awarded during the Falklands War were won by members of the Parachute Regiment who deliberately sacrificed their lives for others. The longer an efficient unit serves together, the more this feature tends to emerge.

One might expect, therefore, that any study of the last stand would contain frequent mention of the world's élites. Certainly, among the examples I have quoted, some are present, including the Grenadiers and Chasseurs of the Old Guard at Waterloo, the Marines who defended Wake Island, and 2nd Battalion The Parachute Regiment at Arnhem Bridge. In the majority of cases, however, it was units of the line, albeit with a well-developed *esprit de corps*, which circumstances presented with a test to destruction. Examples are the US 7th Cavalry at the Little Big Horn, the 24th Regiment, later the South Wales Borderers, at Isandhl-wana and Rorke's Drift, the 2nd Battalion The Rifle Brigade at Outpost Snipe during the Second Battle of Alamein, the 5th Battalion The Hampshire Regiment at Sidi Nsir in Tunisia, the 2nd Battalion West Yorkshire Regiment at the Admin Box in Burma, and the Gloucester-shire Regiment, Royal Northumberland Fusiliers and Royal Ulster Rifles at the Imjin in Korea. Nor should it be forgotten that in first class armies artillerymen accord their guns the status of colours in other branches of the service and fight to the muzzle in their defence.

In two of the episodes the men involved did not even have the distinction of belonging to line regiments. The defenders of The Alamo were volunteers, lacking uniforms or formal training and discipline, and they were regarded by their enemy, the Mexican dictator Santa Anna, as being little better than armed hooligans on the make; yet, they fought in a spirit of unquenchable idealism. Before its epic fight at Camerone the French Foreign Legion was widely viewed, not least in France itself, as being a somewhat disreputable organization which provided a haven for Europe's criminal classes.

In a category entirely their own were the Japanese, to whom the concept of surrender was unintelligible because of a religious conviction that their lives already belonged to the Emperor. In this context I have included their defences of Tarawa Atoll partly because it illustrates the point, and partly because it provides a graphic illustration of the terrifying experience of fighting against troops who are determined to extract the highest possible price before they are killed. For a while, the outcome of this battle hung in the balance and it was only won by the discipline, dogged perseverence and iron determination imbued in its members by the US Marine Corps.

The battles I describe have passed into legend not simply because of the courage and resolve of those making the stand, but also because this was matched by their enemies, who were prepared to accept very severe casualties in order to eliminate them. With one exception, the stand benefited the cause of those who made it, sometimes with redeemed honour, but more often with far wider implications. Most obviously, a stand weakened the enemy, cost him time and disrupted his plans, all of which could be used against him in subsequent engagements. Even if a stand was apparently unsuccessful, the enemy's minor but frequently expensive tactical victory was often counter-productive in that it aroused a fierce desire for revenge not only among the comrades of the defeated troops, but in their homeland as well, a most important consideration in terms of the psychological aspects of warfare. Such was the case in the aftermath of the Little Big Horn, Isandhlwana and the massacre of the patients and staff by the Japanese at the Admin Box's Main Dressing Station. The exception was Tarawa where, although the garrison died in the knowledge that they had inflicted heavy loss, their incredibly tough defence brought no other benefit to Japan; indeed, it was the Americans who were the long-term beneficiaries, for they refined their amphibious assault techniques so that later landings on similar island fortresses succeeded at far lower cost.

Bureaucrats in general, and military bureaucrats in particular, enjoy committing analytic formulae to paper, taking delight in the issue of pamphlets on such subjects as, say, the issue of pamphlets. To the best of my knowledge, however, no army has attempted to incorporate the last stand into its *Field Service Regulations*, for the very good reason that to do so would indicate a singular lack of confidence in its own abilities. Nevertheless, the phenomenon of the last stand is one which merits attention, as its effects, both political and military, clearly extend far beyond the battlefield. There is also good reason to examine the motivations of those who were prepared to make the ultimate sacrifice in hopeless circumstances when surrender might possibly have saved their lives. In the simplest cases, of course, extermination seemed inevitable and life could only be prolonged by continued resistance. But there have also been many other instances where men have been offered honourable terms and even safe conduct but have bluntly rejected them. The purpose of this book, therefore, is to study some of the better known examples of the phenomenon, and a few less well known. All provoke awe, and the reader will draw his own conclusions without further assistance from the author.

CHAPTER 1
The Old Guard at Waterloo
18 JUNE 1815

Despite its comparatively short existence, the Imperial Guard of Napoleon I has become the very symbol of the period in which it served. Containing as it did the finest soldiers of France, its memory still evokes in many Frenchmen a nostalgic retrospection to the days of *La Grande Nation*, when post-revolutionary energy took their forefathers to the most distant corners of Europe, and to the style and spirit of those times, indefinable but best expressed as *La Gloire*. Also remembered, with pride, is that on the stricken field of Waterloo it was the Guard, with one short, defiant, dubious phrase, and by the self-sacrifice and discipline of some of its units, which saved the honour of the French Army. Even today, so long after the event, such uniforms, weapons and other memorabilia of the Guard as have survived are eagerly sought by collectors willing to pay the highest prices for them.

The Guard could trace its roots to two Revolutionary units, the *Garde du Corps Législatif* and the *Garde du Directoire Exécutif*, which, in 1799, were amalgamated under Joachim Murat to form the Consular Guard, consisting of a grenadier battalion, a chasseur company, three light cavalry squadrons and an artillery battery. The function of this was to provide a bodyguard for the three Consuls. Having outmanoeuvred his rivals, however, Napoleon decided that as the Imperial Guard it would play a role of far greater significance. First, it would serve as the model for the entire army, and secondly, on the battlefield it would fight as the ultimate reserve, being committed to retrieve a desperate situation or to deliver the final, decisive attack. Understanding his men as he did, Napoleon offered membership in such an élite as a reward for long and meritorious service in the regiments of the line, although from 1804 onwards the cream of each conscript intake was also trained specifically for the Guard. Because of its élite status, better pay, smarter uniforms and more congenial conditions of service, the Guard never lacked recruits. It expanded steadily until it had become an army within an army, containing infantry and cavalry regiments, foot and horse artillery, engineers, supply train, military police and a naval unit; at one period its more exotic units included a Mameluke cavalry regiment and a scout regiment composed of Tartars. The personal loyalty of Guardsmen to the Emperor was intense, and the prospect of being returned to their units in disgrace ensured that strict discipline was maintained. Within the Guard there were the sub-divisions of the Old, Middle and Young Guards, the ambition of every Guardsman being to work his way upwards into the ranks of the Old Guard. Of this the 1st Grenadiers and 1st Chasseurs were regarded as being the most prestigious of all.

Often, there was no need to commit the Guard. At Austerlitz, Jena, Friedland and even at Borodino the infantry of the Old Guard were not engaged, although their presence, clearly indicated by the mass of tall bearskins, was something no enemy commander could ignore. Believing in their own invincibility, they referred to themselves as the 'Immortals'; so, too, did the rest of the army, because they were so seldom in action. Yet, despite the jealousy of the line regiments, when the army saw the Old or Middle Guard advance it knew that the crisis of the battle had been reached and also that the Guard never failed. The Young Guard was committed more regularly, often to the most critical sector of the fighting, with the deliberate intention that its members should earn their promotion to the Middle Guard.

Because of their tremendous reputation, the soldiers of the Old Guard were permitted liberties which would not have been tolerated in other units. When Napoleon met Tsar Alexander of Russia at Tilsit in 1807 he pointed to a terribly scarred Grenadier. 'What do you think of men who can endure such wounds?' he asked. 'And what do *you* think of men who can inflict them?' replied the Tsar. 'They're all dead!' interjected the Grenadier, settling the issue once and for all. Such familiarities led Napoleon to call them his Old Moaners (*grognards*). They have traditionally been portrayed as grizzled men in their middle years, but in fact they were old in experience rather than years. The majority were aged between 25 and 35; had they been older, comparatively few could have met the physical demands of campaigning. In 1812 the Guard marched into Russia 40,000 strong. Only 5,000 returned, the remainder having either perished in the Russian snows or been captured. Even so, standards of entry were not lowered. To qualify for the Old Guard officers and NCOs had to have twelve years' service, including several campaigns, while Guardsmen in the 1st Grenadiers and 1st Chasseurs required ten years' service, including campaigns.

When, in 1814, Napoleon abdicated, a small contingent of the Guard was permitted to accompany him in his exile on Elba. This included a composite grenadier/chasseur battalion, two squadrons of Polish lancers and 100 artillerymen. Of the rest, only four cavalry regiments and six infantry battalions were retained in the Bourbon Royal Guard, their pay cut by one-third and the private's traditional status as an NCO removed. The remainder were either dispersed or dismissed on half-pay. As if this were not sufficient cause for disgust, Louis XVIII, with an astounding lack of tact, formed his own personal bodyguard, the *Maison Militaire du Roi*, from former emigré nobles, granting its privates the pay and status of officers. Not surprisingly, when Napoleon returned from Elba, his former Guardsmen rallied to him without a second thought.

During the campaign of 1815, for practical purposes, the infantry of the Guard consisted of the Old Guard under Lieutenant-General Count Friant with the 1st and 2nd Grenadiers and the 1st and 2nd Chasseurs, each of two battalions; the Middle Guard under Lieutenant-General Count Morand with the 3rd Grenadiers (two battalions), the 4th Grenadiers (one battalion) and the 3rd and 4th Chasseurs, each of two battalions; and the Young Guard under Lieutenant-General Count Duhesme with the 1st and 2nd Tirailleurs and 1st and 2nd Voltigeurs, each of two battalions.

Napoleon's enemies had rallied quickly against him, hoping to overwhelm him by sheer weight of numbers. The Austrians were advancing towards the Upper Rhine and the Russians towards the Middle Rhine, but he was confident that the frontier defences of eastern France would hold until, with the 125,000 strong Army of the North, he dealt with the more immediate threat posed to Paris by two Allied armies in the Netherlands, the one an Anglo-Dutch-Belgian force under the Duke of Wellington, and the other a Prussian army under Field Marshal Prince Blücher. This he proposed to do by separating them and defeating them in turn.

On 16 June battle was joined. Detaching Marshal Michel Ney with one-third of the army to drive in Wellington's advance guard at Quatre Bras, the Emperor attacked Blücher at Ligny with the rest. The Prussians, while inexperienced, fought doggedly throughout the day. Napoleon had been on the point of committing the Guard, but delayed doing so until the identity of a large body of troops on his left flank had been established; it turned out to be one of his own corps, subjected to order and counter-order, marching uselessly between Ligny and Quatre Bras without contributing to either battle. By the time the Guard went in the evening was well advanced and although the Prussian centre was broken, Blücher's army was able to withdraw.

At Quatre Bras Ney had made no impression on the British who were, nevertheless, obliged to withdraw on 17 June to conform with the Prussians. Napoleon decided to concentrate on the destruction of Wellington's army, but detached Marshal Emmanuel de Grouchy with 33,000 men to pursue Blücher, who was believed to be withdrawing eastwards in the direction of Namur. In fact, as a result of a decision taken by General Count von Gneisenau while Blücher was temporarily incapacitated, the Prussians were marching steadily northwards towards Wavre, and because of the faulty intelligence he had received, Grouchy was unable to regain contact that day. Napoleon, however, had failed in his object of separating the Prussians from the Allies, for during the night a liaison officer from Blücher reached Wellington with a letter promising to effect a junction between their two armies the following day.

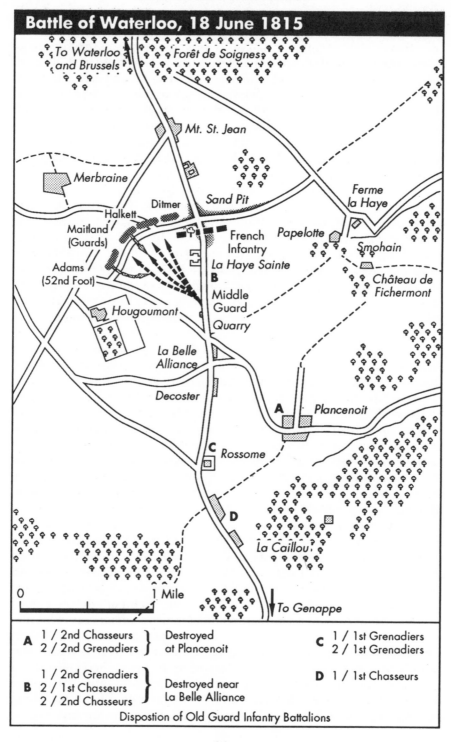

Battle of Waterloo, 18 June 1815

To Waterloo and Brussels

Forêt de Soignes

Mt. St. Jean

Merbraine

Sand Pit

Ferme la Haye

Ditmer

Halkett

Maitland (Guards)

French Infantry

Papelotte

Smohain

La Haye Sainte

Adams (52nd Foot)

B

Middle Guard

Château de Fichermont

Hougoumont

Quarry

La Belle Alliance

Decoster

A Plancenoit

C Rossome

D

La Caillou

0   1 Mile

To Genappe

A	1 / 2nd Chasseurs 2 / 2nd Grenadiers }	Destroyed at Plancenoit	**C**	1 / 1st Grenadiers 2 / 1st Grenadiers
B	1 / 2nd Grenadiers 2 / 1st Chasseurs 2 / 2nd Chasseurs }	Destroyed near La Belle Alliance	**D**	1 / 1st Chasseurs

Dispostion of Old Guard Infantry Battalions

The British withdrawal from Quatre Bras was neatly executed. In contrast, the French follow-up was tardy and further slowed by the onset of torrential rain. By the evening of 17 June both armies were deployed on low ridges opposite each other, separated by a shallow valley, and a major engagement on the morrow was inevitable. The battlefield, four miles wide by two-and-a-quarter miles deep, was ten miles from Brussels and about two miles south of the village of Waterloo in the Forest of Soignes.

Wellington was at the peak of his abilities, but his army was not the magnificent force he had led to victory in the long Peninsular War. Most of the British infantry who had fought in Spain and Portugal had been sent to North America during the final stages of the War of 1812, and many of their replacements were untried, either as individuals or units. On the other hand, their morale was good and they were dependable, as were the Germans of the King's German Legion and most of the contingents from Hanover and Brunswick. The same could not be said of all the Netherlands troops, amounting to almost half the 60,000 men Wellington had present. Some would distinguish themselves, some were unhappy about fighting former comrades among the French, and some were ready to make themselves scarce at the first sign of trouble.

Across the valley, the situation was reversed. The somewhat larger French Army was experienced, highly motivated, possessed tremendous *élan* and could field many more guns. Its Achilles' heel was Napoleon himself who, although he was aged only 43 and was three months younger than Wellington, was past his best both physically and mentally. He is known to have been suffering from piles and cystitis, painful and very personal complaints regarding which he was understandably sensitive. These were doubtless responsible for his morose, irritable manner, but in addition cystitis can induce the symptoms of fever and this may have been the cause of the torpor which affected him for much of the battle. Equally important was the fact that his abilities as a field commander had declined, as he himself had predicted they might, some years earlier. He refused to accept the advice of those of his Marshals who had fought the British in Spain and believed that Wellington's army could be thrown off its ridge by sheer brute force, without recourse to manoeuvre. During the battle itself he revealed that he had lost the ability to co-ordinate the various elements of the army to the best advantage and, above all, that his once brilliant sense of timing had gone.

At dawn the heavy rain which had continued to fall for much of the night was replaced by fitful, watery sunlight, but the ground had been reduced to a quagmire. It was, therefore, necessary to let it dry out a little and it was not until 1120 that the French artillery opened fire. Shortly after, elements of Reille's corps launched an attack on the château of Hougoumont, covering Wellington's right. This was intended as a diversion which would cause Wellington to commit his reserves there, following which an attack would be launched on his centre by D'Erlon's corps. In the event, the diversion became a fierce battle within a battle, lasting until dusk, and absorbed far more French troops than British.

Nevertheless, D'Erlon's corps, 16,000 strong, commenced its advance at about 1400, supported by the fire of 80 guns. It was halted by the disciplined firepower of the British infantry, then routed with a counter-attack delivered by the heavy cavalry of the Household and Union Brigades, who were in turn severely cut up by French cavalry when they pursued too far. D'Erlon attempted to renew his assault but the farm known as La Haye Sainte, covering the left-centre of the British position, remained a thorn in his side. Meanwhile, Grouchy had caught up with the Prussians, but Blücher, mindful of the promise he had given, detached one corps to hold him off while the rest of his army converged on the battlefield from the east. 'It must be done!' he shouted as he rode along the columns of weary, toiling infantry. 'I have given my word to my comrade Wellington! You would not have me break my word?' Bülow's corps, in the lead, was directed against Plancenoit, where it could menace the French right, while Zieten's corps was ordered to join Wellington's line on the ridge. By 1300 the Prussian advance guard was visible and Napoleon was forced to send Lobau's corps from the centre of his line to the right to meet this new threat. It had therefore become imperative that Wellington should be defeated before Blücher could arrive. On the opposite ridge the scarlet ranks were visibly thinning and many men could be seen leaving the Allied line, heading for the Forest of Soignes to their rear. Ney, whom Napoleon had placed in tactical control of the battle, assumed that Wellington's army was on the point of disintegration. Because of this, and the urgency of the situation, he decided to mount a massed cavalry attack in the centre which he felt would complete the rout of the enemy.

Ney's conclusions, however, were wrong. Wellington had merely been pulling back his units beyond the crest so that they would be better protected from the French artillery, and most of those heading for the rear were either wounded or prisoners under escort, although un-doubtedly there were a number of deserters as well. The attack, therefore, would be made against unshaken infantry in secure squares, yet it would itself lack infantry support which could rake the squares and thin their ranks. There was, in fact, very little infantry available, as Reille, D'Erlon and Lobau were all fully occupied and the only remaining source was the Imperial Guard, which Napoleon retained under his personal command. Tacitly, the Emperor concurred with this serious tactical error, although the Cavalry of the Guard was permitted to join in, first the light horsemen of the 1st and 2nd Lancers and the *Chasseurs à Cheval*, and then the heavy *Grenadiers à Cheval*, the Empress' Dragoons and the *Gendarmerie d'Elite*.

The first attack rolled up the slopes at about 1600, passing between La Haye Sainte and Hougoumont. The British artillery remained in action as long as possible, scything great gaps in the advancing squadrons before the gunners ran back across the crest to shelter in the squares, many of which remained invisible until the French had breasted the ridge. Sharp controlled volleys from ranks four-deep emptied saddles and shot down horses by the score. Like a wave, the attack burst round the squares, troopers vainly trying to hack their way through the hedge of bayonets. Units became intermingled and as casualties began to mount control was lost. At this point the British cavalry counter-attacked, bundling the French off the ridge but rallying quickly, and finally the gunners ran out to blast the retreating enemy. Twelve separate attacks of this kind were delivered and similarly repulsed until by 1730 the magnificent French cavalry, cuirassiers, carabiners, dragoons, lancers, hussars and *chasseurs à cheval* alike, had been virtually destroyed; Ney himself had had four horses shot under him. Latterly, the British had welcomed the arrival of the increasingly tired and dispirited horsemen since it provided some relief from the fire of the French artillery which was taking a steady toll.

On the right Lobau was under increasing pressure from Bülow and had lost Plancenoit. With Prussian shells now bursting nearby, Napoleon sent Duhesme with the *Tirailleurs* and *Voltigeurs* of the Young Guard to recapture the village, which they succeeded in doing. The respite gained was only temporary for weight of numbers forced them out. Reluctantly, the Emperor committed two Old Guard Battalions, the 1st/2nd Chasseurs and 2nd/2nd Grenadiers. In two columns thirty files wide they advanced steadily and regardless of loss behind their drummers, then in a wild bayonet charge drove the Prussians through Plancenoit and on for a further 600 yards, all without firing a shot.

Napoleon had sat hunched in an armchair at Rossomme for most of the day, but he had now shaken off his lethargy and come forward to a better viewpoint. Despite the threat to his right, he believed that there was still time to beat Wellington. The key to victory, he perceived, lay in La Haye Sainte, past which the road climbed the ridge to the crossroads in the centre of the Allied position, and Ney was ordered to capture the farm at all costs.

The buildings were grouped around a courtyard, with a garden to the north and an orchard to the south. There was a gate leading on to the road, another by the barn giving access to the fields, and a back door from the house into the garden. During the night the farm had been crowded with men sheltering from the rain, and the barn doors, together with the farm carts and much of the furniture, had vanished into their camp fires. When morning came, therefore, little remained in the buildings from which barricades could be constructed. Responsibility for the defence of La Haye Sainte rested with the 2nd Brigade of the King's German Legion, commanded by Colonel Christian von Ompteda. The Legion, as it was known, consisted in the main of Hanoverian exiles who had fled to England when their country, of which George III was also

King, was occupied by Napoleon in 1803. Most had fought in Spain under Wellington and were accepted by their British comrades as being the only troops on either side who were their equals. Now, after twelve years of soldiering far from home, they had become grizzled veterans noted for their steadiness and marksmanship; for the moment, too, their feelings towards the French were more than usually vindictive because their long-awaited release had been delayed by Napoleon's escape from Elba.

Ompteda detailed the Legion's 2nd Light Battalion, commanded by Major Lewis Baring, to hold the farm while the rest of the brigade remained in position behind, to the west of the crossroads. Of Baring himself little is known save that he played the flute well and was clearly a very competent and professional officer. Fortunately, one of his subalterns, a Scot named George Graeme, has left a graphic account of the defence of La Haye Sainte.

Baring had 360 men under command, but his pioneers had been sent off to help fortify Hougoumont and there were no materials left with which to barricade the farm's gates and doors. Nevertheless, loopholes were knocked in the walls and the Germans had poured a galling fire into the flank of D'Erlon's corps as it advanced, then joined in the pursuit when it was repulsed. The French had then advanced against the farm itself, swarming round the buildings in their efforts to break in. Fighting raged at every door, window and loophole; an attempt to rush the barn's open doorway was met with such heavy fire that the entrance was soon piled high with the bodies of those who had led the attack and those who, possessed of *la rage*, had tried to scramble over them. Then, the straw in the barn had caught fire. Using camp kettles filled from the pond, Baring had led a party which extinguished the blaze and shortly afterwards the French attack faltered. Next, the garrison had fired into the flank of the repeated cavalry attacks which occupied the rest of the afternoon, and must have inflicted serious casualties.

Curiously, both army commanders developed a blind spot regarding La Haye Sainte. Napoleon's massed artillery was only 300 yards distant and could have turned the farm into a heap of rubble if only the order had been given; instead, it continued to engage targets on the ridge. For his part, Wellington failed to keep the garrison supplied with ammunition and, while the immediate responsibility rested with the divisional commander concerned, the Duke was later to comment that he should have seen to it himself but had been unable to think of everything. Certainly, somewhere along the chain of command something had gone wrong, although just what has never been determined. Seriously worried by his heavy ammunition expenditure, Baring had dispatched no fewer than four messengers back to the ridge to request fresh supplies, without result. David Haworth, in his unsurpassed account of the battle, suggests a possible explanation was that the garrison's Baker rifles had a bore of 0.615-inch which was obviously not compatible with the 0.75-inch

18

Brown Bess musket arming the bulk of the infantry, and that the Germans' reserve ammunition was in a wagon which had overturned on the road from Brussels. At 1600 Baring sent a fifth messenger back with a warning that unless supplies were received immediately the farm would fall. The living among his men were now outnumbered by the dead, but by stripping the pouches of the killed and wounded they managed to produce four rounds per man. Even so, they had no thought other than to fight it out.

At about the same time that Baring was dispatching his last messenger, Ney was forming up infantry and engineers from D'Erlon's corps, now rallied somewhat, for his own assault on the farm. As the column approached, the deadly fire from the walls slowly spluttered into silence. The reason was immediately apparent to the French, who surged forward, smashing down the gate with axes and fighting their way into the yard. Baring gave the order to abandon the position and escape through the rear door of the house into the garden, but for most this was impossible. Ensign Frank, wounded in the arm, hid under a bed, where he remained for the rest of the battle; shortly after he had concealed himself the French burst into the room and shot two wounded men. In the narrow hall of the house a French officer grappled with Lieutenant Graeme. The subaltern threw him off, parried several bayonet thrusts then escaped by the rear door with musket balls cracking past his head. He succeeded in reaching the ridge, where he was joined by Baring and a mere 39 men.

Ney immediately brought up a battery which opened fire on the Allied line, only 300 yards distant, while a cloud of skirmishers pressed even closer. Stubbornly disregarding advice that a unit of French cuirassiers had arrived in the lee of the farm, the 22-year-old Prince of Orange ordered Ompteda to deploy another Legion battalion in line and advance to disperse the skirmishers. It did so, but was wiped out in less than a minute when the cuirassiers charged. Ompteda, who had led the counter-attack in person, jumped his horse into the garden of La Haye Sainte and was seen slashing at the enemy before he was shot down.

It was too much for some of the Allied units. A neighbouring Hanoverian brigade withdrew out of range and a Nassau brigade fled. Led by their Colonel, the fashionable Cumberland Hussars – a Hanoverian regiment, named after a son of George II – rode off and did not halt until they reached Brussels, where they spread the news that the battle was lost. And so it appeared, for a yawning gap had opened in the Allied line around the vital crossroads. Ney knew that he had only to drive into it and Wellington would be defeated, but his men were exhausted and the need for fresh troops was critical. This was, in fact, just the sort of situation for which the Imperial Guard had been created, and as yet most of its infantry had barely been touched by the battle.

The officer best suited to delivering Ney's request should have been of a rank senior enough to have talked back to the Emperor in his morose state of mind. Instead, Ney sent a Colonel Heymès, to whom Napoleon reacted with a sarcastic tirade. *'Des troupes! Ou voulez-vous que j'en prenne? Voulez-vous que j'en fasse?'* (Troops! Where do you want me to get them? Do you want me to make them?)

Slowly but inexorably, the window of opportunity began to close. At 1900 the Imperial Guard could have broken the Allied centre with ease, but with every minute that passed Wellington was marching men into the gap and Zieten's corps was closing from the east to strengthen the line. There could, however, be no denying the justice of Ney's request. Having satisfied himself that the situation at Plancenoit was again under control, Napoleon took two decisive steps. First, he sent an officer to gallop along the front with the news that it was Grouchy's army, not Blücher's, which had appeared on the right. The effect on morale was electric, for victory now seemed assured; as to what the reaction might be when the truth was discovered no thought had been given. Secondly, at about 1930, the Emperor personally led forward six battalions of the Middle Guard and three of the Old Guard. Although, traditionally, artists have painted them in full dress, they were wearing their blue greatcoats, their parade dress being carried in their packs and their long plumes strapped in waterproof covers to the scabbards of their short swords, ready for the triumphal march into Brussels. As the columns of nodding bearskins marched towards La Haye Sainte they were fittingly played into action by 150 musicians to the stirring strains of the March of Marengo which, prior to that battle had been known as the March of the Consular Guard.

It was a spectacle befitting a moment of truth. The entire French Army responded, knowing that the crisis of the battle had been reached; the Guard was going in, and the Guard never failed. There was cheering everywhere as men and units who thought they had no more to give fell in on the flanks to join in this last tremendous assault. Napoleon, dissauded from going any further by his staff, turned aside into a quarry. Surprised and a little angry that the Emperor had decided not to lead them personally, the Guard marched past, paying its compliments in stony silence. The 2nd/3rd Grenadiers were detached to form a firm base, but the rest of the Middle Guard was handed over to Ney, now hatless, splattered with mud and riding his fifth horse, as the leading wave of the assault. The three Old Guard battalions were retained by Napoleon as a second wave, should it be needed.

For reasons which have never been satisfactorily explained, the advance of the Middle Guard did not take it past La Haye Sainte and on to the crossroads. Instead, it inclined left just short of the farm, a route which was unsuitable for a number of reasons. First, the French troops in and around La Haye Sainte would be unable to support the attack with their fire. Secondly, although the French cavalry had overrun the British guns many times, they had not thought to spike them, and now they were back in action, sending round shot through the ranks of the Guardsmen, followed by grape and canister as they drew closer. Thirdly, the ground had been churned into a morass by repeated cavalry attacks and was thickly strewn with dead and wounded men and horses, all of which made the going difficult. Fourthly, the left flank of the attack would be exposed to enfilade fire from Hougoumont. Fifthly, the attack was not delivered as a concentrated hammer-blow which would smash through the Allied line, but with four battalions in column and one in square, moving along roughly parallel axes with two horse artillery guns in each of the intervals between battalions; inevitably, given the nature of the going, this meant that battalion attacks would be made piecemeal with greatly diminished effect. Sixthly, and most important, the attack was not being directed against what Ney knew to be the weakest part of the Allied line, but against an unknown quantity which, in the event, proved to be the sector best able to withstand it.

Behind the crest the Allied infantry was sheltering from the redoubled fire of the French artillery, but it knew that the Guard was on its way as ample warning had been given by a deserter. To their front the British guns were hammering away at unseen targets, their drifting smoke producing a fog which became thicker by the minute. From beyond came the steady beat of scores of drums sounding the *pas de charge*, accompanied by shouts of '*Vive l'Empereur!*' Wellington, riding along the ridge, watched the progress of the advance and calculated that its leading elements would strike Major-General Peregrine Maitland's 1st Brigade, consisting of the 2nd and 3rd Battalions 1st Foot Guards. The brigade was screened by a bank which ran along the lateral track at this point, but Wellington, who believed that cavalry would support the French attack, ordered Maitland to adopt a more secure formation four ranks deep. Then, having told the men to lie down, he positioned himself behind them to await developments.

During their advance two battalions of the Guard, the 1st and 2nd of the 3rd Chasseurs, had converged so that their front was now some sixty files wide. They had incurred heavy losses from the British artillery fire but had closed the gaps in their ranks and marched on without pause. Led by their officers, they passed through the now abandoned gun positions and emerged from the smoke expecting to see their foe break and run, as they always had, but all that was visible was a small group of senior officers, watching them impassively. 'Now, Maitland! Now's your time!' called Wellington when the French were within 40 yards. 'Up, Guards!' came the order, and suddenly the Chasseurs were presented with ranks of scarlet infantry, rising from the earth before them. 'Make ready!' The muskets came up into the aim. 'Fire!' In one terrible minute of precise, close-range volley fire 300 Chasseurs went down. Those at the rear of the column tried to fire back over the heads of those in front, and some tried to extend into a firing line, to no avail. Then, suddenly, the British came on with the bayonet and the entire column broke and fled.

On the left of Maitland's men was the 5th Brigade, commanded by Major-General Sir Colin Halkett. The brigade had suffered so severely during the French cavalry attacks that two of its battalions, the 30th (Cambridgeshire) and 73rd (Highland) were, in effect, lying dead in their squares. At 1930, by which time the 73rd's survivors were commanded by a subaltern, the colours of both were sent to the rear. Nevertheless, Halkett decided that he would cover the exposed left flank of Maitland's counter-attack with his two remaining battalions, the 33rd (West Riding) and 69th (South Lincolnshire), little realizing that his advance placed him on a direct collision course with the 1st/3rd and 4th Grenadiers. As the bearskins loomed out of the smoke, they were stopped in their tracks by a volley. However, the accompanying French horse artillery immediately began firing grapeshot into the British line. Halkett ordered his men back behind the crest, but during this move he was wounded and control was lost when his two battalions became intermixed. While Major Kelly of Wellington's staff restored order, a potentially dangerous situation was averted by the French reluctance to resume their advance. When their officers did get them moving again, they came on cautiously behind a ragged fire, and had clearly not expected to meet determined opposition. Kelly held his own fire until the Grenadiers had reached the crest, then shot away their leading ranks with a concentrated volley. The French, still deployed in column, could not match the fire of the 33rd and 69th, who were fighting in line, and they began to give way. To the British left the guns of a Dutch brigade, recently pushed into the line by Wellington to close the gap in his centre, also opened up on the column's right flank with grapeshot. Unable to stand more, the Grenadiers bolted.

Meanwhile, Maitland's Foot Guards had halted their pursuit and returned to the ridge when they observed another French column advancing up the slope to their right. The column, nominally consisting of one battalion of the 4th Chasseurs, had been swelled by men from the rear ranks of the defeated 3rd Chasseurs, and it was moving in the most determined manner against Major-General Sir Frederick Adams' 3rd (Light) Brigade. On the right of the brigade, however, was the 1st Battalion 52nd (Oxfordshire) Regiment, commanded by Colonel Sir John Colborne, who had no intention of waiting passively for the assault. Having obtained Adams' approval, he waited for the French to reach the crest then wheeled his battalion until it was parallel with the left flank of their column and opened fire. The Chasseurs, already engaged to their front, halted and formed a firing line towards him. In the ensuing firefight more than 150 of the 52nd were killed or wounded in less than four minutes, but the French loss was greater. As the range closed Colborne gave the order to charge. Cheering, his men surged forward, their bayonets levelled. The column broke in wild confusion, disintegrating as it fled towards La Haye Sainte. Reforming, the 52nd continued to march across the forward slope of the ridge, eliminating the last vestiges of resistance.

In the valley below and on each flank, every Frenchman who could had watched the advance of the Guard's columns. They had seen them disappear into the smoke and heard the musketry rise to a climactic roar which signified that the issue was being resolved. Then, from the pall hanging over the summit, figures of running Guardsmen emerged, first in small groups, then in hundreds. At first there was total disbelief, then, as the terrible truth dawned, the news spread like wildfire along the front – 'La Garde recule!' It was a cry of despair, for if the Guard had failed, what hope was there for the rest of the army? The remnants of Reille's and D'Erlon's corps, on the point of renewing their attacks, began shredding away towards the rear.

Within fifteen minutes of the repulse of the Guard, the Army of the North was in full retreat. Zieten's corps had entered the battle and Bülow, reinforced by Pirch's corps, had finally broken through at Plancenoit and was driving the wreckage of Lobau's divisions before him. Now the full effects of Napoleon's deceit made themselves felt. There were shouts of 'Nous sommes trahis!' and the retreat became a wild stampede. On the ridge, the scarlet lines emerged from the smoke into a fine sunlit evening as Wellington ordered a general advance across the battlefield.

Perhaps the Middle Guard had failed because, too used to easy victories, it no longer knew how to cope with a tough, unshaken enemy. The Old Guard, however, was made of sterner stuff. Napoleon had not committed the second wave of his assault and now he formed its three battalions, the 1st/2nd Grenadiers, the 2nd/1st and 2nd/2nd Chasseurs, into squares which retired steadily from La Haye Sainte, scorning the flood of fugitives which swept past. Islands of discipline in a sea of roaring confusion, they provided a temporary refuge for the Emperor, who was hurried away with a small escort provided by a remnant of the Guard cavalry. Soon, the British hussars were swarming round the squares, then infantry, but they continued to withdraw in good order, halting from time to time to beat off attacks and dress their thinning ranks. They succeeded in reaching their own side of the valley, only to find the whole area covered with a panic-stricken mob fleeing from the converging British and Prussian advance. The hussars rode off to sabre at will among them, but the squares were now beset by combined infantry and artillery fire. At length, although they continued to move majesically through the terrified remnant of a once mighty army, their numbers had dwindled so much that they were forced to form smaller triangles. These, in turn, were reduced to isolated groups and, near La Belle Alliance, they were finally destroyed.

Some minutes before the end a British officer had approached the

2nd/1st Chasseurs, shouting that they had done enough and could now surrender with honour. The response of their commander, General Pierre Cambronne, was confined to a single epithet, '*Merde!*' A moment later he was struck on the forehead by a spent ball and, stunned, he tumbled from his horse. When he came to the square had moved off and he stumbled after it. He was spotted by Colonel Hew Halkett, the commander of a Hanoverian brigade, who rode at him and was about to cut him down when he surrendered. At this point Halkett's horse was shot dead and Cambronne made off again. He was still groggy, however, and Halkett experienced no difficulty in catching him on foot and sending him under escort to the rear.

At Rossomme, the site of his former headquarters, Napoleon found the two battalions of the 1st Grenadiers under General Petit. Forming square on each side of the road, they maintained a steady retreat, fending off the pursuit, which had now been taken up by the Prussian cavalry, and giving short shrift to such of the fugitives as got in their way. The Emperor, with several of his senior officers, including Soult, Lobau, Bertrand and Drouot, rode with them and at Le Caillou picked up the 1st/1st Chasseurs, which had been left to guard the Imperial baggage. Napoleon then rode ahead in the hope that a stand could be made at the village of Genappe, two miles to the south, but here the remnant of the army, crazed by the contagion of its own fear, was tearing itself to pieces. Men were killing each other in their desperation to cross the narrow bridge spanning the little River Dyle, which was a mere ten feet wide and just three feet feep. The tailback jammed the village street and its approaches, so that it took the Emperor's escort an hour to clear a path for him.

Yet, those in Genappe were in no immediate danger. One-and-a-half miles short of the village, Petit was able to break up his squares and continue the retreat in column of march. Contemptuous of the struggling mob in the village, he marched his three battalions round its eastern outskirts and forded the stream without the slightest difficulty. Rejoining the road, the remnant of the Old Guard marched on through the darkness of a midsummer night, its duty done. Behind, in Genappe, new heights of horror were reached when the Prussian cavalry arrived, slashing its way into the struggling mass.

Napoleon's defeat was total, his power broken forever. Perversely, Frenchmen would forgive him for the lost opportunities, the mistakes and the lies which were his responsibility alone, and they would blame Grouchy for the disaster, although he had succeeded in extricating his portion of the army from its difficult situation. Searching for some crumb of comfort, they seized upon the stand of the Old Guard, and in particular on a story in which Cambronne had imperiously rejected the call to surrender with the phrase, '*La Garde meurt, mais ne se rend pas!*' (The Guard dies, but never surrenders!). Despite Cambronne's denials that he had ever used such a phrase, the story became an article of faith.

It was actually the brainchild of a Paris journalist and, of course, it was wonderful copy, providing as it did just what his readers wanted. The probability is that it had its roots in Brussels society, which contained a group of ladies of a certain age known as La Vieille Garde. The ladies were members of the Prince of Orange's intimate circle, and of them it was said unkindly, '*Elles ne meurent pas et se rendent toujours!*' (They never die and always surrender!) Such gossip would easily have been picked up from British officers when Wellington's army entered Paris, or even before, and the journalist's imagination did the rest. In fact, the Old Guard's actions at Waterloo did not require the embellishment of noble phrases; they spoke for themselves.

CHAPTER 2
Remember the Alamo!
23 FEBRUARY TO 6 MARCH 1836

Although the Spanish colonial authorities in Mexico had made periodic attempts to settle the province of Tejas since 1690 they enjoyed little success, for few people wished to live in the vast empty land far to the north. Such settlements as there were tended to be concentrated around the widely scattered missions established by the Catholic Church, the military garrisons and the centres of civil administration, as much for mutual protection against fierce bands of roving Indians as to diminish their sense of isolation. During its dying days, however, the Spanish administration decided to award land grants to the numerous Americans who were only too anxious to settle, the only provisos being that they should accept Mexican citizenship and become Roman Catholics. By 1835 there were some 28,000 Americans living in Tejas, or, to give it its Anglicized form, Texas, reducing the native population to a small minority.

In 1821 Mexico fought for, and won, her independence from Spain. The principal architect of the Mexican victory was General Agustin de Iturbide, who had himself crowned Emperor the following year. This was not acceptable to the more liberal shades of Mexican opinion and in 1823 he was ousted by a republican coup in which one of the principal participants was Antonio López de Santa Anna Pérez de Lebrón, a former oficer in the Spanish Army who had thrown in his lot with the Mexicans. In 1824 a Constitution was adopted guaranteeing the rights, freedoms and privileges of all Mexican citizens.

During the years which followed, Santa Anna, essentially a devious, corrupt and ruthless politician who possessed a degree of military skill, steadily increased his influence until in 1833 he was elected President. It was soon apparent that his liberal professions were merely a pose and that his real interest lay in wielding absolute power, for he soon dissolved the national Congress and began dismantling the federal structure of government which had been copied from the United States.

The reaction of the American colonists in Texas, who referred to themselves as Texians, was predictable. They were already aware that the Mexican concept of rights, freedoms and privileges differed radically from their own and they resented the fact that, despite their numbers, Texas was still administratively subordinate to the state of Coahuila, which did not represent their interests. Most of the Americans simply wanted to live their lives in peace, but the President's actions were in contravention of the 1824 Constitution and looked dangerously like those of a would-be tyrant. Some were for immediate armed rebellion, others for secession, but, for the moment, calmer counsels prevailed.

Meanwhile, Santa Anna was fully engaged in putting down revolts which had flared up in no fewer than eight states. In June 1835 the Americans intercepted a dispatch addressed to the President's brother-in-law, General Martin Perfecto de Cós, who was restoring order in Coahulia, declaring that civil government had been suspended and that Santa Anna intended dealing personally with the vocal and potentially dangerous colonists. The threat could not be ignored and it became inevitable that, sooner or later, the simmering discontent of the Americans would erupt into violence.

Cós, with 1400 men, established a base at San Antonio de Bexar, on the River San Antonio. Here, east of the town and across the river, was the Alamo, a former mission and barracks, consisting of the old conventual buildings with a large, semi-fortified walled enclosure to the west. The largest and most impressive of the buildings was the church, work on which had begun in 1756 following the collapse of an earlier structure, although it had not been completed by the time the mission was withdrawn in 1793 and still lacked a roof. In 1801 a Spanish cavalry unit occupied the buildings, being replaced by Mexican troops in 1821. Some sources suggest that the complex derived its title from the Spanish soldiers, who came from Alamo de Parras and named their barracks the Pueblo de San José y Santiago del Alamo; equally, it may simply have taken its name from the grove of cottonwood trees (*alamos*) growing nearby.

As a fortress, the Alamo left a great deal to be desired and Cós expended some effort in putting it into a defensible state, constructing cannon emplacements approached by ramps in the chancel of the old church and at other suitable points around the walls, as well as enclosing the vulnerable angle between the church and the south-east corner of the compound behind a low earthwork topped by a palisade. It seems that his troops were of poor quality and contained a large criminal element, but he no doubt believed that they would perform adequately enough against such civilian opposition as they would encounter. He also seemed determined to provoke an incident which would justify opening hostilities against the settlers, demanding the return of an ancient and completely useless cannon which had been lent to the town of Gonzales some years previously to scare off marauding Indians. The citizens of Gonzales, defiantly flying a banner inscribed '*Come and Take It*', refused to hand it back, claiming that it was state property and therefore had nothing to do with the central government. Cós sent a detachment to secure the gun, but on 2 October 1835 this was ambushed as it approached the town and forced into an ignominious retreat, one

Mexican being killed in the exchange.

These shots signalled the start of the War of Texan Independence, and for neither side could there be any turning back. The settlers began forming an army at Gonzales, but at first it numbered only 500 and attempted to conduct its affairs in an atmosphere of democracy gone crazy. An appeal for help to the United States was received sympathetically but there was nothing that could be done officially as, quite properly, the Washington administration regarded the dispute as an internal Mexican problem in which it could not become involved. On the other hand, there was widespread popular support for the settlers, and Washington did nothing to prevent the dispatch of funds, munitions and supplies to the settlers, nor did it discourage volunteers from joining them, either as individuals or in groups. Some of the volunteers were veterans of the War of 1812, others were deserters from the US Army seeking action and adventure, and others, like the New Orleans Greys, marched into Texas having been raised and equipped specifically for the purpose.

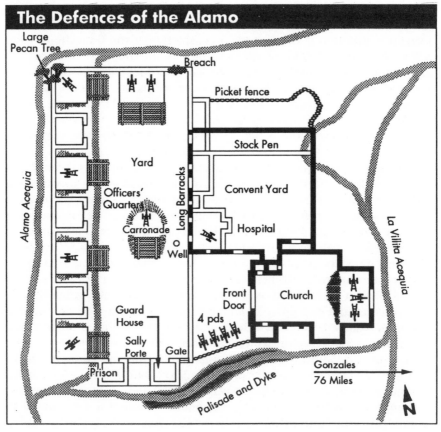

The Defences of the Alamo

Large Pecan Tree

Breach

Picket fence

Stock Pen

Yard

Alamo Acequia

La Villita Acequia

Long Barracks

Convent Yard

Officers' Quarters

Carronade

Hospital

Well

Front Door

Church

Guard House

4 pds

Sally Porte

Gate

Gonzales 76 Miles

Prison

Palisade and Dyke

N

Meanwhile, at Gonzales the democratic process had resulted in a decision to attack San Antonio. Command of the advance guard was given to James Bowie, a businessman who had made a fortune in land speculation and was also a noted duellist, famed for the use of the knife which bore his name. His business had brought him to Texas, where he had married the daughter of the Provincial Vice-Governor, becoming a Mexican citizen in 1830. Three years later his wife and children had died during a cholera epidemic, and, desolated, he had turned to drink for consolation with the result that his health began to break down. He was, however, an early convert to the cause of Texan Independence and this had restored some purpose to his life.

On 27 October Bowie's men found themselves confronted by a much larger body of Mexicans some two miles south of San Antonio. The Texans, who lost only one man during the subsequent engagement, were much the better marksmen, killing 67 of their opponents and wounding a similar number. Shaken, the Mexicans withdrew into San Antonio, while the settlers, too few in number to launch an assault, settled down to await reinforcements. With the onset of winter, some began to drift home and others, feeling that they were accomplishing nothing, suggested withdrawal. However, the recently arrived American volunteers, including the New Orleans Greys, wanted more positive action. The argument was resolved by a Kentuckian named Ben Milam, recently escaped from the Mexican gaol in which he had been incarcerated for his republican views since Iturbide's days. On 6 December he persuaded the 300 men still present to follow him in an attack on the town. The fighting, from house to house and street to street, raged for four days until Cós, despite the fact that he still retained the Alamo, requested terms. He and his men were paroled on the condition that they would not fight against the 1824 Constitution, and were permitted to march off, retaining sufficient arms to defend themselves against Indian attack.

The Texans had performed a remarkable feat of arms, but the immediate consequences of their victory were almost as bad as a defeat. Many, believing the war was over, went home. Others, returning to Gonzalez with their appetites for action whetted, became involved in a disastrous invasion of Mexican territory. Only 104 men under Colonel James C. Neill were left at the Alamo and they set about improving the defences as far as possible. It was immediately clear that the perimeter of the complex, a circuit of almost 500 yards, could not be defended by so small a garrison, but Cós had left behind some 20 guns and the best of these, ranging from a pair of 3-pounders to one 18-pounder and a carronade, were emplaced where they would do most good, the majority being 4-pounder field guns. The carronade, a shipboard weapon designed for close-quarter battering, was also a fearful man-killer when loaded with grapeshot; one source records it as having been sited on a mound in the centre of the walled enclosure, where it could be used against any attackers who broke through the defences; another shows it emplaced in the centre of the west wall; and a third shows two 8-pounder guns on the central mound, placed specifically to cover the interior of the south gate. This apparent contradiction suggests that some re-deployment of the more important artillery weapons took place while the Alamo was under siege, dictated by changing circumstances. It is also probable that fire steps were constructed around the wall of the enclosure where these were not immediately available on the roofs of barracks and stables.

Despite this effort, it was not the intention of the Texans' commander-in-chief, General Samuel Houston, that the Alamo should be defended. Houston had crammed a great deal into his 39 years. A lawyer by profession, he had been wounded twice during the War of 1812, was a former Governor of Tennessee and General of Militia, and had lived among the Cherokee Indians. He had been in Texas since 1832 and was a natural choice for command, although the task was a thankless one. Simultaneously, he was required to raise, train, equip and supply the army, decide such matters as its establishment, drill, uniform, the granting of commissions and, above all, establish a coherent strategy in a climate in which his subordinate commanders declined to obey him because they either felt bound by the democratic decisions of their men, or believed they were answerable only to the legislative council which had been formed. He was aware that Santa Anna was assembling an army for the invasion of Texas, and that it consisted of far better troops than those that had been defeated at San Antonio. For the moment, he had no intention of committing his enthusiastic amateurs to a pitched battle; instead, he decided to harass the Mexicans, withdrawing steadily before them until their lines of communications were over-extended, then attack when the enemy was weakest.

To succeed, he would need every man he could assemble. Bowie, now appointed Colonel, was dispatched to the Alamo with 30 men and instructions to abandon the post and dismantle its defences. On arrival, he found that a fifth of Neill's garrison had deserted and that the remainder were on the verge of starvation. Using his business contacts among the local community, he procured supplies and morale improved. After discussing the overall situation with Neill, Bowie decided to ignore Houston's order, although the decision was not taken in any wilful spirit. Rather, it stemmed from the realization that Santa Anna's invasion route would pass directly through San Antonio; that before he continued his advance Santa Anna would have to subdue the Alamo; and that the longer he took about it, the more time Houston would have to lick his own army into shape. Houston was so angered by this latest act of disobedience that he came close to resigning, but Governor Harvey Smith smoothed him down, sent him on leave and, agreeing with Bowie, arranged for the dispatch of such reinforcements as were available.

The first of these, thirty men under Lieutenant-Colonel William B. Travis, a young South Carolinian lawyer given to flamboyant dress and theatrical declamations, arrived on 3 February 1836. On 8 February the small Tennessee Company of Mounted Volunteers rode in, commanded by Colonel David Crockett, former hunter, Indian fighter, Congressman, Militia officer and teller of tall tales, already a legend in his own lifetime. 'I have come', he told Neill, Bowie and Travis, 'to aid you all I can in your noble cause. All the honour I desire is that of defending the liberties of our common country.'

Shortly after, Neill departed on leave, turning command of the Alamo over to Travis, the senior regular officer present. This was understandably resented by Bowie who, despite his nominal superiority, held only a volunteer commission. The two bickered openly and Bowie embarked on an ill-tempered and protracted drinking bout which effectively destroyed what remained of his health. Travis, conscious of Bowie's record and aware that the volunteers present believed him to be the better leader, offered to share command with him, and this was accepted. Few doubted that they were in for a hard fight and, while his men prepared for a siege, Travis dispatched a request for assistance to Colonel James W. Fannin, who was at Goliad (La Bahia), some 90 miles downstream, with the best of the Texan troops.

Santa Anna's army, consisting of one cavalry and two infantry brigades, artillery and engineers, included a high proportion of regular units and was in every way a more formidable force than that which had made such a miserable showing under Cós. It left Saltillo on 1 February and marched north, picking up reinforcements as it crossed the Rio Grande. Santa Anna pushed his men hard, putting them on half rations when the rudimentary supply system broke down. An outbreak of dysentery decimated the ranks, but on 23 February the army had its reward, reaching San Antonio a full month before it was expected. Surprised, Travis withdrew his troops, and those of their dependants who were present, into the Alamo. He rejected a call to surrender and in response Santa Anna hoisted a red flag on the belfry of the church of San Fernando, situated in the centre of the town, indicating that no quarter would be given. Unimpressed, Travis fired a shot at it with his long-range 18-pounder, emplaced at the south-eastern corner of the defences. He then sent further appeals for help to Goliad and Gonzales.

Aware that the Texans possessed considerable firepower, Santa Anna did not launch an immediate assault. Instead, he began constructing siege batteries, which were moved closer to the walls as the siege progressed, and opened a slow but steady bombardment. He lacked resources to mount a close investment and instead established a cordon of pickets, the intervals between which were patrolled by his cavalry. Notwithstanding these, messengers leaving or entering the Alamo experienced little difficulty in doing so.

31

Bowie was now so seriously ill that on the morning of 24 February he took to his bed. Travis resumed sole command and drafted his now famous appeal addressed to 'the people of Texas and all Americans in the world'. After describing the course of events thus far, he declared: 'Our flag still waves proudly from the walls. *I shall never surrender or retreat.* Then, I call on you in the name of Liberty, of patriotism and everything dear to the American Character, to come to our aid with all despatch . . . If this call is neglected, I am determined to sustain myself as long as possible and die like a soldier who never forgets what is due to his own honour and that of his country. *Victory or Death.*' He added a short postscript: 'The Lord is on our side – When the enemy appeared in sight we had not three bushels of corn – We have since found in deserted houses 80 or 90 bushels and got into the walls 20 or 30 head of Beeves.'

The flag referred to, which was flown above the church, is believed to have been the Mexican tricolor with the black numerals 1824 replacing the national arms in the central panel, signifying that the Texans remained loyal to the Constitution of that date. A second flag, of gold-fringed blue silk with a spread eagle in the centre above the legend '*God & Liberty*', emblazoned in black overall '*First Company of Texan Volunteers From New Orleans*', flew above the unit's barracks.

The slow Mexican bombardment continued, knocking a few stones out of the walls but otherwise doing little harm. On 25 February Santa Anna decided to harass the garrison further and sent his sharpshooters into a group of shacks east of the river, from which they began sniping at the southern defences. They were answered by Crockett and his men, whose long rifles were as accurate at 300 yards as smoothbore muskets at one-third the range, supported by gunfire from the church and the lunette covering the south gate. Soon, the Mexicans had had enough and a sortie, executed without loss, burned the shacks to prevent their future use by the enemy. That evening, Travis sent out another dramatic appeal ending, 'Give me help, oh my Country!' The following day a party gathering wood east of the fort clashed with a Mexican patrol but returned safely. Fannin set out with a relief column from Goliad, but his heart was not in the enterprise and when a wagon broke down after covering less than a mile he delayed for 24 hours and then postponed the advance indefinitely.

On the 27th the Mexicans tried to deprive the garrison of water by cutting the irrigation channel flowing into the Alamo from the north, but were driven off. Even had the attempt succeeded, the Texans still had access to two wells, one in the former cloisters and the other in the large enclosure. On the other hand, the enemy had begun using the hours of darkness to maintain his policy of harassment and numerous alarms deprived the defenders of sleep. Worried by the lack of communication, Travis sent Captain James B. Bonham, another South Carolinian lawyer, to emphasize the gravity of the situation. Throughout 28 February the

Mexican bombardment was continuous. The effects of this, combined with a depressing drizzle, lowered the spirits of the garrison. Crockett suggested that what was needed was some music and he set to with his fiddle, taking turns with John McGregor, a Scot from Nacogdoches, who had brought his bagpipes with him; and, no doubt, there were men willing to contribute a song and join in a chorus or two. At the end of it, everyone felt much better.

So far, Santa Anna's prosecution of the siege could hardly be described as energetic, but on the morning after the concert it was observed that, overnight, new batteries had been constructed closer to the fort. This, coupled with the appearance of Santa Anna and his staff, riding just beyond cannon shot and surveying the defences through their telescopes, indicated that the siege had entered a new and more dangerous phase. It did not escape Santa Anna's notice that not only was the north wall of the enclosure less heavily defended than other sectors, but also that its approaches could not be covered by flanking fire from other positions within the defences.

During the early hours of 1 March, the eighth day of the siege, the 32 men of the Gonzales Ranging Company of Mounted Volunteers, led by Lieutenant George Kimball, a hatter from New York, rode into the Alamo. Here, at last, was proof that Travis's appeals were being heeded. The Texans, now in good heart, celebrated by firing two cannon-balls at the house which they thought to be Santa Anna's headquarters. This was located in the plaza of San Antonio, so it was a long shot, but one of the rounds reached its target. The cumulative effects of the bombardment were now beginning to make themselves felt and the garrison spent much of its time patching up the damage. On 2 March the Texan Assembly, meeting at Washington-on-the-Brazos, issued its Declaration of Independence. Those in the Alamo, who were technically fighting in defence of the Mexican Constitution of 1824, remained unaware that they were now soldiers of the new Republic.

On 3 March Captain Bonham returned from Goliad, pursued by the enemy, who were checked by fire from the walls. The news he brought Travis was sombre. Fannin, a prey to indecision, had decided to march to the relief of the embattled fort, but had again postponed his advance indefinitely. In the light of this, and the sight of Mexican reinforcements reaching Santa Anna's camp, Travis accepted that the end was probably near. That night he sent a dispatch to Governor Smith, declaring that: 'The victory will cost the enemy so dear, that it will be worse for him than a defeat.'

Dawn on 4 March revealed that a Mexican battery had been established within 250 yards of the north wall of the enclosure. Travis, wishing to conserve his powder and ammunition to meet the inevitable assault, severely restricted the return fire from the Alamo's cannon. This was the signal Santa Anna had been waiting for, since it revealed that

33

the Texans had expended most of their munitions. Accordingly, he began work on the detailed planning of his attack. Once more, a sense of gloom hung over the fort. Several of the Mexican-born defenders slipped away and Travis, wishing to be fair to the rest of his men, assembled them on 5 March and offered them the chance to escape. Legend has it that he drew a line in the dust with his sword, declaring that he intended remaining in the Alamo to inflict the maximum possible loss on the enemy, and that those who wished to say with him were to cross the line. It is said that Bowie had himself carried over the line in his bed and that the rest followed, all save a veteran of Napoleon's army named Louis Rose, who made good his escape; later, Rose's claim that he had been a member of the Alamo's garrison was not believed. Other versions are less certain as to details, but whatever the truth of the matter, the fact is that the men decided to remain with Travis at a time when escape was clearly still possible.

The Mexican guns had been firing all day and by evening had opened a breach in the north wall of the enclosure. When they ceased fire at 2200 the garrison attempted to close this by erecting a stockade on top of the piled rubble. Travis sent out what was to be his last appeal to Fannin, commenting that as a result of the enemy's close-quarter fire, '. . . every shot goes through, as the walls are weak'. Even Crockett, normally optimistic, suggested that they should march out and die in the open, rather than remain cooped up behind the battered walls.

Altogether, Santa Anna now had some 2,000 men available, of which he intended employing 1,800 in four assault columns plus a reserve. The south face of the defences was to be attacked by the light companies of the Matamoros, Jiménez and San Luis Battalions, under Colonel Juan Morales; the eastern defences by the fusilier companies of the Matamoros and Jiménez Battalions, under Colonel José Maria Romero; and the main assault was to be delivered against the vulnerable northern perimeter by two columns, that on the north-eastern sector consisting of the Toluca and part of the San Luis Battalions under Colonel Francisco Duca, that on the north-western sector by the Aldama and three companies of the San Luis Battalions under Cós, who apparently no longer considered himself bound by his parole. All columns were equipped with scaling ladders, axes and crowbars. The reserve, consisting of the grenadier companies of the five battalions and the engineers, was retained by Santa Anna under his personal command. During the early hours of 6 March the columns moved into position. Shortly after 0500, in the pre-dawn darkness, their buglers sounded the Advance and they moved forward in open order.

Afterwards, only the Mexicans were able to describe the general course of events, but it is known that the alarm was given by Captain John J. Baugh, Travis's second in command and adjutant, and that Travis ran to the north wall armed with a shotgun. It is known, too, that many of the Texans had several weapons loaded and ready on the firesteps and they blazed away with these while the cannon fired until they could be depressed no further. The north-eastern attack column was torn apart and its commander, Duca, was killed. Cós's men reached the wall and began raising their ladders, only to be beaten back, but during their repulse Travis was shot through the head and died almost immediately. Morales' attack against the southern defences was also held. That by Romero on the eastern sector sustained such serious casualties that the survivors drew off to the north, joining the remnant of Duca's column.

While General Manuel Castrillon reorganized the northern attack force, Santa Anna ordered his band to strike up. It was, of course, quite usual for bands to play their troops into action, but on this occasion Santa Anna's choice of music was intended to convey a message to both sides, for it was the '*Deguello*', believed to have had its origins in a trumpet call used during the Spanish wars against the Moors, signifying a fight to the death. Certainly, its implications would have been quite clear to the few native-born Mexicans remaining in the Alamo, but to most of those present the distant notes would merely have sounded mournful, and perhaps a little creepy.

A second assault was launched, and thrown back. It seems probable that at this point Santa Anna reinforced his columns with units of the reserve, for when the third assault came in it possessed a drive almost certainly imparted by the grenadier companies, the best soldiers in their battalions. Curiously, the commander of the engineers, Colonel de la Peña, later remarked that the reserve was not needed, although this is clearly not the same as saying it was not committed.

Simultaneously, Cós's column forced a barricaded postern at the north-western angle of the defences, smashed their way through the flimsy stockade covering the breach, and overwhelmed the defenders of the north wall. At the same time, Morales' men obtained a footing at the south-western corner of the enclosure, capturing the 18-pounder gun, and were quickly reinforced. With the Mexican tidal wave pouring into the compound from north and south, Baugh ordered the defenders back from the walls to the western portion of the old conventual buildings, known as the Long Barracks, which had been prepared as a secondary line of defence. Crockett and his men, who had farthest to run, were cut off and killed, fighting with clubbed rifles against the more numerous bayonets of the Mexicans. Despite galling fire from the church and the convent, Morales then cleared the Low Barracks on each side of the main gate, but it seems likely that the defenders of the Long Barracks imposed a temporary check on Cós, inflicting unexpectedly heavy loss with their fire and forcing the Mexicans to seek refuge in the water-course running the length of the enclosure. This was soon resolved, however, for the cannon on the walls were swung round and battered breaches in the thin walls. The Mexicans swarmed through these and a savage struggle ensued in which the Texans were overwhelmed. Bowie, fighting with pistols and knife from his bed, was bayonetted repeatedly. A few of the defenders attempted to escape, probably over the east wall, but the Mexican cavalry were waiting and they were cut down.

There remained the church, where Captain Almeron Dickinson, the garrison's principal artillery officer, held out with Bonham and a few men. The door was blasted in with the 18-pounder and the final Mexican rush spared none save the garrison's dependants. An attempt to explode the remaining stock of gunpowder was frustrated. 'On top of the church building I saw eleven Texians,' recalled Sergeant Becerra, whose squad had captured a cannon. 'They had some small pieces of artillery and were firing on the cavalry and on those engaged in making the escalade. Their ammunition was exhausted and they were loading with pieces of iron and nails. The captured piece was placed in a position to reach them, doubly charged, and fired with so much effect that they ceased working their pieces.'

By 0630 the fighting, if not the killing, was over, the capture of the Alamo having taken some 90 minutes to complete. The Mexicans loss was in the region of 600, of whom approximately one-third were killed. A similar proportion would have been seriously wounded and, because of the primitive medical services of the day, a large number of them would have died or been unfit for further service. Becerra's squad was among those detailed to collect the Mexican dead and wounded. 'It was a fearful sight. Our lifeless soldiers covered the ground surrounding the Alamo. They were heaped inside the fortress . . . The killed were generally struck in the head. The wounds were in the neck, or shoulder, seldom below that. The firing of the besieged was fearfully precise. When a Texas rifle was levelled on a Mexican he was considered as good as dead. All this indicates the dauntless bravery and the cool self-possession of the men who were engaged in a hopeless conflict.'

Given that an overall casualty return of one-third had not been anticipated, the courage of the Mexicans in pressing their assault was undeniable but, as Colonel Juan Almonte remarked, 'Another such victory and we are ruined.' Travis had been as good as his word.

Santa Anna rode in and ordered the local Alcalde to point out the bodies of Travis, Bowie and Crockett. Seven prisoners were then dragged before him. One, a Mexican named Brigido Guerrero, managed to convince his captors that he had been held prisoner by the Texans, but the remaining six were killed on the spot. The women and children present were treated courteously by Santa Anna and his officers and allowed to leave, as was Travis's Negro servant John, who was technically a non-combatant. The bodies of the garrison were then burned, the defences of the Alamo dismantled, and the cannon buried after their trunnions had been smashed off.

The garrison of the Alamo were not professional soldiers, although some had military experience. A small number owned property in Texas but most had little to gain from the conflict, even if they were victorious. Yet, they deliberately chose to sacrifice themselves. Of the 189 men who served in the Alamo, the birthplace of all but twenty are known. One was a Dane, two were Germans and at least nine were native-born Mexicans. Those born in the United States numbered 128, the largest contingents coming from Tennessee with thirty-three, Virginia with thirteen, Kentucky with twelve and Pennsylvania with ten, the majority of their names revealing Anglo-Saxon or Celtic roots. Of the remainder, twelve were born in England, twelve in Ireland, four in Scotland and one in Wales. Thus, most of those present were heirs to democratic ideals which had been fought for on both sides of the Atlantic. They belonged to an age in which freedom and liberty were tangible rather abstract concepts and, because Travis and Crockett were able to inspire them, they fought for their beliefs.

Following the fall of the Alamo, Santa Anna split his army into several columns which advanced deeper into Texan territory. Houston was forced into a hasty withdrawl from Gonzales. Fannin, having abandoned Goliad, marched to join him but was caught in the open and forced to surrender. He and more than 300 of his men were marched back to Goliad and on 27 March were massacred in cold blood.

The new republic had entered its darkest hour, but help was on the way. The American public had been stirred by Travis's appeals, roused by the defence of the Alamo, shocked by Crockett's death and deeply angered by the massacres. More volunteers, arms and money arrived and Houston was at last able to concentrate and train the army under his own supervision. By the third week of April Santa Anna's own column had become dangerously isolated. This was the situation Houston had been waiting for, and by means of forced marches he brought his own army, consisting of about 800 men and two guns, within striking distance. During the afternoon of 21 April, while the Mexicans were taking their siesta, he launched an attack on their camp beside the River San Jacinto. Advancing with shouts of 'Remember the Alamo! Remember Goliad!' the furious Texans burst into the camp and in eighteen minutes routed the enemy for the loss of two men killed and 23 wounded. About 600 Mexicans were killed and 730 were captured. At the height of the slaughter pleas of 'Me no Alamo!' availed little; the Aldama, Matamoros and Toluca Battalions were present in the camp, and they had contributed their share to the massacre at the Alamo.

The real culprit, Santa Anna, escaped the battle but was captured the following day in disguise. Many would gladly have lynched him there and then and several attempts were made on his life. Recognizing that his survival depended upon it, he concluded an armistice with Houston, under the terms of which the remaining Mexican troops left Texas. The Mexican Government repudiated the agreement but on 4 July the new republic was formally recognized by the United States and ten years later was absorbed into the Union.

CHAPTER 3
The Demons of Camerone
30 APRIL 1863

In 1831 Paris was a powder keg ready to explode. The city was not only a Mecca for political dissidents from all over Europe, but was also riven by the factional rivalries of Bourbon absolutists, Bonapartists, anti-clericalists, conservatives, liberals and a starving mob only too anxious to loot and riot against a less than popular administration. By far the most dangerous element of this volatile population were former members of the Royal Swiss Guard and the Regiment of Hohenlohe, also recruited from foreigners, which had been disbanded when Charles X was replaced on the throne by his more liberal cousin, Louis-Philippe, the previous year. These men, trained, disciplined, resentful and unemployed, were willing participants in the rioting and posed a serious threat to the political establishment. The problem was, what to with them without resorting to violence or upsetting delicate sensibilities?

After one particularly serious riot involving the disbanded mercenaries the veteran Minister of War, Marshal Soult, is said to have mused: 'So they wish to fight? Then let them bleed or shovel sand in the conquest of North Africa!' And so, with Royal Assent, the Foreign Legion was conceived, initially as a mercenary force which would be employed beyond the boundaries of France.

Men joined the Legion for a variety of reasons. Some, as Soult had intended, were mercenaries seeking re-employment; some were poltical refugees; some sought escape from their wives or their debts; some, down on their luck, wanted a fresh start and time to sort themselves out; and some were simple adventurers attracted by the prospect of soldiering in exotic lands. If the Legion liked the look of a man if would permit him to engage under a *nomme de guerre* and preserve his anonymity but, contrary to popular fiction, it was not a refuge for criminals nor were those convicted of crimes permitted to engage as an alternative to penal servitude. The truth was that the Legion was anything but a soft option. Many of the original recruits were a rough lot, requiring the firmest handling before they were knocked into shape, and the tradition of strict discipline has been maintained ever since.

A considerable body of French opinion regarded the formation of the Legion as a national disgrace and was deeply offended that mercenaries should be employed to fight France's battles for her. For the same reason, the Regular Army was inclined to distance itself from the Legion, although it ensured that if there were a dirty job to be done, it would be the Legion that did it. Already isolated from family, home, country and even from Europe itself, the Legion was soon aware that it was also despised by the very people for whom it was fighting. Naturally, it turned inwards upon itself and soon developed a fierce *esprit de corps* best expressed by its unofficial motto 'Legio Patria Nostra' – The Legion is Our Country. It was to the Legion that the soldier's loyalty lay, not to France.

The Legion served the first years of its life in Algeria, but in 1835 was cynically made available to the Spanish Government for service in the Carlist War. Few survived, but the concept had proved so successful that it was reformed in France and immediately sent back to Africa. In 1848 Louis-Philippe was forced to abdicate and was succeeded by Prince Louis Napoleon, a nephew of Napoleon Bonaparte, first as President of the Second Republic, and then as Napoleon III, Emperor of the French. It was to be France's misfortune that while Napoleon possessed the ambitions of his uncle, his abilities were markedly inferior. He was, in fact, viewed by the elder statesmen of Europe as a dangerous parvenu whose devious intrigues posed a serious threat to international security.

During the Crimean War elements of the Legion took part in the Battles of the Alma and Inkerman as well as the Siege of Sevastopol. In 1859, during the war between France and Piedmont on the one hand and the Austro-Hungarian Empire on the other, Legion regiments fought at the Battles of Magenta and Solferino, the latter being so sanguinary that it led directly to the founding of the International Red Cross movement. Thus far, the Legion had proved itself the equal of any infantry in the world, but it had yet to prove that it was in a class of its own. The opportunity to do so occurred in Mexico.

A civil war had ravaged Mexico from 1857 to 1860, damaging the economy so seriously that the new President, Benito Juarez, suspended payment of foreign debts. The countries with most to lose, the United Kingdom, France and Spain, mounted a joint expedition which occupied Vera Cruz in December 1861. The British and Spanish, recognizing that blood could not be got from a stone, withdrew the following April, leaving Napoleon free to pursue one of the most astonishing conspiracies in history. His aim was nothing less than establishing a puppet French empire in Mexico, and since the United States was involved in its own Civil War there was no one to deny him. He had even acquired a monarch, the Archduke Maximilian, brother of the Austrian Kaiser Franz Joseph, to occupy the throne he had created. Franz Joseph attempted to dissuade Maximilian but the latter, a sincere if simple man, believed that he had a duty to serve and intended to fulfil it. Unfortunately, no one had consulted the Mexicans, and they soon made it plain that they had no intention of having a foreign master thrust upon them. When French troops attempted to march inland towards Mexico City they were sharply checked at Puebla on 5 May 1862 and forced to retire. It was clear that substantial reinforcements would be required before the advance could be resumed and in September an additional 30,000 men began arriving at Vera Cruz.

At first, the Legion was not involved and, somewhat unsubordinately, its junior officers sent a petition directly to Napoleon requesting active service in the campaign. Unknown to them, the devious Emperor was already considering a plan which involved seconding the Legion to Maximilian for a period of ten years, but their suggestion was accepted just the same, albeit accompanied by a sharp reprimand for daring to go over the heads of the generals. The Legion's first contingent, a composite regiment consisting of two battalions and a headquarters company, commanded by Colonel Pierre Jeanningros, reached Vera Cruz on 28 March 1863.

The previous month the French army had again pushed inland, leaving the sweltering heat of the foetid coastal plain as it climbed steadily into the cooler, healthier uplands of the central plateau. At Puebla the Mexicans again made a stand and the French were compelled to invest the town. Immediately, their 150-mile-long line of communication was subjected to attack by guerrilla bands. It required large numbers of troops to protect it and the Commander-in-Chief, General Elie-Frederic Forey, made no bones about the task he had set the recent arrivals: 'I preferred to leave foreigners rather than Frenchmen to guard the most unhealthy area, the tropical zone from Vera Cruz to Cordoba, where the malaria reigns.' It came as no surprise to the legionnaires to find that they had been given yet another dirty job. Philosophically, they set up fortified posts along the route and began escorting convoys between them. Soon, however, the over-heated swamplands began exacting their toll and daily the ranks were thinned by yellow fever, typhus and malaria.

Meanwhile, Forey had requested heavy artillery with which to smash the defences of Puebla. The guns, together with ammunition and other supplies, including the army's pay chests filled with gold, left Vera Cruz on 15 April in a convoy consisting of 64 horse-drawn vehicles. Surrounded as it was by a bitterly hostile population, neither presence of the convoy nor its nature could be kept secret from the Mexican authorities, and since its progress amounted to little more than a painful crawl, the probability was that it would be attacked in strength. Its security was a matter of grave concern to Colonel Jeanningros, who had established his regimental headquarters at Chiquihuite in the foothills of the central plateau, and on 27 April he sent back two companies to reinforce the escort.

The French were not quite blind as far as intelligence-gathering was concerned, having attracted some support among the local Indians. On 29 April an Indian arrived at Jeanningros' headquarters and confirmed that the Mexicans were indeed planning to attack the convoy. Furthermore, they attached such importance to the operation that, in addition to guerrilla bands, they were employing regular army units which included several cavalry squadrons and three infantry battalions. The only details which the scout could not supply were the time and place of the attack, but as the Mexicans were already on the march it was obviously imminent.

Jeanningros' men were already stretched very thin on the ground by the nature of their employment, but he decided to send his 1st Battalion's Third Company on a reconnaissance in force back down the Vera Cruz road to the hamlet of Palo Verde, some twenty miles distant. The precise location of the convoy was unknown, but, if met, the company was to join the escort. If, on the other hand, neither the convoy nor the enemy had been encountered by the time Palo Verde was reached, it was to return to Chiquihuite. The one contingency which had not been allowed for was meeting the enemy on the march back.

The Third Company had a nominal strength of 120, but disease had reduced this to a mere 62 fit men. Some of the legionnaires were native-born Frenchmen, the rest being Poles, Italians, Germans and Spaniards. There was also one legionnaire, Peter Dicken, whose name suggests that his origins may have been British, or possibly American. In age the men varied between grizzled senior NCOs approaching their middle years and two 17-year-old recruits. Naturally, some had an interesting history. Corporal Berg, for example, had formerly held a commission in the French Army and had served in North Africa and Syria. Cashiered for misconduct, he had begun to rebuild his life by enlisting as a private soldier in the Legion.

As the Third Company's officers were all sick, Jeanningros detailed the battalion adjutant, Captain Jean Danjou, to lead the patrol, accompanied by Second-Lieutenant Napoleon Villain, the paymaster, and Second-Lieutenant Maudet, also of Headquarters Company. Danjou was an officer of wide experience who had served in North Africa, the Crimea and Italy. In place of his left hand, which he had lost in the Crimea, he wore a wooden hand with flexible joints, held in position by a leather cuff. Villain and Maudet were also long-service professionals who had worked their way through the ranks to become sergeant-majors and then been commissioned. Villain had been decorated for gallantry at Magenta and Maudet had been awarded the British Crimean Medal for his part in the Battle of Inkerman.

The company left Chiquihuite at about midnight, its reserve ammunition and rations carried on pack mules. At 0230 it reached a post held by the battalion's grenadier company at Paso del Macho and halted briefly to brew coffee. The grenadiers' commander, a Captain Saussier, worried by Danjou's lack of numbers, offered to reinforce the company with a platoon of his own. Danjou, however, was anxious to cover as much ground as possible in the cool of the night and, rather than wait

41

for the men to be roused, he declined. The march was resumed and, shortly before 0700 the company passed an abandoned and partially ruined hacienda named Camerone. It attracted little attention, since there were many such deserted farmsteads along the road. A mile or two beyond lay the hamlet of Palo Verde, equally deserted and ruinous. This was the limit of the patrol and, after posting sentries, Danjou permitted his men a rest during which they began to brew coffee. There had been no contact with the enemy during the march, nor was there any sign of the convoy.

Hardly had the camp kettles begun to boil than dust clouds were seen approaching from the foothills to the west. The volume of dust indicated cavalry which, in the circumstances, could only be hostile. Danjou was now faced with a number of difficult decisions. Given the overall context of his mission, he might have considered dispatching one of the subalterns on his own horse to find and warn the convoy. He did not do so and in the final analysis it mattered little, as the convoy commander was already aware of the increased threat and had halted at Soledad, some twenty miles distant, to await further reinforcement. As far as the Third Company was concerned, Danjou had three alternatives to consider. The first was to continue along the Soledad road in the hope that he would reach the convoy before he was run down in the open, but this course was fraught with too many risks and would have been rejected immediately. The second was to stand and fight in the limited cover available at Palo Verde, an alternative which would almost certainly result in the destruction of the company. The third, which he adopted, involved the company trying to work its way westward past the

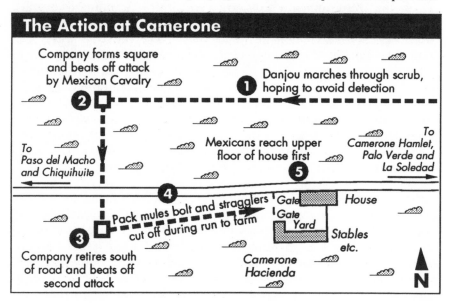

The Action at Camerone

Company forms square and beats off attack by Mexican Cavalry

1 Danjou marches through scrub, hoping to avoid detection

2

To Paso del Macho and Chiquihuite

Mexicans reach upper floor of house first
5

To Camerone Hamlet, Palo Verde and La Soledad

4 Pack mules bolt and stragglers cut off during run to farm

Gate House
Gate Yard
Stables etc.

3 Company retires south of road and beats off second attack

Camerone Hacienda

N

advancing cavalry by taking advantage of the tall, thick scrub which covered the country. The plan was hazardous, but at least the vegetation provided some concealment and made it difficult for the horsemen to deploy.

The mules were hastily packed and the company moved into the scrub to the north of the road. It then began marching westwards with scouts out ahead, the main body almost certainly moving in two parallel platoon columns which could quickly be formed into a single square if the need arose. All went well until the company neared Camerone, where a shot cracked out and one of the scouts was wounded. A number of legionnaires rushed the hacienda only to find that the sniper had vanished. Danjou resumed the march with the intention of trying to reach a nearby Indian village and had covered a further mile when the Mexican cavalry, alerted by the shot, cantered into view.

The horsemen, some of whom were lancers, spotted the Legion company at once and deployed to attack. Danjou ordered his men to form square. Two squadrons advanced simultaneously to attack from different directions, walking their horses to within 75 yards of the Legion ranks before they charged. This sort of thing was all in a day's work to the veterans of Algeria. Danjou held his fire until the enemy had closed to within fifty yards, then ordered two volleys followed by independent fire. Saddles were emptied and horses went down. The Mexicans, their attack blunted, wheeled away, but began circling the little square. Appreciating that there was nothing to be gained by remaining where they were, Danjou decided that they would fight their way back to Camerone. This was easier said than done, for the high scrub presented as much of an obstacle to the passage of a formed square as it did to the ranks of the cavalry. Inevitably, gaps appeared in the hedge of bayonets and the horsemen spurred in to cut off stragglers. Frightened by the firing, the company's mules bolted, taking with them the reserve ammunition, rations and, worst of all, the water. The matter should have ended there and then, for the Mexican commander, who had 800 men at his disposal, could have sent a squadron galloping to Camerone and so denied its use to the legionnaires. A few of his troops certainly used their initiative and had established themselves in the upper storey of the hacienda by the time the company reached the buildings.

Sixteen men had been lost during the retreat, leaving Danjou with two officers and forty-six legionnaires, some of whom were already wounded; Legionnaire Lai, the company drummer, staggered in with no less than seven lance wounds. The precarious refuge consisted of nothing more than the farmhouse and a walled courtyard in one corner of which was a ramshackle lean-to stable block, but the men set to erecting barricades and improvising loopholes for themselves. They were harassed immediately by the Mexicans on the upper floor of the house, but attempts to eject the latter failed as there was no direct access to them.

This meant that a portion of the company's strength always had to be directed against the enemy within, whose fire covered most of the courtyard.

There followed a protracted fire fight, interspersed with attempts by groups of dismounted cavalrymen to rush the more tumbledown sections of the wall. None came close to success. At about 0930 a Mexican lieutenant came forward under a flag of truce and spoke to Danjou. He pointed out that the company was now surrounded by 2,000 men and recommended an honourable surrender as an alternative to further pointless loss of life. Despite assurances that he and his men would be decently treated as prisoners of war, Danjou was immovable, commenting that he had plenty of ammunition and that there would be no surrender.

This was not mere death-or-glory bravado. By now, Danjou was clearly aware that the Mexicans were the force which had been assembled for the attack on the convoy. Furthermore, because of the casualties they had sustained, they had allowed themselves to become embroiled in a pointless battle with a half-strength Legion company which should simply have been contained while the primary mission continued. Surrounded in the hacienda under the blazing tropical sun, the legionnaires presented no serious threat to the operation and in due course thirst would have compelled them to surrender without another shot being fired. That, however, was not the enemy's inclination and Danjou decided that it would be to the convoy's ultimate benefit if he continued to absorb their entire attention as well as writing down their strength to the best of his ability. As he visited each area of the defences in turn he extracted a personal oath from every man that he would fight to the bitter end.

The fight continued. At approximately 1100, while darting across the courtyard, Danjou was hit by sniper fire from the upper storey of the house. Two of his men dragged him to safety, but he died five minutes later, and command devolved upon the senior of the two subalterns, Second-Lieutenant Villain. Shortly after, the distant sound of a bugle call was heard. Hopes that it was Jeannigros at the head of a relief force were quickly dashed when Sergeant Morzycki, who had established himself in a vantage point on the stable roof, shouted that the Mexican cavalry had been joined by about 1,000 infantry.

The commander of the force detailed to attack the convoy, Colonel Francisco Milan, had arrived with three battalions, and the numbers surrounding the hacienda were further swelled by local *guerrilleros*. The odds against the Legion company, already impossible, had reached absurd proportions. Furthermore, the Mexican regulars were armed with modern American carbines and rifles. Nevertheless, Villain rejected a further summons to surrender. His men repulsed several more assaults, but the sheer volume of fire being directed at them was producing a steady toll of casualties. By now the sun had turned the interior of the courtyard into an oven and the legionnaires, having drained the last contents of the water-bottles, were beginning to suffer the agonies of thirst. Some of the wounded, old African hands, appreciated the importance of retaining fluid and drank their own urine. At 1400 Villain was shot dead and Maudet assumed command. Ammunition was beginning to run low, but, using rounds taken from the pouches of the dead and wounded, the survivors fought back. Some of the Mexicans who had succeeded in reaching the wall began to knock holes in it. Others brought up straw bales and set fire to them, the acrid smoke adding to the legionnaires' torment. Still the defence held.

At 1700 Milan, angered by the militarily preposterous situation which had developed, harangued his men fiercely on the subject of their own and the national honour. When Maudet, who had only twelve men left on their feet, rejected a final call to surrender, a concerted assault was launched. After an hour's fighting the Mexicans were in control of the entire house and an outbuilding, leaving Maudet and five unhurt legionnaires penned in the stable. Their ammunition was all but expended and the end had clearly come, but true to the promise they had given Danjou, they refused to give up. Instead, they wrenched a barricade aside and launched a desperate bayonet charge into the mass of Mexican infantry. Maudet was mortally wounded at once and Legionnaire Katau, attempting to shield him, was riddled with nineteen bullets; Legionnaire Leonhart also sustained moral wounds. The three survivors, Corporal Maine, Legionnaire Constantin and the less seriously wounded Legionnaire Wenzel, stood back to back, expecting death and prepared to kill, their bayonets circling warily at the circle of dark faces around them. The Mexicans seemed awed, and for the moment none of them was prepared to make the first move. Then one of their senior officers thrust his way forward and approached Maine. 'Will you surrender now?' he asked quietly.

'On condition we keep our weapons and you look after our officer,' replied Maine. 'To men such as you one refuses nothing.' The three were brought to Colonel Milan, who found difficulty in accepting that they were the only survivors. When convinced that this was the case, he exploded: *'Pero, non son hombres – son demonios!'* (Truly, these aren't men – they're demons!).

The Mexicans were as good as their word. The buildings were searched for the wounded, who were well treated. Seven, including Maudet, died in captivity, but sixteen survived and, together with the sixteen who had been cut off and captured during the retreat to the farm, were exchanged for an equal number of Mexican prisoners about a month after the battle. In the interim, Milan permitted Corporal Berg to send a short note to Jeanningros: 'The Third Company of the 1st is dead, *mon Colonel*, but it did enough to make those who speak of it say, "It had nothing but good soldiers."' This was not the first news that Jeanningros had had of the lost company, nor were those in Mexican hands the only survivors. Indian reports of a battle lasting all day, and the failure of any of Danjou's men to return, must have prepared him for the worst. On 1 May he led a force to Camerone and a mile short of the hacienda came upon a heavily bloodstained figure in Legion uniform lying beside the road. It was Lai, the drummer, who, in addition to the multiple wounds he had sustained from the Mexican lancers, had also been shot twice during the defence of the farm. He had been left for dead when the wounded were removed and was lying under several bodies when he regained consciousness. After dragging himself along the road his strength had finally given out.

From Lai, Jeanningros learned the details of the engagement and also the enemy's strength. He reached the hacienda, now pock-marked by thousands of bullets, to find that it had been cleared by the enemy, who had placed the dead legionnaires in a ditch. Conscious that Milan's force might still be in the area, and not wishing to share the fate of the Third Company, he returned to Chiquihuite, using the scrub for cover. Two days later he was back with every man he could muster to meet the convoy at Palo Verde. The dead of Camerone were buried, a task so grim that not even Danjou's body could be identified, so thoroughly had the vultures and coyotes performed their grisly work.

The self-sacrificial stand of the Third Company had its reward. The precise number of casualties sustained by the Mexicans at Camerone remains unknown, although 300 is the most common estimate, of which not less than one-third were killed. The encounter seems to have shaken Milan so badly that he made no serious attempt to dispute the passage of the convoy through Legion-controlled territory. The arrival of the guns at Puebla proved decisive. The fortress fell on 17 May and the road to Mexico City was open. Maximilian was enthroned the following month, but a bitter guerrilla war continued for four years, at the end of which Napoleon, threatened with intervention by the United States, withdrew his support and his army. Typically, Maximilian refused to desert the few Mexicans who remained loyal to him. He was captured by the Juaristas and executed by firing squad on 19 June 1867.

During the rest of the period that the French Army remained in Mexico, its units were ordered to halt and present arms whenever they marched past Camerone. Later, most of the site was cleared when a railway line was built over it, but in 1893 the Mexican Government permitted a monument to be erected nearby. Little is known of what became of the Third Company's survivors. Corporal Maine was commissioned on his release from captivity and rose to the rank of Captain. Corporal Berg also received an immediate commission but was killed in a duel with another subaltern two years later; one story has it that his opponent was Maine. Shortly after the battle a local farmer, rooting in the ruins of Camerone, came across Danjou's wooden hand. He kept it as a curiosity for two years then, having learned something of its history, offered to sell it to General Achille Bazaine, who had succeeded Forey as the French Commander-in-Chief in Mexico. Bazaine, who had once served with the Legion himself, bought it for a nominal sum. It became the Legion's most treasured possession and was housed in the Hall of Honour at Sidi Bel Abbes until 1962, when it was moved to the Legion's new depot at Aubagne, near Marseilles.

Camerone established the Legion's reputation as one of the world's élite fighting units, and it remains the yardstick by which it measures itself. Every recruit learns the story and is taught that this is the standard to which he must aspire. Every year the anniversary of the battle is celebrated by Legionnaires, wherever they are serving, but for members of the 1st Regiment the event has a special significance, for along its ranks is paraded a glass-sided casket containing the wooden hand of Jean Danjou, the only tangible relic of a courageous, capable and determined officer who, reading the wider implications of the battle in which he was involved, recognized that the sacrifice of himself and his few men would benefit the Legion and the French Army as a whole.

CHAPTER 4
The Little Big Horn
25–26 JUNE 1876

On 4 July 1876 the United States of America commemorated its first centennial. It was a moment of supreme optimism in which men could put behind them the tragedy of the recent Civil War and look to a future bright with the promise of a young nation already emerging as one of the great powers of the world. Eager immigrants were arriving daily to swell the population, the national wealth was growing steadily and, above all, the old frontier was being pushed further and further west as new lands were opened up. For those willing to work and possessing the will to succeed, the possiblities offered by the next century seemed limitless.

The country celebrated its birthday in style. Among the few who remained at work throughout the festivities were the duty telegraph operators, and shortly before midnight on 5 July they prepared to receive a long transmission datelined Bismarck, Dakota Territory. The clattering key's first sentence left them dumbfounded: *'General Custer attacked the Indians June 25 and he with every officer and man in five companies were killed.'* The dispatch which followed provided brief details of a battle on the River Little Big Horn during which Major-General George Armstrong Custer, *beau sbreur* of the Civil War and veteran Indian fighter, together with more than 200 men of his famous 7th Cavalry, had ridden to their deaths. Naturally, the news cast a dismal shadow over the festivities and an outraged public demanded vengeance so vociferously that Congress sanctioned the expansion of the cavalry by permitting the enlistment of an additional 2,500 recruits.

Since then, the engagement on the Little Big Horn has generated more controversy, discussion, books, articles, television documentaries and films than any other event in American military history. Yet, by Civil War standards, it was the merest scuffle and was not even the first occasion on which regular troops had been worsted by Indians, although it did mark a turning-point in the long succession of Indian Wars. Much of the fascination derives from the complex character of Custer himself, and from the fact that he died on a stricken field like some monarch from the Age of Chivalry, surrounded by his kinsmen and men-at-arms, none of whom lived to tell the story. The only witness to the end of Custer and his men were Indians and when, at length, they spoke, their version was fragmented and delivered in an idiom difficult to relate to precise events.

Even today, after a long century's examination of the written and oral evidence available, supplemented by detailed archaeological examination of the site, the battlefield still clings to many secrets, although the main course of the engagement has been somewhat clarified.

Few would claim that George Custer was an intellectual soldier. The truth was, in temperament he had more in common with the medieval knight than with the professional cavalry officer of the mid-nineteenth century. He graduated from West Point bottom of his class at the outbreak of the Civil War and served as a subaltern with the 5th Cavalry at the First Battle of Bull Run. He quickly demonstrated that he was courageous, dashing and had a sharp eye for the tactical battle, and in 1862 he was promoted captain. Altogether, he was breveted five times for gallantry and by 1865 he had become a Major-General of Volunteers, commanding the Michigan Cavalry, which he led during the final phases of the war. He played an important part in the engagements culminating in Lee's surrender at Appomattox Court House, for which he was presented with Lee's flag of truce; one story has it that he also made off with the table on which Grant and Lee signed their historic undertaking.

Before his Volunteer cavalry regiments disbanded he told them: 'You have never lost a gun, never lost a colour, and never been defeated; and notwithstanding the numerous engagements in which you have borne a prominent part, you have captured every piece of artillery which the enemy has dared to open upon you.' The admiration was not altogether mutual for, while unsparing of himself, he was a demanding leader and imposed so harsh a discipline that one of his brigades was brought to the verge of mutiny.

In fact, the Boy General, as he was dubbed at the time, had several serious failings. Of these the most obvious was a marked tendency to over-project his personality, evidenced by the unathorized black velvet uniforms he designed for himself, adorned with galloons of gold braid, which were clearly symptomatic of a desire to present a certain image to superiors and subordinates alike. Rather more serious was his inclination to pursue objectives without paying due regard to the details by which they were to be achieved. That his objectives were, nevertheless, attained, he was inclined to ascribe laughingly to 'Custer's Luck'. There was of course no guarantee that such luck would last forever. Again, it was significant that while he was prepared to impose discipline, he was selective in its application to himself. For example, having once ordered the summary execution of twelve soldiers for desertion, he later absented himself without leave to visit his beautiful wife. There were limits to the Army's patience and in 1867 he was court-martialled for this and sundry other offences, the sentence being suspension from duty without pay for one year.

After the war, Custer had reverted to his substantive rank of lieutenant-colonel, although he continued to be addressed as General as a matter of courtesy. He commanded the 7th Cavalry on the frontier, where the Plains Indians were fiercely resisting the inexorable westward pressure of settlers. The conflict was inevitable, as the nomadic lifestyle of the Indians was not compatible with a settled agricultural and industrial economy, a situation further aggravated when white hunters all but destroyed the immense buffalo herds on which the Indians depended for survival. The government attempted to bring the situation under control by establishing reservations and agencies which were responsible for feeding the tribes, but many Indians regarded this as demeaning and longed for their old freedoms. Some braves remained on the reservations during the hard months of winter and then left to hunt or raid according to the inclinations. This state of friction was more or less constant along the frontier, despite peace treaties the principal effects of which merely reduced the number of atrocities committed by both sides.

Numbers and weapons apart, the Indians could not hope to win in the long term, and many of them recognized the fact. Their style of warfare involved raids and ambushes, between which they were forced to feed themselves, and they were most vulnerable when they retired to their lodges for the winter. The army, however, while less mobile, fed itself and campaigned throughout the year. Custer, for one, immediately saw the advantage of launching ruthless dawn attacks on Indian villages during the winter months. He personally ordered his men to hang any brave who was not killed in the fighting, to make prisoners of their women and children, to slaughter the tribe's pony herd and to burn every tepee. This may or may not have been his own inclination, but it was certainly that of his superior, Lieutenant General Philip H. Sheridan, commander of the Military Division of the Missouri, who was prepared to pursue a policy of extermination to solve the Indian problem. To his victims, Custer was known as Yellow Hair because of the golden locks which fell to his collar; it was no compliment, for he was feared and hated and many longed for the day when that particular scalp would be nailed to a lodge pole.

Custer produced results and saw to it that his exploits were fully reported for the benefit of an admiring public. To his credit, he also worked hard to establish the reputation of his regiment. The Seventh was fortunate in that, unlike the majority of cavalry regiments on the frontier, its troops served together for most of the time, and it was thus able to establish an *esprit de corps*. On parade, the regiment presented a smart appearance as Custer followed the old European tradition of grouping horses of the same colour in troops; at one period the Seventh is known to have contained one troop each of greys, chestnuts and blacks, three of sorrels and four of bays. He also added to the regimental identity by adopting a catchy tune which was used when the troops marched past in review order or were played into action; this was the jig 'Garry Owen', the rhythm of which was suited to a fine, bouncy canter, and is said to have been introduced by one of his troop commanders, Captain Myles Keogh, an Irishman who had served previously in the Papal Zouaves. Despite its title, the regiment's role had more in common with that of mounted infantry, and this was reflected in its arms, which were the Springfield carbine, supplemented by the Colt revolver for close-quarter work. Comparatively little use had been made of sabres during the Civil War, and even less on the frontier, and as their rattling could alert an enemy Custer withdrew them into storage, where they remained until needed for ceremonial occasions.

To an outsider, all might appear well with the Seventh, but tensions existed among the regiment's officers. The causes of these were somewhat more sinister than the usual friction between old hands who had learned their business in the Civil War and the new generation of West Pointers, for this was present throughout the army and was disappearing with the passage of time. As might be expected, they were generated by Custer himself, who demanded not merely loyalty but also admiration from his subordinates. From many he received it, and their reward was to be admitted to the charmed inner circle over which he and his wife presided at Fort Abraham Lincoln; for good measure, the circle contained members of his own family, including his brother, Captain Thomas Custer, and his sister's husband, Lieutenant James Calhoun. Excluded were those who perceived his faults, refused to be impressed, or in some imagined way detracted from the regiment's glamorous image, and these men he treated almost as enemies.

One such was Major Marcus A. Reno, who was to serve as Custer's second in command during the 1876 campaign, and another was Captain Frederick W. Benteen, the regiment's senior captain. Reno had graduated from West Point in 1857 and was a veteran of a score of Civil War battles, breveted three times for gallantry and attaining the rank of Brevet Brigadier General of Volunteers in 1865. Since the war he had held a variety of appointments, many of them extra-regimental, and his record was one of useful if unspectacular service. Benteen was not a West Pointer. He had been granted a Volunteer commission in the 10th Missouri Cavalry in 1861 and enjoyed steady promotion, becoming the regiment's lieutenant colonel in 1864. He had ended his Civil War service as a colonel commanding an infantry regiment and in 1866 was accepted by the Regular Army as a captain in the 7th Cavalry. And that, as far as Custer was concerned, was where his career ended. Ten years later, Benteen had grown prematurely grey and embittered.

Ironically, shortly before the Seventh embarked on the march which would take it to the banks of the Little Big Horn, Custer had come within a whisker of losing his command. With the best of intentions, he had dipped his toe into the muddy water of politics, giving evidence to Congress with regard to corruption in high places, notably in the

Secretary of War's office and in the Indian agencies. Unfortunately, his testimony was based on hearsay and President Grant, whose personal integrity was not in question, was extremely annoyed, since some of it implicated his own brother Orvil. The President gave orders that Custer be suspended from active duty and the latter was forced to plead with his immediate superior, Major General Alfred H. Terry, commanding the Department of Dakota, for his intercession. Terry was able to enlist the support of General William Sherman and the decision was reversed, with the proviso that Custer's part in the coming campaign was restricted to command of his own regiment. Custer returned from Washington shaken by the experience but determined to restore his dented reputation with some spectacular coup.

The proximate cause of the 1876 campaign lay in the Black Hills of Wyoming and South Dakota. These formed the favourite hunting grounds of the Sioux and Cheyenne and had been unequivocally ceded to them by the government in 1868 as part of their reservation. Since then, gold had been discovered in the hills and, despite the efforts of the army to keep them out, large numbers of prospectors had converged on the area. The Indians declind to sell the mineral rights for the sum offered by Washington, and, understandably, began to regard the 1868 treaty as worthless. In 1875 they started hunting and raiding in the unceded territories beyond the boundaries of the reservation. Alarmed, the government issued a proclamation on 3 December of that year, informing the Sioux and Cheyenne that those who remained outside the reservation after 31 January 1876 would be treated as hostile. It was ignored. In March an attempt to enforce the order was foiled partly by severe weather, although an engagement on the Powder River left little doubt that the Indians were in an ugly mood and were prepared to fight.

It was decided to try again in May, using larger forces. Intelligence regarding the Indians was patchy and unreliable. They were known to be in the vast area lying between the River Yellowstone and the Big Horn Mountains, probably camped on one or more of the tributary rivers which flowed into the Yellowstone from the south: the Powder, the Tongue, the Rosebud or the Big Horn. As to their strength, the Indian Bureau believed that the absent bands could produce perhaps 800 braves, but as they moved to fresh grazing and hunting grounds every few days it was thought unlikely that so many would be met at any one time. The Bureau, however, had seriously under-estimated the numbers absent from the reservation; moreover, for once the tribes were travelling together, and they were able to field an absolute minimum of 1,500 warriors.

The architect of the campaign was Terry, who was clearly unaware of the enemy's true strength; had it been otherwise, Sherman was to comment, his plans would have taken a different form. As it was, Terry envisaged the converging advance of three columns, each capable of dealing with a force of the size estimated by the Indian Bureau, the collective action of which would be to round up the Indians and compel their return to the reservation. One column, commanded by Colonel John Gibbon and consisting of six companies of the 7th Infantry and four troops of the 2nd Cavalry, a total of 450 men, had already left Fort Ellis, Montana, on 30 March and was marching east along the northern bank of the Yellowstone. The second column, commanded by Terry himself, consisted of twelve troops of the 7th Cavalry, two companies of the 17th and one of the 6th Infantry, plus a detachment of 20th Infantry manning three Gatling machine-guns. This column, 925 strong, left Fort Abraham Lincoln on 17 May and marched westward to the Yellowstone, where it effected a junction with Gibbon's force. The third column, commanded by Brigadier General George Crook, consisting of five troops of the 2nd and ten of the 3rd Cavalry, plus two companies of the 4th and three of the 9th Infantry, a total of more than 1,000 men, left Fort Fetterman on 29 May and began penetrating the disputed area from the south.

The theory was that the Indians would be trapped between the northern and southern elements of the expedition as they converged inwards and, faced with the 2,500 men available to Terry, they would be forced to submit. The major obstacle to this was the sheer size of the operational area: as the crow flies, Fort Ellis was almost 500 miles from Fort Abraham Lincoln; Fort Abraham Lincoln was 375 miles from Fort Fetterman; and Fort Fetterman was 340 miles from Fort Ellis. A number of things therefore became apparent. First, Terry's apparent numerical superiority was widely dispersed within this immense triangle. Secondly, the northern and southern elements were unable to provide mutual support for each other's operations, nor were they able to communicate directly. And thirdly, the Indians, already concentrated, enjoyed interior lines and were thus able to attack each of Terry's columns in turn.

Terry's Crow scouts suggested that no hostiles were present east of the Rosebud and on 10 June Major Reno and six troops of the 7th Cavalry were sent off on a reconnaissance in force to verify the fact. Reno was ordered to ride up the valley of the Powder then cross to that of the Tongue, by which he would return to the Yellowstone. On 17 June however, he exceeded his instructions and continued westwards into the valley of the Rosebud, where he discovered a heavily used Indian trail leading across the hills towards the Little Big Horn river, a tributary of the Big Horn. He then returned to the Yellowstone where, despite the positive information he had obtained, he was petulantly criticized by Terry on the grounds that his presence on the Rosebud might have alerted the hostiles; the same, of course, was true of his presence on the Powder and the Tongue, had the scouts' intelligence proved inaccurate.

On 21 June Terry held an orders group aboard his floating head-quarters, the river steamer *Far West*. Present were Gibbon, Custer and Major James Brisbin, commanding the four troops of 2nd Cavalry. The

Crow scouts had observed smoke rising from the Little Big Horn valley, which coupled with the trail found by Reno, suggested that this was where the major part of the hostiles were encamped. Terry was anxious to entrap them there and to this end he devised a plan which involved Custer and his regiment marching up the Rosebud, then crossing the watershed to drive down the Little Big Horn valley; simultaneously, Gibbon was to be ferried across the Yellowstone to the mouth of the Big Horn, from where he was to march into the Little Big Horn valley from the north, so providing a blocking force. Gibbon calculated that he would not be in position until 26 June and since timing was crucial, Custer was ordered *not* to use the trail discovered by Reno, but to ascend the Rosebud to its head before turning down the Little Big Horn. Such a move, Terry felt, would not only inhibit premature springing of the trap, but would also prevent the hostiles escaping to the south. He offered Custer the three Gatling machine-guns, but these were declined on the grounds that they would slow the rate of march; he also offered to reinforce 7th Cavalry with Brisbin's four troops, but this too was declined, undoubtedly because Custer was determined that such credit as was to be earned would be his and the Seventh's alone. Once the details had been agreed, Terry's chief of staff translated them into written orders, in which Custer's copy contained the following paragraph: *'The Department Commander places too much confidence in your zeal, energy and ability to wish to impose upon you precise orders which might hamper your action when nearly in contact with the enemy.'* Naturally, Custer was delighted, for within the overall operational concept he had thus been permitted the widest possible latitude.

None of those present at Terry's orders group knew it at the time, but the entire plan was already based on a faulty premise, namely that Crook's column was still bringing pressure to bear on the hostiles from the south. The unpleasant truth, of which everyone remained in ignorance for some days to come, was that on 17 June Crook had fought a six-hour engagement against the Sioux and Cheyenne on the headwaters of the Rosebud. He had barely succeeded in holding his own and had since retired towards his base, declining to renew his advance until he received reinforcements. For their part, the hostiles were cock-a-hoop and looked forward with enthusiasm to the prospect of killing yet more soldiers.

At noon on 22 June, with the band playing *Garry Owen*, Custer led the 7th Cavalry out of camp past Terry and Gibbon. He was dressed, as was his custom when campaigning on the frontier, in a fringed buckskin suit, a planter's broad-brimmed hat and red bandana; some noted, with interest, that his yellow locks had been shorn to a less flamboyant length. As he drew level with the senior officers Gibbon called out: 'Now, Custer, don't be greedy! You wait for us!' 'No, I won't!' replied Custer, and one could make of that what one would.

The Seventh swung into the Rosebud valley and vanished from view. The regiment, followed by a pack train with fifteen days' ammunition and rations, was riding heavy; each horse, in addition to his rider and the latter's personal weapons, canteen and saddle roll, carried 100 rounds of carbine and 24 rounds of revolver ammunition, plus a 12-pound sack of oats. Despite this, Custer set a gruelling pace in intense heat. On 23 June the column marched 35 miles. The following day, it was in the saddle continuously from 0500 until 1200, covering a further 45 miles. Custer then granted his weary men and horses a three-hour respite, but had no intention of halting for the night. By now he had reached the Indian trail discovered by Reno, which he was specifically ordered to cross and proceed towards the upper reaches of the Rosebud. However, placing the widest possible interpretation on the discretionary powers granted him by Terry, he decided to follow it. At 2000 he summoned his officers and informed them that the march would continue, but that the regiment would rest the following day and attack early on the 26th, as Terry had ordered.

The night march lasted five hours, covering a mere ten miles before Custer called a halt in a ravine close to the watershed of the Wolf Mountains, the range dividing the Rosebud from the Little Big Horn. At dawn the column's Indian scouts climbed the Crow's Nest, a high feature on the ridge, from which they could look into the Little Big Horn valley, some fifteen miles distant. They observed a huge pony herd, and also smoke rising from numerous breakfast fires, although distance and the morning mist concealed the size of the village itself. Nevertheless, taking together the heavily used trail and the size of the herd, the scouts were able to inform Custer that the hostile concentration was far larger than anyone had anticipated. On the basis of this, Custer might well have stuck to his declared intention of resting that day and attacking on the morrow, had he not received a second piece of vital intelligence. During the night march a mule had shed its load and at first light a Sergeant Curtis was sent back to recover it. He had found a party of Sioux examining the packs, but when he appeared they had mounted and ridden off. While returning to the bivouac, he had observed more Indians watching the regiment from high ground.

From this point onwards, Custer knew that his every move would be known to the hostiles. A prudent commander, recognizing that he had lost the element of surprise, would have secured a sound position for his troops while he sought accurate information on the enemy's strength and dispositions, and only then embarked upon positive action if he considered it justified the risks. Custer, however, was distracted by the problems of restoring his own reputation and was concerned that the hostiles, having learned of his presence, would decamp and escape from the trap which Terry had set for them. If that happened, the responsibility would be his alone and he would be sharply censured for diverting from the route Terry had set him, thereby provoking premature contact with the enemy. He therefore decided to attack the village, notwithstanding the warning he had received regarding the hostiles' numbers and the fact that his own troops, men and horses alike, were worn out by the exertions of the previous two days. This decision not only revealed a deep contempt for his enemies, but also ignored the alternatives open to them now that they were aware of his presence. These were either to decamp, in which case the regiment would become involved solely with their rearguard, or to stand on ground of their own choosing, which would involve the Seventh in heavy fighting.

Custer was already on the shakiest possible ground, but he might have escaped some of the worst consequences of his actions had he not committed the cardinal sin of dividing his force without accurate

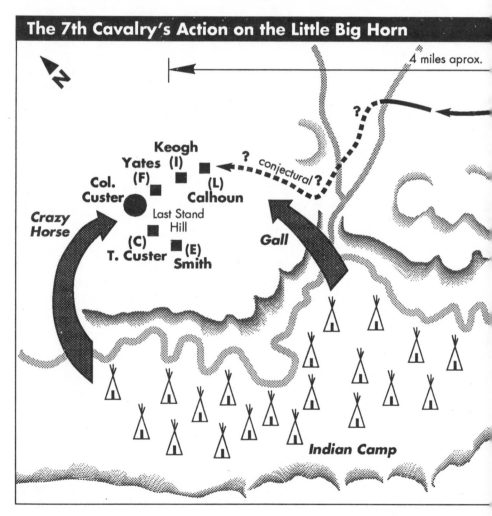

The 7th Cavalry's Action on the Little Big Horn

knowledge of the enemy's strength or precise whereabouts. His plan, attempting as it did to cover every contingency, relied too heavily on 'Custer's Luck', and was in fact a recipe for disaster. Captain Benteen, with three troops, was to carry out a reconnaissance over the bluffs to the south, the object being to ensure that the Indians were not escaping, and 'to pitch into anything' he might find or return to the regiment's principal axis of advance, depending upon circumstances; Major Reno, with another three troops, was to cross the Little Big Horn and mount a strong diversionary attack on the southern end of the village; while this was in progress Custer, with five troops under his personal command, would launch the main attack on the opposite end of the village from behind the hills to the east; the pack train, escorted by the remaining troop under Captain Thomas McDougall, was to follow Benteen.

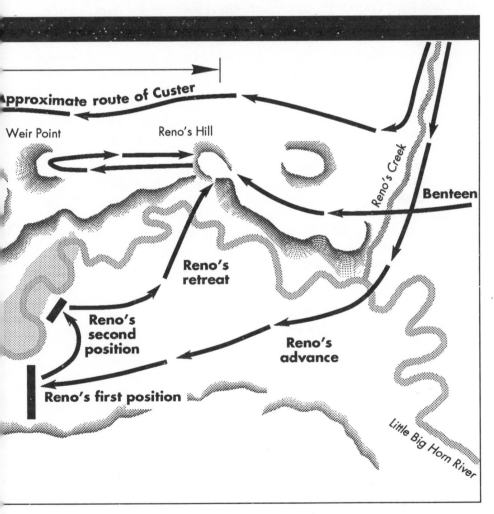

By noon the regiment had crossed the watershed and for nine miles Custer's and Reno's columns followed opposite banks of the stream later known as Benteen's Creek. At about 1400 Custer's column halted to examine an abandoned tepee containing a dead Indian. Shortly after, a party of Sioux, some forty strong, were seen galloping away down the valley. Custer immediately sent his adjutant, Lieutenant W. Cooke, splashing across the stream with orders for Reno. As Reno remembered them, they were '. . . to move forward at as rapid a gait as prudent, and to charge afterward, and that the whole outfit would support me'. In fairness to Custer, it must be stated that the contemporary meaning of the word support did not imply an advance along the same axis, as it does today, but rather a simultaneous attack in another part of the field.

The two columns diverged, Custer's on to the high ground to the right and Reno's down the stream until it met the Little Big Horn. Reno's troops forded the river, hampered by its strong current and soft bottom, and then halted briefly to tighten their saddle girths before moving north along the floodplain. The advance was made initially with two troops in line and one in reserve, but as the tepees came into view Reno brought the third troop forward into line. It was now approximately 1500 and, having seen the attack launched, Cooke left to return to the main column. At about this time, on the bluff later named Weir's Hill, Custer was seen waving his hat in encouragement; it was the last sight anyone beyond his immediate battlefield was to have of him.

Oddly, despite the numerous blunders which had already been made, Reno achieved complete tactical surprise. The chiefs of the assembled Sioux tribes – the Hunkpapa, Blackfoot, Miniconjou, Brule and Oglala – and of the Cheyenne, were well aware of the Seventh's presence, but their collective opinion was that only a fool would dream of attacking them while they were concentrated; they could certainly not have foreseen that the enemy commander would sub-divide his force to do so. The only warning the Indians received came from the party of braves sighted near the abandoned tepee, who galloped into the Hunkpapa circle only minutes before Reno came into view.

Be that as it may, the Indian response was swift and dramatic. Hardly had the Charge sounded than hundreds of warriors, many of them naked, swarmed out of the village. Reno, immediately recognizing that his 112 men would ride to their deaths if they continued, halted his attack and formed a dismounted skirmish line. The Indians rapidly turned his open left flank and compelled him to withdraw into a copse beside the river. This was quickly seen as a death-trap in which the three troops would soon be isolated and cut to pieces. Reno was therefore forced to accept the unpalatable truth that his command's survival depended upon reaching the high ground across the river. He led a disorderly retreat back towards the ford, found his path blocked by the enemy and swung left, reaching a second ford. Here the river bank was six feet deep and many horses refused until forced over the edge by pressure from behind. It was during this period of the engagement, while the troopers were running the gauntlet intermingled with the Indians, and in the mêlée above the ford, that the heaviest casualties were incurred. Somehow, the survivors crossed the river and dragged their mounts up the steep slopes of the flat-topped bluff which became known as Reno's Hill. On the summit, shaken, breathless and exhausted as they were, they rallied and prepared to defend themselves, but, for the moment, few of the Indians followed them. Reno was hatless, his face and tunic covered with the blood and brains of a Ree scout who had been killed at his side; believing that he had been wounded, he tied a bandana round his head. The extent of his loss was soon apparent: three officers and 29 troopers and scouts had been killed, seven were wounded, and fifteen were missing. Of Custer there was no sign, nor would there be. For the moment, Reno was entirely alone.

Custer's column was known to have ridden along the ridge which bordered the Little Big Horn, planning to descend its northern slopes and attack the lower end of the village. His own diversion to the bluff from which he watched the start of Reno's attack would have revealed the true size of the village and, anticipating heavy ammunition expenditure, he sent back Sergeant Daniel Kanipe with a request that the pack train be hurried forward to join him. A few moments later Cooke rejoined the column and Custered ordered a second messenger to be dispatched. The adjutant scribbled a hasty note and handed it to Trumpeter John Martin, a recently arrived immigrant whose real name was Giovanni Martini.

Kanipe's ride was uneventful and he reached Benteen an hour later. Benteen sent him on to McDougall and as the sergeant rode past the ranks he shouted, 'We've got 'em boys, we've got 'em!' Martin, however, was ambushed by Indians as he rode along the reverse slope of the ridge, his mount being hit in the withers, although he managed to complete his mission. The note he delivered read: '*Benteen. Come on. Big village. Be quick. Bring packs. W. W. Cooke. PS Bring pacs.*' This was the final message received from Custer, but there was nothing in it to suggest that anything was amiss. The emphasis of the two messages received by Benteen was on ammunition rather than reinforcement, and Custer's location was not even mentioned. Furthermore, Martin, like Kanipe, indicated that the engagement was going well. He said that the Indians were 'skeedadling' and, despite his still limited command of the language, this could only mean that the hostiles were on the run. Benteen may have been concerned by the ambush through which the trumpeter had ridden, but in view of the contacts early that morning he probably did not regard it as unduly significant.

Numerous theories exist regarding the fate of Custer and his men, but of these the most probable was put forward by Brigadier General S. L. A. Marshall, the American military historian and battlefield analyst.

The majority of their bodies were found lying by troops along the ridge and in a ravine leading down to the river, and a few more were scattered across the hills as though shot down while trying to escape. It seems that Custer's column was detected and its intentions correctly interpreted. While Reno's assault was being repulsed, a counter-attack was mounted on Custer, and the architect of this is generally regarded as having been Chief Crazy Horse. Appreciating that the column intended to descend the northern end of the ridge, Crazy Horse quickly sent a blocking force there, sending more of his braves round to the reverse slopes of the ridge while yet more swarmed up the ravines from the river. Checked frontally, the column, strung out over three-quarters of a mile, halted. The Indians, the majority fighting on foot, closed in using every scrap of cover and the troopers dismounted to return their fire. The fire fight was one-sided, for although the majority of the Indians were armed with bows, about one-third possessed firearms, including about 200 Winchester and Henry repeating rifles, which alone were capable of a heavier volume of fire than all the single-shot carbines of Custer's men. They were, too, the better shots, and they fired prone from cover while, initially at least, the soldiers, some four in ten of whom were recently joined recruits, stood or knelt on the open upper slopes. Even so, the Seventh seems to have repulsed one mounted attack delivered across the crest from the east; although the Indians soon rallied and came on again.

For a while, there was a possibility that the column's two rearmost troops, Calhoun's 'L' and Keogh's 'I', might have been able to extricate themselves, but this quickly passed with the arrival of yet more warriors, flushed with their victory over Reno. The horse-holders quickly became targets and many of the cavalry mounts were stampeded. For the Indians, the battle then became a matter of whittling down the strength of each troop and closing in to finish off the survivors. Only one avenue of escape seemed to present itself, and that was down a steep ravine which split the line of sheer bluffs fronting the river. Two troops, Lieutenant A. E. Smith's 'E' and Captain Thomas Custer's 'C', desperately tried to fight their way down this, possibly on the instructions of Custer himself, who may have intended covering their breakout by a self-sacrificial stand with Captain G. W. Yates' 'F' Troop. The attempt failed and those who could retired up the slopes to join Custer and Yates on what became known as Last Stand Hill, which also marked the point at which the column had been halted by Crazy Horse. As no cover was available the remaining horses were shot for use as breastworks. There, under incessant fire, the men waited for the end, which was not long in coming. The column had come under attack at approximately 1545, about the time Reno was fighting his way back across the river, and the battle lasted about an hour. The Indians had reached such a pitch of frenzy that they killed several of their own number in the close-quarter fighting. Afterwards, they continued to cavort across the battlefield, firing into the bodies, scalping, mutilating and stripping them of their uniforms, which they burned or carried off as trophies.

More than 200 men perished with Custer, but the exact figure will never be known. Custer himself died from bullet wounds in the left side and left temple, either of which would have been fatal. He had fought with exemplary bravery and it was due to this, plus the fact that they did not recognize him because of his shorter hair, that the Indians did not disfigure him as they did the others. With him died his brother Thomas, a second brother, Boston, serving as a civilian guide, their young nephew Harry Reed, who was simply along for the ride, and Custer's brother-in-law, Lieutenant James Calhoun.

Estimates of Indian casualties vary, but most sources agree that about 50 were killed outright and that a larger number died of the wounds they received. Because their perspective tended to be personal, few Indians could provide a coherent narrative of the battle. As the Sioux warrior Hump put it, 'They made such short work of killing them that no man could give any correct account of it.' Red Horse recalled that following Reno's repulse many of those involved joined in the attack on Custer; that some soldiers tried to surrender and were promptly killed, but that the remainder made five brave stands; and that '. . . had the soldiers not divided, they would have killed many Sioux'. Of the five lost troops, Crow King commented: 'They kept in order and fought like brave warriors as long as they had a man left.' Chief Sitting Bull, the tribes' spiritual leader, did not take part in the fighting, but his verdict on Custer was that he was a 'great chief' and also 'a fool who rode to his death'. Custer's own Indian scouts tended to agree. They had refused to accompany his column along the ridge and, without witnessing the battle, were aware of its outcome and had ridden off; one of them reached Terry with the exaggerated news that the entire 7th Cavalry had been wiped out.

In 1983 a fierce brush fire swept across the battlefield and this exposed many areas which had not already been plundered by visitors to the site. Using archaeological techniques, more than 4,000 artefacts were discovered, of which the most significant were large quantities of spent rounds and cartridge cases. Together, ballistic science and computer technology permitted a detailed analysis to be made, from which it became possible to trace the movement of individual weapons around the battlefield. The result tends to support General Marshall's view that, save for the abortive foray down the ravine, the soldiers remained in their positions while the Indians converged to overrun one troop after another. Nevertheless, many questions remain unanswered, and are likely to remain so. Why were the bodies of two subalterns, the medical officer and most of 'E' Troop never found? Did they survive the battle to become the grisly playthings of the squaws at the campfire celebrations that night? Why was the body of a sergeant found one-and-a-half miles south of the battlefield? Clearly, he had been killed after his tired mount had been run into the ground, but did he escape from the massacre on his own initiative, or did Custer dispatch him to summon assistance? As to whether the firepower of the three Gatlings, or the presence of Major Brisbin's four troops of 2nd Cavalry, or the issue of sabres, would have made any difference, such considerations remain as speculative as the outcome of the campaign had Custer followed his orders.

In the final analysis, the death of Custer and his men was but the ending of the second act in the drama of the Little Big Horn. The final act was played some four miles to the south, around the hill to which Reno and his battered command had retired. Benteen, coming on fast, was drawn to the spot by firing from the summit and arrived at about 1615, followed by the pack train. Reno was still in a state of shock, as were some of his men, and his intention was to remain on the defensive. However, the sound of distant fighting could be heard along the ridge and some officers were for pushing on and joining Custer. Marshall, quite rightly, regards this as a 'thought for simpletons'. Custer had expected to become heavily engaged. For those on Reno's Hill, there was no indication whatever that he required assistance. Furthermore, while Reno now had a total of seven troops at his disposal, his three original troops were shattered and, for the moment, quite incapable of acting offensively. Finally, although none could have been aware of the fact, the Custer battle was in its dying moments and had Reno succumbed to pressure he would merely have contributed to the tragedy.

This undisciplined wrangle among the officers ended when Captain Thomas Weir, one of Benteen's troop leaders, insubordinately took his troop off, to be followed in turn by others. They reached the bluff from which Custer had watched Reno's initial attack develop, subsequently named Weir's Hill. From here the Custer battlefield was visible, some two miles distant, enveloped in dust clouds in which galloping Indians could be seen, although no detail could be discerned. The Indians, however, could see Weir and they swarmed to the attack. A hastily formed skirmish line could not withstand the pressure and soon the troopers were engaged in a second headlong retreat to Reno Hill, where they were forced to fight for their lives. They dug in using knives to loosen the earth and mess kits to shovel it and, when lulls permitted, piled ration and ammunition boxes from the mules into makeshift breastworks. By the time the Indian attacks slackened at sunset, another eighteen men had been killed and forty-three wounded.

During the long hours of darkness the plight of the wounded became grievous. Nineteen men volunteered to undertake the hazardous descent to the Little Big Horn to fill canteens, all being later decorated with the Medal of Honor. Lieutenant De Rudio, another former Papal Zouave, and several troopers who had remained hidden in the copse beside the river since Reno's retreat, also managed to reach the hill safely. The sounds of revelry from the Indian village continued far into the night, punctuated by biasts blown on a captured trumpet, which raised false hopes of relief in many.

On the morning of 26 June the Indians returned to the attack, two determined attempts to overrun the summit being repulsed. During the afternoon the tribes broke camp and the Indian horde moved off in the direction of the Big Horn Mountains, setting fire to the grass as they left. For the moment, Reno's command held its position.

Terry and Gibbon entered the Little Big Horn valley from the north during the morning of 27 June. Only then did the Seventh's survivors learn the fate of their comrades on a battlefield which presented 'a scene of sickening, ghastly horror'. The dead were lightly covered pending reinterment and the wounded were conveyed down-river to the steamboat *Far West*.

The mauling of the 7th Cavalry marked a turning-point in the history of the Indian Wars. Because their nomadic lifestyle made it difficult for the tribes to remain together for long, the Sioux and Cheyenne soon dispersed. Many of them understood instinctively that their great victory would never be forgiven. Some bands sought sanctuary in Canada, others were hounded back to the reservations, and a few returned sullenly of their own accord. The army fought a number of successful engagements against them in the months that followed although the vengeance demanded by an outraged public in the east proved ever elusive. Even so, the scale of the response convinced many Indians of the hopelessness of their position. Never again would the tribes take the warpath in such numbers, and never again would they win such a victory.

The Battle of the Little Big Horn was to claim one further victim, and that was Major Marcus A. Reno. The Seventh's rank and file made it quite clear where they stood when, within a week of the engagement, to a man they signed a petition to the President and Congress requesting his promotion and that of Benteen. Their request was not granted, although Reno remained in command of the regiment until October 1876. Yet already, a whispering campaign against him was being conducted by surviving officers of the pro-Custer faction. With a viciousness surprising in a man who had spent much of the time hiding in a wood, De Rudio declaimed: 'If we had not been commanded by a coward, we should all have been killed.' No doubt Weir, who deserved a Court Martial, was also ready to contribute his two-pennyworth. When Custer's first biographer, who was clearly prepared to accept mess gossip at face value, actually blamed Reno for the disaster, the latter was compelled to request a Court of Inquiry. Far from clearing his name, the Court damned him with faint praise: 'While subordinates, in some instances, did more for the safety of the command than did Major Reno, there was nothing in his conduct that requires animadversion.' Reno's fall was steady and sustained. In 1877 he was court-martialled for slandering and attempting to seduce the wife of another officer who was absent on duty, and was sentenced to dismissal, this being commuted by the President to two years' suspension without pay in recognition of his previous service. Reinstated in 1879, he assumed command of Fort Meade, Dakota, but the following year was again court-martialled for conduct unbecoming an officer and a gentleman, the charges specifying repeated drunkenness and brawling in a saloon, and he was dismissed the service. The army later acknowledged that the punishment was excessive, but he died in poverty in 1889 and was buried in the military cemetery at the Little Big Horn.

Benteen's subsequent career was more straightforward but his prospects may have been affected by his antipathy to Custer and his association with Reno. He was not promoted major until December 1882 and, still bitter, retired in that rank six years later. In 1890 the army honoured him with the brevet rank of brigadier general for his conduct during the defence of Reno Hill.

Defeat inevitably begets acrimony, but for one participant in the battle, who saw all but could tell nothing, the story had a happy ending. Captain Keogh's charger Comanche was found standing beside the body of his master on the battlefield, bleeding from numerous bullet and arrow wounds and with his saddle hanging beneath his belly. He was led gently down to the *Far West* and when the steamer reached Bismarck he was carried in a wagon to Fort Abraham Lincoln. There he spent a year supported by slings in his stall and on his recovery was granted the freedom of the post. He grazed where he liked, was never saddled or ridden again, and, led by a mounted trooper, paraded in a place of honour on ceremonial occasions. Sometimes, when he saw his old troop at drill, he would trot over and take his accustomed position at its head. On pay days, the troopers treated him to a bucket of beer.

CHAPTER 5
Isandhlwana and Rorke's Drift
22 JANUARY 1879

Most wars are complex in their origins, but the Zulu War of 1879 was not and at its simplest can be regarded as a preemptive strike deliberately engineered by Sir Henry Bartle Frere, the United Kingdom's High Commissioner in South Africa. Frere believed that, sooner or later, the formidable Zulu standing army would launch an invasion of the territories for which he was responsible and, that being the case, the best way to handle the situation was to destroy that army at the earliest possible opportunity.

The Zulu nation certainly possessed the most efficient and potentially dangerous native army in Africa. Its soldiers, fit, athletic and trained for war from boyhood, were conscripted into regiments, and were not allowed to marry until they had proved themselves. As a result of this the younger units possessed a keen psychological edge induced by frustration and were naturally inclined to welcome war as a means of ending their enforced celibacy. The regiments were well organized, strictly disciplined and developed a high *esprit de corps* which they demonstrated with individual titles, distinctive head plumes, shield markings and other adornments. On the march, regiments moved at a ground-devouring lope which often disrupted their opponents' plans before they were fully laid, and over broken country they could move faster than a horse. Their commanders were adept at concealing large bodies of men until the moment chosen for the attack had arrived. Their strategy was entirely offensive and their most favoured tactic was based on the image of the bull. On approaching the enemy, each wing of the army would push out fast moving horns which would envelope the flanks and rear of their opponents; the enemy's main body would then be crushed against the Zulu centre, which formed the bull's chest, behind which lay the reserve or loins. Each warrior carried a hide shield, several long assegais for throwing and one shorter stabbing assegai or a hard wooden club known as a knobkerrie. Some had acquired firearms, which they handled less efficiently, but the majority preferred to close with and kill their enemies in the traditional manner. Despite enjoying mixed fortunes against laagered or mounted Boer marksmen, for generations they had carried all before them and inspired mortal fear in their African neighbours.

Frere's personal knowledge of the Zulus and their king, Cetewayo, was based on hearsay and be believed, incorrectly, that they were blood-crazed savages who, at the first excuse would pour across the Natal frontier to indulge in an orgy of killing, burning and rape. For what other purpose than expansion, he reasoned, would a large and powerful tribal grouping maintain a standing army of 40,000 men when its neighbours were simply concerned with settling and improving the land? The truth was that Cetewayo was well aware of the resources which the Great White Queen had at her disposal and took the pragmatic view that his own and his nation's interests were best served by maintaining friendly relations with the British. Furthermore, Zulu mores were, in some respects, more puritanical than the most strictly enforced Victorian codes and the penalty for breaching them was often death. As for the army, it was central to the Zulu way of life and without it the very fabric of society would be unrecognizable. Frere, however, took the view that the business of the army was war and that, no matter how quiet the Zulus might be at present, sooner or later it would exercise that function. He therefore began seeking the means by which a decisive conflict could be provoked, contrary to the advice of many who had first-hand knowledge of the Zulus and their ways.

In 1877 the insolvent Transvaal Republic was annexed by the United Kingdom, and in the process the British inherited a border dispute between Boer settlers and the Zulus. A commission established to examine the problem found in favour of the latter. This did not suit Frere at all and he decided to set aside its verdict until he could impose a solution of his own. Then, during 1878, a series of incidents occurred which played right into his hands. First, in July two wives of a Zulu chief named Sirayo escaped to Natal with their lovers. Adultery being a capital crime among the Zulus, they were pursued by Sirayo's sons, brought back and executed. That there had been a frontier violation was undeniable and the Governor of Natal demanded that the culprits be handed over, together with a fine of 500 cattle. Cetewayo, in a difficult situation, commented that the young men had acted foolishly and in the heat of the moment, but he apologized and offered the sum of £50. Then, in October, two government surveyors were arrested and detained for a while by the Zulus, who pointed out correctly that they were carrying out unauthorized work beyond their own border. Finally, a number of missionaries complained that their work in Zululand was being hindered by the King and his men, who, it was alleged in a series of lurid but unsubstantiated tales, killed converts and generally imposed their cruel will on a hapless people. Curiously, none of the missionaries had personally sustained the slightest harm at the hands of this 'godless despot'. Quite possibly, having seen the way events were moving, they had decided to get out while the going was good and, having abandoned their erstwhile if sublimely indifferent parishioners, were anxious to save face. Be that as it may, they found a willing and most sympathetic audience in the High Commissioner.

Whether viewed singly or collectively, none of these incidents provided adequate grounds for war, but Frere decided that the moment was ripe for Cetewayo to be taught his lesson and wrote to London requesting additional troops. He had no reason to suspect that his request would be denied, for thus far the Government had supported him. Recently however, international relations had deteriorated to the point at which a war with Russia seemed possible, and a major campaign was in progress in Afghanistan. The Government, therefore, informed Frere that war with Cetewayo was to be avoided. Unfortunately, its instructions arrived just too late, for Frere had already gone too far to turn back.

On 11 December 1878 Cetewayo's representatives were informed of the boundary commission's verdict. The Zulus' title to the disputed lands was recognized, but they were not permitted to occupy them. Then, even before the shock of this had sunk in, the King's councillors were presented with an ultimatum demanding, within twenty days, the disbandment of the Zulu army; the establishment of a formal British Residency in the King's capital; the surrender of Sirayo's sons and the payment of the outstanding fine of 500 cattle. Such terms would have been unacceptable to any self-respecting ruler and Frere knew it. Cetewayo offered to pay the fine but in other respects stood his ground. Aware of British military preparations across the frontier, he began concentrating his troops, hoping to avoid a confrontation yet determined to defend himself if the need arose. On 6 January 1879 British troops began crossing into Zululand and Frere had his war. It was to be a very bloody business and much of the blood spilled so needlessly was British.

Frere's Commander-in-Chief was Lieutenant-General Lord Chelmsford, who had previously served in Abyssinia in 1867 and against the Ashanti in 1874. Chelmsford's abilities as a general can fairly be described as pedestrian, his principal faults being under-estimation of the enemy, lack of imagination and the inability to read a battle beyond the range of his binoculars. He had available some 6,000 Regulars and colonial volunteers, plus 9,000 native levies, amply supported by twenty field guns and ten rocket-launchers. His plan of campaign envisaged three columns penetrating Zululand from Natal and the Transvaal, then converging on Cetewayo's capital, Ulundi, where the Zulu army would be destroyed by disciplined firepower. In its early stages it bore a startling similarity to that which had foundered on the banks of the Little Big Horn less than three years previously.

We are concerned solely with the Central or No. 3 Column, which crossed into Zululand at Rorke's Drift on the Buffalo River, as the upper reach of the Tugela was called. The column was commanded by Colonel Richard Glyn of the 24th Regiment (later The South Wales Borderers), and consisted of the 1st and 2nd Battalions, 24th Regiment; 'N' Battery 5th Brigade Royal Artillery with six 7-pounder guns; mounted infantry

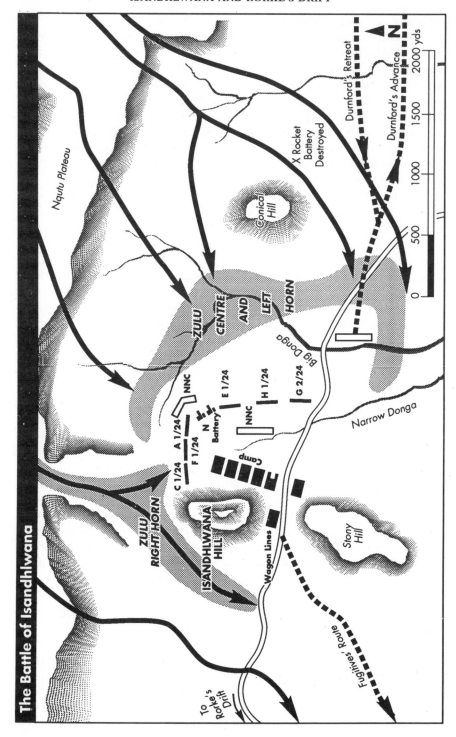

The Battle of Isandhlwana

and local volunteer units, engineers and two native battalions; together with a train of cumbrous and slow-moving ox wagons: a total of more than 4,700 men of whom 1,852 were Europeans. It was Glyn's misfortune that Chelmsford and his staff had decided to accompany him, for Chelmsford, not content with being Commander-in-Chief, also behaved as though he were column commander. Today, a battle group leader, having received his orders, would probably tell his general he was in the way if he attempted to interfere in their detailed execution, but a century ago it was different. Chelmsford, instead of deciding what had to be done and telling Glyn to get on with it, used Glyn's troops and did the job himself.

There was some preliminary skirmishing, but it was the state of the road which delayed the advance until the engineers could put it into a condition which would support the guns and wagons. By 20 January, however, the column had advanced ten miles and established a camp beneath the high, rocky kopje of Isandhlwana, so named because its outline resembled a wrist and clenched fist, although to the men of the 24th it also bore a striking similarity to their own sphynx badge. From the camp the road passed over a nek or col westwards towards Rorke's Drift, while to the north a spur connected the kopje with the escarpment of the Nqutu Plateau. To the east lay an open plain intersected by a donga (watercourse), beyond which lay a conical hill. Chelmsford was pleased with the position, as it offered excellent observation and a good field of fire over the plain, across which he believed the Zulu army would advance from Ulundi, should its commanders decide to attack him. On the other hand, he did not take the elementary precaution of laagering the wagons, contrary to his own Field Force Regulations and the personal advice of Paul Kruger, because he did not believe it to be necessary. Likewise, he ignored the advice of another veteran Zulu fighter, J. J. Uys, who arrived while the camp was being pitched: 'Place your spies far out . . . The Zulus are more dangerous than you think.' Thus, the wagons were parked uselessly behind the tent lines, no pickets were posted on the summit of Isandhlwana or its reverse slopes, and cavalry vedettes posted on top of the Nqutu escarpment by the Natal Mounted Police were called in by a staff officer on the grounds that they were 'far too far away and were of no use up there'. It was a situation which caused serious concern to many officers in the camp.

Early on the 21st, Chelmsford decided to send out a strong patrol to the south-east, in the direction of the stronghold of a Zulu chief named Matyana, some twelve miles distant. The patrol was commanded by Major John Dartnell, a former officer who had emigrated to South Africa and established the Natal Mounted Police as an efficient force, and was 150 strong, consisting of some of his own men, augmented by members of volunteer units. He was instructed to return in daylight. Shortly after, two battalions of the Natal Native Contingent under Commandant Rupert

Lonsdale, who had previously held a commission in a Highland regiment, were sent out to support him. During the afternoon Chelmsford rode up the Nqutu escarpment. He spotted a dozen mounted Zulus who turned and disappeared over the brow of a hill a mile distant. As he was returning to camp he was met by a messenger from Dartnell, who confirmed that he was in contact with the enemy and was remaining out, simultaneously requesting the dispatch of two regular infantry companies so that he could attack Matyana's men in the morning. Annoyed by Dartnell's disregard of his orders, Chelmsford declined the request for reinforcements but sent out blankets and provisions.

That night the General's sleep was disturbed when a second message arrived from Dartnell at 0130. It had been written before dusk, but the messenger had experienced difficulty in finding his way. The enemy confronting the reconnaissance force, it seemed, had been reinforced and now numbered approximately 2,000. This placed Chelmsford in something of a dilemma, for Dartnell's command was too small on its own to accomplish anything, yet was large enough to provide a tempting target for the enemy. Furthermore, the NNC element could not be relied on for, while its British officers were most experienced, its locally recruited European NCOs were, to put it bluntly, a rough lot and the rank and file dreaded the Zulus, were jumpy, badly armed and poor shots to boot. On the other hand, had they been in any immediate danger, Dartnell and Lonsdale could have fallen back on the camp. Nevertheless, Chelmsford was not prepared to risk the destruction of 1,600 of his men although, ironically, the decisions he now took were ultimately to result in the deaths of a somewhat larger number.

First, he decided to form a relief column which would march to Dartnell's aid immediately. This consisted of the 2nd/24th, less one company still on outpost duty, plus four of 'N' Battery's six 7-pounder guns. The column was to be commanded by Colonel Glyn, but, as Chelmsford and his staff were to accompany it, the appointment tended to be nominal. Command of the troops remaining in the camp, whose strength now numbered less than half the original, devolved upon Lieutenant-Colonel Henry Pulleine of the 1st/24th, whose instructions were to remain strictly upon the defensive. To make up Pulleine's numbers, Chelmsford also ordered up a force known as No. 2 Column, commanded by Colonel Anthony Durnford, from Rorke's Drift. This consisted of 300 mounted Basutos, several NNC companies and a rocket detachment, and had hitherto been employed protecting the line of communication. The order was written at 0200 by Lieutenant-Colonel John Crealock, Chelmsford's military secretary, and carried to Durnford by Lieutenant Horace Smith-Dorrien of the 95th Regiment (Sherwood Foresters), who was employed on transport duties. The actual text of the message is important, for in the recriminations which followed the ensuing disaster a determined and largely successful attempt was made to lay responsibility for it at Durnford's door. Crealock, something of a stuffed shirt, maintained that the relevant passage of the order had read: 'Move up to Isandhlwana camp at once with all your mounted men and rocket battery; take command of it . . .' The order itself was never found, but the order book into which the original was copied was discovered some months later on the battlefield and revealed that the text had been: 'You are to march to this camp *at once* with all the force you have with you of No. 2 Column . . .' For sheer sloppiness this almost equals the scrap of paper that sent the Light Brigade into the Valley of Death; it does *not* tell Durnford he is to take command, nor does it hint at what he should do when he reached Isandhlwana. On the other hand, it presumed that Durnford would automatically assume command, since he was senior to Pulleine. In such circumstances it can be argued that he would inherit the order given to Pulleine to maintain a defensive stance. Against this, however, if the overall situation changed Durnford was entitled to exercise his judgement and it would have been quite unreasonable to expect him to have done otherwise.

Cursing the ways of generals, Glyn's relief column shrugged into its equipment, formed ranks, and at 0430 marched out eastwards across the still dark plain. Chelmsford rode ahead and made contact with the surprised Dartnell and Lonsdale who, far from being embattled, had passed a nervous but otherwise untroubled night. As the dawn mist cleared some Zulus were spotted on a nearby ridge and chased off. A number of them were killed, Matyana himself narrowly escaping capture. At 0930 Chelmsford ordered a halt for breakfast, during which he decided that the Central Column was to shift its camp from Isandhlwana to the banks of the nearby Mangeni, a tributary of the Buffalo. This was a curious decision, since all the information obtained from prisoners indicated that the main Zulu army had been marching towards him and was probably in the vicinity. Nevertheless, without knowing the enemy's whereabouts, he chose to act as though the troops were engaged in peacetime manoeuvres. Yet, with the information at his disposal, it should have been possible for him to have formed an appreciation of the very dangerous situation which was developing. The Zulus were not at the head of the plain, and since the country to the south was open the probability was that they were approaching Isandhlwana under cover of the reverse slopes of the Nqutu plateau, which now lay to the left rear of the relief column.

This was exactly what the Zulu commanders, the veteran Tshingwayo and the younger Mavumengwana, had decided to do. They had much the better intelligence system and, whereas Chelmsford did not even know where they were, they were quickly advised of his every move. They were pleased to learn that Dartnell and Lonsdale had left Isandhlwana on the 21st since it would make their attack on the camp that much easier; and they were delighted when Chelmsford led out half the remaining garrison next morning. The army had been in the area of Matyana's stronghold early on 21 January, but the generals declined the chief's suggestion that they should attack Dartnell and Lonsdale since they had much larger fish to fry. That morning the army, 20,000 strong, had marched to the northern edge of the Nqutu plateau and concealed itself silently in a valley. The generals were against attacking the camp on the 22nd because of the new moon, which was regarded as unpropitious, and decided to launch their assault the following day. The irony was that, but for an accident, the camp at Isandhlwana would already have been abandoned.

Chelmsford sent an order to Pulleine telling him to strike camp and move forward, and an NNC battalion under Commandant G. Hamilton-Browne was sent back to assist with the work. At about 1000 a startling message was received from Pulleine himself, timed at 0805 and reading: 'Staff Officer – Report just come in that the Zulus are advancing in force from left front of camp.' The general's naval liaision officer – a Naval Brigade had been formed for service in the war – climbed a tree on a nearby hilltop and surveyed the distant camp through his telescope. The tents were standing and nothing untoward seemed to be happening. Satisfied, Chelmsford sent off the mounted infantry on a sweep to the north and decided to press on to the new camp site and wait for Pulleine and Durnford to come up.

At about noon, Commandant Lonsdale told a staff officer that he was returning to Isandhlwana to obtain provisions for the NNC, as the rations sent out the previous night were insufficient and some of the men were exhausted, not having eaten for two days. Some fifteen minutes later the mounted infantry brought in two prisoners, who confirmed that the Zulu army was expected to reach Isandhlwana that day. Ominously, while they were being interrogated, the faint boom of gunfire was heard from the direction of the camp. Chelmsford and his staff rode up a hill from which their binoculars revealed shell-bursts on the Nqutu escarpment. Some of the older hands noted with disquiet that the oxen had been driven into the camp, generally a sign of serious trouble, but the General remained confident that Durnford had joined Pulleine at Isandhlwana and that the camp was capable for standing off an attack.

Meanwhile, Hamilton-Browne's NNC battalion, plodding its way back to the camp, had also taken a prisoner who confirmed that there were twelve Zulu regiments on the plateau. When shells were seen bursting on the escarpment the men refused to go further. Hamilton-Browne rode on alone to within four miles of the camp and, to his horror, observed the huge black wave of the Zulu army pouring over the edge of the plateau. He had already dispatched two warning notes to Chelmsford and now he sent off a third, desperate it its urgency: 'For God's sake come back with all your men. The camp is surrounded and must be taken unless helped.'

It is probable that Chelmsford and his staff regarded these warnings as exaggerations. The major business of the day, the establishment of the new camp site on the Mangeni, continued, and Glyn's troops were ordered to converge there. Some element of doubt nevertheless remained and shortly after 1400 the General decided to ride back towards Isandhlwana with a mounted infantry escort and see for himself just what was going on. On the way, he received two messages from Pulleine which reassured him. The first read: 'Staff Officer. Heavy firing to the left of our camp. Cannot move camp at present.' The second, also addressed to a staff officer, contained slightly more detail: 'Heavy firing near left of camp. Shepstone [one of Durnford's officers] has come back in for reinforcements and reports that Zulus are falling back. The whole force at camp turned out and fighting about one mile to left flank.' The implications were obviously that Durnford's column had reached the camp and that the situation was under control.

At 1500 Chelmsford reached the halted NNC battalion but refused to countenance Hamilton-Browne's suggestion that the camp had fallen. He rode on and five miles short of Isandhlwana was met by a rider on a foundering horse. It was Lonsdale, in a state of shock, and he had a terrible tale to tell. Tired out by two days' exertions and a night without sleep, he had been dozing in the saddle when he reached the camp at about 1400. He was jerked awake when a shot cracked past his ears and, looking about, saw that the men in scarlet jackets with green facings were black. They were Zulus, engaged in looting the tents and wagons. The camp itself was a slaughterhouse, thickly strewn with the intermingled bodies of British, Kafir and Zulu soldiers, sprawled in every conceivable attitude of death. Pursued by flying assegais and rifle bullets, Lonsdale had escaped by the skin of his teeth. His equally exhausted mount had collapsed once since leaving the camp and had taken over two hours to stagger the remaining distance. Stunned, Chelmsford could only mutter: 'I can't understand it. I left a thousand men there.'

Isandhlwana had fallen because the mistakes made outside the camp had been compounded by those made within it. Following the pre-dawn departure of Chelmsford and Glyn, the troops left in camp consisted of five companies of the 1st/24th, one company of the 2nd/24th which had been on outpost duty when the column left, six NNC companies, most of the Natal Mounted Police and the two remaining 7-pounders of 'N' Battery. In round figures, this amounted to 600 British infantry, 600 native infantry, 100 cavalry and 70 gunners. The 24th, which provided the backbone of the defence, was a typical line regiment consisting of long-service regulars. The men, drawn from town and country back-grounds, were tough mentally and physically, and in outlook were stoic, phlegmatic and stolid. Subject to strict discipline, they had inherited the long British tradition of firing aimed, precise and controlled volleys which had blown great gaps in their enemies' ranks the world over. In contrast to their fathers, who had fought in the Crimea with the muzzle-loading Tower musket, capable of firing two rounds a minute, they were armed with the breech-loading Martini-Henry rifle, producing a five-fold increase in the rate of fire, plus greatly improved range and accuracy.

At 0730 the buglers had sounded 'Cook House' and the men lined up at their field kitchens. Thirty minutes later, before the meal had been completed, a trooper galloped in from the police vedette on the Nqutu escarpment and informed Pulleine that the Zulus were present in strength on the plateau. 'Fall In!' was sounded and the companies stood to in front of the camp, joined by Lieutenant Charles Pope's 'G' Company 2nd/24th, which had been manning the outpost line. Pulleine scribbled his first note to Chelmsford. For an hour nothing happened, then a marching body of Zulus was spotted some miles away on the edge of the escarpment; they then disappeared from sight. A second messenger from the vedette arrived and reported that of the three Zulu groups which it had been observing, one had moved away to the north-west and two to the north-east. As there was clearly no immediate threat to the camp, Pulleine allowed his men to stand down but kept them under arms and in position.

This was the situation when, at 1000, Colonel Anthony Durnford arrived from Rorke's Drift with five troops of Natal Mounted Natives, three NNC companies, a rocket battery and sufficient reserve ammunition to bring the camp's stock to half a million rounds. Durnford had originally been commissioned into the Royal Engineers, although in temperament he was more suited to the cavalry. He had been in South Africa since 1872 and taken part in the suppression of several native uprisings, in one of which he had lost the use of his left arm. Something of an extrovert in the Custer mould, he wore his own version of campaign dress, including a slouch hat with crimson puggaree, and was hung about with revolver, ammunition belts and a hunting-knife. He was a dedicated soldier and an inspiring leader who had brought his Basuto horsemen to a high pitch of efficiency. Perhaps, more than any officer present, he understood the vital importance of deep reconnaissance. Against this, he was an awkward subordinate who tended to know better than his superiors, and he was given to the unauthorized use of his own initiative, a trait which had already earned him a sharp rebuke from Lord Chelmsford.

It has sometimes been suggested that a coolness existed between Durnford and Pulleine regarding command of the camp, but this is something of an exaggeration. Durnford permitted the troops to finish their breakfast and he and Pulleine did likewise in the latter's tent. While they were eating, a third trooper arrived from the vedette. Unfortunately, the man was unable to deliver an intelligible message and Pulleine sent an NNC officer, Lieutenant Higginson, to find out what was going on. Durnford also dispatched two troops of his Basutos to carry out a thorough reconnaissance of the entire plateau, Captain Barton with Lieutenant Roberts' troops to the north-west and Captain Shepstone with Lieutenant Raw's troop to the north-east.

Higginson returned with the news that the Zulus seen earlier were moving off in an easterly direction, that is, in the direction taken by Chelmsford and the relief column. This put a different complexion on the matter and Durnford decided to use his own column to protect the General's left flank. He asked for two companies of the 24th to accompany him but Pulleine demurred, pointing out that his orders were to defend the camp, although he would comply with the request if ordered to do so. Durnford did not press the point, although he did suggest reinforcement of the isolated NCC company on the spur connecting Isandhlwana kopje with the plateau. Pulleine sent up Captain C. W. Cavaye's 'A' Company 1st/24th, which took position on the left of the NNC, with Lieutenant E. Dyson's platoon acting as flank guard a further 500 yards to the left. Finally, Durnford ordered Higginson back up the escarpment with orders for Roberts' and Raw's mounted troops to drive the Zulus along the plateau and conform to his own movements on the plain. At approximately 1100 he led his column out of the camp, leaving Pulleine once more in command.

For a while, all went according to plan. Then, some of Raw's Basuto troopers chased after a Zulu party driving cattle. The pursuit took one of them to the edge of a rocky valley on the northern edge of the plateau, where he reined in. From below, 20,000 pairs of hostile eyes glared at him. Then, with a roar, the Zulu army sprang from its haunches, surged up the slope and on to the plateau. Once its hiding-place had been discovered the phases of the moon counted for nothing; the assault on Isandhlwana had begun.

As the black wave, more than a mile wide, surged forward, Shepstone dispatched a trooper over the escarpment to warn Durnford, ordered Roberts and Raw to fall back on the spur, imposing as much delay as they could, then galloped for the camp, pausing only to alert Cavaye and the NNC on the spur itself. When he arrived he was breathless, agitated and unable to convince Pulleine of the full horror of what he had seen. Simultaneously, Chelmsford's order to move the camp arrived and the crash of volleys from the spur indicated that Cavaye was heavily engaged. Dispatching his second note to Chelmsford, Pulleine had the Alarm sounded and the troops stood to again. Because of the heavy firing from the spur, he also sent Captain A. F. Mostyn's 'F' Company 1st/24th to support Cavaye, and this took position on the latter's left.

It was now approximately noon. On Pulleine's behalf a staff officer scribbled the third message received by Chelmsford, already quoted above. Clearly, the reference to the Zulus falling back was utter nonsense and the officer was confusing them with the Basutos. It was sadly typical of the staff work of the period, but in the final analysis it was already too late to matter. For the moment, the enemy was not yet within sight of the camp and Pulleine had obviously not grasped the seriousness of the situation; had he done so, he would not have acted as he did. His companies were drawn up not less than 1,000 yards from the camp, facing east, far removed from their reserve ammunition wagons. On the right was Pope's 'G' Company 2nd/24th, then Captain G. V. Wardell's 'H' Company 1st/24th, then Lieutenant F. P. Porteous' 'E' Company 1st/24th, with Major Stuart Smith's two 7-pounder guns on the left, aimed at the escarpment. Up on the spur the NCC company had soon had enough and retreated towards the camp, rallying inconveniently in front of the guns, where it was joined by a second NCC company which had been performing outpost duty. Cavaye, Mostyn, Roberts and Raw, now reinforced by Captain R. Younghusband's 'C' Company 1st/24th on their left, had inflicted serious casualties on the enemy but were unable to check their advance and were retiring steadily and in good order down the spur towards the camp, so prolonging the British line into an L-shape with the guns at the exterior angle. As yet there was no cause for serious alarm and, within the camp, the bandsmen were being detailed to the companies as stretcher-bearers, the drummer boys were reporting to the quartermasters as ammunition runners, and the remaining NNC units were forming up as a reserve. Yet, it does not require the benefit of hindsight to appreciate the inherent weakness of Pulleine's dispositions. The perimeter he had chosen to hold might have been suitable if the entire Central Column had been present, but was far too long for the troops he had available. On the eastern face, particularly, the companies were spread very thin and there were gaps of 200–300 yards between them. Had Pulleine appreciated the danger he would doubtless have contracted his perimeter around the camp itself. The effect of this would have been to concentrate his firepower in a continuous line, maintain the ammunition supply to the companies and restrict the frontage of the Zulu attack. In such circumstances the probability is that the camp would not have fallen.

Tshingwayo, on the other hand, had planned his attack well and his regimental commanders knew exactly what was expected of them. The right horn was to swing round behind the spur and Isandhlwana kopje to cut the road between the camp and Rorke's Drift. The left horn was to advance rapidly across the plain and effect a junction with it on the nek behind the camp. The centre was to advance directly on the camp. Now fully extended, the Zulu army was deployed twelve deep on a front of several miles, each regiment easily distinguished from its neighbours. Its inner right flank was already engaged with the troops on the spur and, as the main body burst over the edge of the escarpment like a tidal wave, shells from Smith's two 7-pounders began to burst in its ranks. Durnford's little column, still moving east across the plain, had reached a point beyond the conical hill and was almost buried under the onrush of the Zulu left horn. The rocket battery managed to get off one round and was then overrun; three men of the 24th, serving with the battery's escort, were speared and trampled in the rush but survived and later managed to escape. Durnford, imposing such checks as he could, retired towards the camp and reached the donga at a point to the right front of Pope's company. Here, his Basutos maintained a heavy, accurate fire which halted the Zulus to their front and impeded the passage of the left horn towards the nek.

Elsewhere, the Zulus were swarming down the spur and crossing the plain swiftly with their effortless run. To their front was the thin, scarlet line of the 24th, two ranks deep with the front rank kneeling. Suddenly, the line flickered with flame and blue smoke drifted above it as the first volleys crashed out. Individuals pitched to the ground. Then, as the range closed, gaps opened in the ranks as groups went down, their places quickly filled from the rear. Finally, with whole ranks being torn apart by disciplined musketry augmented by 7-pounder case-shot, the assault slowed to a walk then stopped. The Zulus lay down. On the spur, they had been halted 300 yards from the firing line; on the plain, where firepower was less concentrated, perhaps half that distance. And still the dreadful volleys continued to rake the huddled mass. Had he chosen, Pulleine could still have contracted his perimeter, but the line was holding and he saw no reason to do so. The 24th Company, veterans of the recent Ninth Kafir War, were perfectly steady and, it is said, were expecting the enemy to break any minute. That the Zulus were severely shaken is beyond doubt, and there was indeed a definite movement to the rear, but this was sharply checked by the thundrous bellows of a senior officer: 'The King didn't send us here to run away!'

The crisis of the battle had been reached. All, however, was far from well with Pulleine's command. The supply of ammunition reaching the companies had not kept pace with the prodigious expenditure, thanks largely to a situation beggaring belief which had developed at the reserve ammunition wagons. All quartermasters are brought up in the hard school of accountability and to some this becomes an end in itself. Such a man was Quartermaster Bloomfield of the 2nd/24th, who, with a battle raging, declined to issue ammunition to anyone other than runners from Pope's company of his own battalion, sending the runners from the 1st/ 24th companies to their own quartermaster, Pullen, whose wagon was located an additional 500 yards to the south. Needless to say, neither would issue ammunition to Durnford's Basutos, who were by now becoming desperate. Lieutenant Smith-Dorrien, who had returned to Isandhlwana after contacting Durnford at Rorke's Drift, was sufficiently disgusted by their stupidity to organize a party which began opening 2nd/ 24th ammunition boxes of its own accord. When the outraged Bloomfield protested, Smith-Dorrien angrily asked him whether he wanted a requisition. Unfortunately, the boxes themselves gave as much trouble as the quartermasters for, unlike subsequent designs, their lids were closed not by knock-off clamps, or even by nails which could be levered out with a bayonet, but by screws. As if this were not bad enough, there were few screwdrivers available and as the boxes had been deliberately designed to withstand rough handling, they were difficult to break into.

Naturally, the companies began to run short of ammunition. The interval between volleys became longer and the Zulus seensed that something was amiss. It was now approximately 1300 and shortly afterwards the moon passed between the earth and the sun, cloaking the events that followed in an eerie penumbra. On the right, Durnford's troopers, their ammunition expended, mounted their horses and galloped back to the nek. The Zulu left horn, consisting of the Ngobamokosi and Mbonambi Regiments, swarmed across the donga in hot pursuit. Pope's right was now turned and he swung back the exposed flank of his company to meet the threat. Thus encouraged, the rest of the Zulu line edged forward to within 60 yards of the British position and began hurling assegai. The 24th's spluttering response told them what they wanted to know and they quickly generated a killing frenzy, stamping, beating their shields, chanting 'uSuthu!' (the war cry of Cetewayo's faction in the civil war which had brought him to power) and hissing 'Si-gi-di!' (Kill!) It was too much for the two NNC companies covering the exposed angle in the British line. They should never have been left there and the wonder is that they stuck it out as long as they did. Now, they bolted for the camp. With a great roar, the Zulu host surged forward, pouring through the gaps in the line. Within minutes, the companies had been reduced to struggling scarlet knots submerged in a sea of stabbing, clubbing black. None survived, but the details of their stand are known from Zulu accounts and subsequent examination of the site. The Zulus quickly discovered that the fixed bayonet, well handled, was more than a match for the stabbing spear and, after the initial clash, drew back leaving the bodies of comrades squirming beneath the steel hedges. Thereafter, they hurled bodies and rained throwing assegais into the ranks before closing in for the kill. Even then, they worked in pairs, one Zulu engaging a soldier in front while a second stabbed or clubbed him from behind. 'Ah, those red soldiers at Isandhlwana,' recalled a Zulu warrior after the war. 'How few they were, and how they fought! They fell like stones – each man in his place.'

The fight surged into the camp, where an orgy of slaughter took place. The NNC reserve had broken at once and, with the wagon drivers and camp followers, had fled pell-mell for the nek in the hope of reaching Rorke's Drift, only to find the road blocked by the Zulu right horn. They swerved to the left, making for the Buffalo, ten miles distant, but were pursued and hunted down every step of the way. Somehow, Smith had limbered his guns and got them over the nek but they became stuck in a gully and were overrun. Pulleine, knowing all was lost, handed the

Queen's Colour of the 1st/24th to the battalion's adjutant, Lieutenant Teignmouth Melville, with orders to save it; the Regimental Colour had been left behind in Helpmakaar. Together with Lieutenant Neville Coghill, Melville reached the swollen river but was swept off his exhausted horse and lost his grip on the Colour. Coghill returned from the far bank and rescued him but the two were quickly surrounded and killed, taking several of their opponents with them. In 1907 both were posthumously awarded the Victoria Cross. The Colour floated downstream and was later recovered from the bottom of a pool; it hangs today in Brecon Cathedral, adorned with a wreath of immortelles placed upon it by Queen Victoria in memory of the events of that day.

About 350 men managed to escape across what became known as Fugitives' Drift, the great majority of them being members of the NNC or Kafir drivers and camp-followers. Only five British officers reached safety, including Smith-Dorrien (who became an army commander during the First World War); they were all wearing blue patrol jackets, and this coincidence may have saved their lives, for Cetewayo had told his warriors to concentrate on killing red soldiers, the rest being of little account. Only six privates of the 24th survived, and none of them had been present with the rifle companies; they included two bandsmen, Glyn's batman and the three wounded men who had played dead when the rocket battery was overrun.

That any escaped was due to Durnford's mounted men, who had held off the Zulu left horn while the fugitives streamed over the nek, fighting with pistols, clubbed rifles and hunting-knives until overwhelmed. Pope's company had fought its way back towards them and the bodies of its men were found nearby. On the left flank, about 60 men of Younghusband's company had scrambled up the rocks of the kopje and had died one by one as they were picked off. By 1330 the camp was in Zulu hands and the fighting was over, save for one nameless rifleman who concealed himself in a rocky fissure and continued to pick off Zulus for several hours. At length, several of them surrounded the crack and fired into it together; then there was silence.

During the battle and the pursuit the British and colonial units lost a total of 52 officers and 1,277 other ranks killed, of which 21 officers and 578 other ranks belonged to the 24th Regiment. No wounded survived. The lowest estimate of Zulu dead amounted to 2,000, the highest 3,000. To this must be added a comparable figure of seriously wounded, who were removed after the battle by their comrades. Some of the dead, too numerous to carry off, were piled in dongas and roughly covered with rocks. Then, as night fell, the Zulu army left Isandhlwana in sober mood and dispersed into the hills.

Chelmsford spent the afternoon collecting Glyn's footsore column. He was honest with the men and told them what had happened, adding that their task was now to recapture the camp and then fight their way through to Rorke's Drift. The column reached the camp at 2000 to find it silent and deserted. The men, forbidden to enter the camp itself, settled down to snatch a few hours' rest on the nek, which was itself thick with multilated corpses. Several officers wandered among the tents and were sickened by what they saw. There were stripped bodies everywhere, their stomachs slashed open by the Zulus to release the spirit; soldiers' heads, arranged in a ghastly circle; a drummer boy with his throat cut, hanging upside down from a wagon wheel. Oxen, horses and even an officer's dog had been slaughtered, and the looted contents of the wagons lay strewn in every direction.

On the hills around flickered the camp fires of the Zulu army, but what concerned Chelmsford most was the bright glow of a major conflagration in the direction of Rorke's Drift. Long before dawn he had the troops roused and began marching towards the little post, dreading what he might find.

Rorke's Drift was a Swedish mission station consisting of two single-storey, stone-built, thatched buildings. One, the missionary's house, was in use as a hospital and contained 35 patients, including a number wounded during the early skirmishes; the other, sometimes referred to as the barn, had formerly been used as a church and was now a storehouse containing mealie sacks and boxes of biscuit and meat. The senior officer present was Major Henry Spalding, who was responsible for the Central Column's line of communications. Available for the

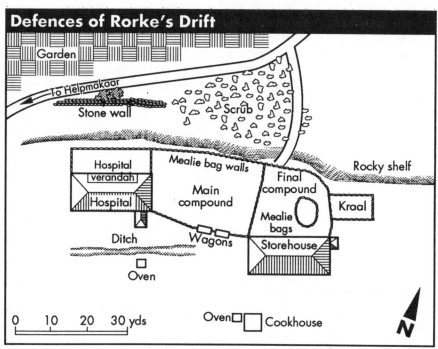

80

defence of the post were Lieutenant Gonville Bromhead's 'B' Company 2nd/24th, plus an NNC company under a Captain George Stephenson. Also present were Lieutenant John Chard of the Royal Engineers, Surgeon-Major James Reynolds, Assistant-Commissary James Dalton, who had formerly been an infantry sergeant-major, the Revd. George Smith, a missionary who had volunteered his services as chaplain, and Mr Otto Witt, the incumbent missionary.

Following the departure of Durnford's column the previous day, the morning had passed quietly at the post. After breakfast Chard rode over to Isandhlwana and returned about noon. During lunch the sound of heavy firing was heard but this evoked little comment, as Chelmsford was known to have left the camp expecting trouble. At 1400 Spalding left for Helpmakaar, looking for a company of the 1st/24th which was to reinforce the post but was two days overdue. This left Chard in command, as he was three years senior to Bromhead, and Stephenson, as an irregular, was not eligible. In the light of events, it is surprising to note that neither Chard nor Bromhead were regarded by their superiors as possessing anything more than average ability. Both were, in fact, rather elderly for their rank, Chard being 32 and Bromhead a year older; in addition, Bromhead suffered from a serious hearing defect which had begun to affect his career. Against this, both were experienced, sound and sensible officers.

At about 1515 two NNC officers on lathered horses splashed through the river with the shattering news that Isandhlwana had fallen and that one horn of the Zulu army was advancing rapidly on Rorke's Drift. One, Lieutenant James Adendorff, volunteered to assist in the defence of the post, and the second galloped off to warn the inhabitants of Helpmakaar. A third horseman, carrying a message from a staff officer who had escaped across Fugitives' Drift, arrived shortly after and confirmed the details. Bromhead had the tents struck and briefly considered loading the wounded aboard the wagons with a view to retiring on Helpmakaar. Dalton, however, pointed out that since the Zulus would quickly overtake the slow-moving column the only possible choice was to stand and fight. Chard agreed and the entire garrison began putting the post into a defensible state.

While loopholes were knocked in the walls of the buildings a barricade of mealie bags was erected around the perimeter. The area thus enclosed ran from the north-west corner of the hospital to a rocky ledge running along the front of the post, then back to the north-eastern corner of the store house; on the southern face a shorter barricade, supplemented by two wagons with biscuit boxes between the wheels, joined the storehouse and the hospital; abutting the eastern face of the barricade was a small stone cattle kraal which it was also decided to defend. The work was hard, since each mealie sack weighed 200 pounds and each ration box 112 pounds, but it continued at remarkable speed.

At about 1530 approximately 100 of Durnford's mounted Basutos arrived. They had been escorting his wagons to Isandhlwana and although they had escaped the débâcle they knew exactly what had happened and were clearly shaken. Nevertheless, their officer asked for orders and Chard sent them out as vedettes to cover the approach of the Zulus. Meanwhile, the Revd. Smith, Mr Witt and Private Wall had climbed a hill known as the Oskarberg to the south of the post, and suddenly they saw the massed ranks of the enemy, some 4,500 strong, breasting the river to the east with their arms linked against the current. As the observers raced down the slope, Wall yelled a warning: 'Here they come – black as hell and thick as grass!'

Mr Witt had seen enough and quickly vanished in the direction of Helpmakaar. He was followed by the Basuto vedettes, who galloped away after firing a few shots; they had already survived one horrible ordeal, and their real loyalty was to the dead Durnford, so perhaps their conduct is understandable if not excusable. Next, Stephenson's 300-strong NNC company panicked and fled, accompanied by their officer. Furious, several of Bromhead's men snatched up their rifles and fired at the retreating backs. Their principal target was the NNC's European sergeant, who pitched forward, dead. Neither Chard nor Bromhead felt inclined to make an issue of the matter.

It was now 1620 and in the space of a few minutes Chard's command had been reduced from more than 500 to 139, of whom 35 were sick or wounded. Realizing that he would now be unable to defend the entire perimeter, at least for long, he had an additional barricade constructed from the north-west corner of the store to the ledge, cutting the defences in two. The hospital was to be evacuated and, under pressure, the garrison would retire into the area surrounding the store. There was little or no time to carry out these orders for at 1630, a mere 75 minutes after Adendorff's arrival, the Zulu attack began. Rorke's Drift had not been one of Tshingwayo's objectives, and indeed Cetewayo was himself opposed to incursions into Natal, but at Isandhlwana the three regiments of the right horn, commanded by Dabulamanzi, the king's brother, had not washed their spears. The post at Rorke's Drift offered them that opportunity and, since apparently there was little risk involved, Dabula-manzi was prepared to place a wide interpretation on his orders.

What followed was a soldiers' battle in which both sides displayed supreme courage and utter determination. Once more the terrible musketry tore holes in the advancing ranks, and once more the Zulu wave surged over its own dead, eager to come to grips. The chest-high barricades, however, provided the protection the little garrison needed, while those Zulus who reached them were forced to use at least one hand in their attempts to scramble over, and were promptly spitted on the long bayonets. Fighting raged continuously around the perimeter as attack followed attack, blurring recollections of the struggle into a series of kaleidoscopic impressions: of Chard and Bromhead, the latter sometimes fighting with rifle and bayonet, forming one tiny reserve after another and rushing with it to reinforce threatened sectors; of the Revd. George Smith, walking the length of the firing line with words of encouragement and fresh ammunition for all, conduct which won him a commission in the Army Chaplains Department; of Commissary Dalton, a tower of strength in the firing line, shot through the shoulder at close range; of the wounded Corporal Friedrich Schiess of the NNC, leaving the hospital and, terrible in his wrath, taking his place at the mealie bags to shoot, bayonet and bludgeon any Zulu within reach, despite sustaining a second wound; of a galling fire from Zulu riflemen on the Oskarberg, largely inaccurate but still capable of dropping a man here and there; of shouted orders, incessant firing, the murderous look on the enemy's face but inches away, the clash of bayonet on assegai, death screams, blood and the acrid smell of drifting smoke; of a day that slipped unnoticed into night, and darkness illuminated by the blazing roof of the hospital.

It was in the hospital that some of the most heroic acts of the engagement took place. Those patients that could had already left the building and were playing an active part in the defence of the post. Others assisted fit men firing through the loopholes, but a number of seriously ill patients remained. At about 1700 the Zulus were swarming round the building, but Bromhead led several counter-attacks which drove them back. At this point Chard decided that he must abandon the western half of the defences and the troops outside retired behind the cross-wall. The men in the hospital were now on their own, and their position was complicated by the fact that the rooms all had barricaded external doors but were not inter-connected internally. When the Zulus broke into the end room and set fire to the thatch they faced the task of cutting holes in three partition walls with a pickaxe, dragging the patients through these and lowering them from a window in the wall facing the storehouse, while simultaneously holding the enemy at bay. In the process, Private Joseph Williams, after killing several Zulus battering their way through a door, was himself seized and hacked to death, as were Private Horrigan and two patients caught on the wrong side of the first hole. The remainder, including Corporal William Allan and Private Frederick Hitch, who were already wounded, Privates Henry Hook, John Williams, William and Robert Jones, continued their desperate work under the blazing roof and eventually they and ten of their twelve charges reached the storehouse, covered by fire from the cross-wall. Of the two remaining patients one, delirious, refused to leave the hospital and was killed when the Zulus finally broke through; the second was speared as he attempted to cross the thirty yards to the storehouse alone.

At about 1800 Chard decided to abandon the cattle kraal at the eastern end of the defences. The garrison was now concentrated in the storehouse compound, in which the remaining mealie bags were piled into a redoubt where a last stand was to be made, if the need arose. In the meantime, the wounded were placed inside and it also served as a platform for marksmen. The flames from the blazing hospital were seen not only by Chelmsford at Isandhlwana, but by Spalding, who was bringing up the missing company from Helpmakaar. By now fully aware of the disaster which had befallen Pulleine, he assumed that the post had fallen and, spotting a large body of Zulus across his path, turned his men about. It was a wise decision for, in the open, the company would have stood no chance at all.

Meanwhile, attacks continued with unremitting fury on the shrunken perimeter. Altogether, six major attacks were identified, and each was repulsed with heavy loss. At midnight, Chard led a sortie which recovered a water cart lying outside the barricade and his men were able to slake their terrible thirst. At 0200 the Zulus seemed to lose heart. The garrison had been fighting for its survival, but they had been fighting for personal gratification, and there was none to be had in this place. For a while, they contented themselves with firing into the defences or flinging assegais from cover, but by 0400 they had gone. Chard and Bromhead dared not let their men sleep, for they would be impossible to wake if the enemy launched a surprise attack. Instead, they worked them hard, knocking down the walls of the smouldering hospital to prevent their being used as cover, stripping the vulnerable thatch from the storehouse, and gathering up the thousands of weapons which lay on the body-strewn ground around the defences. At 0700 a large body of Zulus was seen on the hills overlooking the post, but it soon moved off out of sight.

As Chelmsford marched steadily towards the column of smoke which marked the position of Rorke's Drift a strange incident took place. Marching in the opposite direction, and within shouting distance, was the flank of Dabulamanzi's force. A mere 24 hours earlier each side would eagerly have gone for the other, but now they simply glared balefully and went their separate ways; for the moment, they were prepared to live and let live. The mounted infantry vanguard of Chelmsford's column approached the post at 0800 dreading what they might find, but suddenly set spurs to their horses when a man was seen waving a signal flag from the roof of the storehouse. More men, haggard, grimy and exhausted, were climbing on to heaped mealie bags, cheering wildly and waving their helmets. Zulu bodies lay thick in every direction.

Chelmsford came up and Chard made his report. It was incredible, but the facts were undeniable. His little garrison had sustained the loss of only fifteen dead and twelve seriously wounded, two of them mortally. Now, the survivors sprawled in the sun in their shirtsleeves, sleeping or puffing their pipes. Hook, who had led the fight in the hospital, was brewing tea; ordered to report to Bromhead just as he was, he found himself talking to the General with his braces dangling while a staff officer took details of the story. Nearly 400 enemy bodies were found in the immediate vicinity of the post, and another hundred had been carried by the Zulus as far as the drift; more still were found on the Oskarberg and in the bush around the post. The exact number of Zulus killed has never been established and must again have been paralleled by the number of seriously wounded.

Eleven Victoria Crosses were won by the defenders of Rorke's Drift, being awarded to Lieutenants Chard and Bromhead; Surgeon-Major Reynolds; Commissary Dalton; Corporals Allen and Schiess; Privates Hitch, Hook, William and Robert Jones and John Williams. Had it then been the custom to award the decoration posthumously, the number would have been even larger. In addition, Chard and Bromhead, the elderly subalterns once considered unpromising, became brevet-majors and were summoned to a personal audience with Queen Victoria. The astonishing defence of their post against odds of twenty to one went far to deaden the shock of Isandhlwana and its fame quickly spread around the world. The Kaiser, deeply impressed by the story of inspired junior leadership, determination and expert improvisation, ordered the details to be read at the head of every regiment in his army.

For the Zulus, Isandhlwana was a victory terrible in its consequences. Cetewayo himself likened it to a spear thrust into the belly of the nation, and the defence of Rorke's Drift had twisted that spear. In the kraals, the wails of mourning continued for a fortnight. One tenth of the Zulu manhood was dead, and a similar number lay seriously wounded in their huts. But the moral damage sustained at Isandhlwana and Rorke's Drift was far greater than the physical. If so few men could kill so many in the face of overwhelming odds, what hope was there of victory when the British returned in greater numbers, as they surely would? The self-confidence of the Zulus had been broken and, although they continued to fight with exemplary courage, on 4 July Chelmsford won the decisive battle he had sought at Ulundi.

As for Sir Bartle Frere, who had engineered so much needless bloodshed, the Government was less than pleased that he had provoked the war it had specifically forbidden, and even less pleased by having to dispatch urgent reinforcements in the wake of the Isandhlwana disaster. He was sharply reprimanded, then publicly humiliated by the restriction of his authority to Cape Colony, which might be considered little enough in the circumstances. In his defence he could argue that the Zulu threat (if, indeed, it had ever existed under Cetewayo's rule) had been eliminated once and for all.

CHAPTER 6
Fighting to the Muzzle
ARTILLERY ACTIONS 1914–1918

The First World War was primarily an artillery war. More than 58 per cent of British casualties on the Western Front were sustained as a result of artillery fire, and the proportion incurred by other armies was very similar. Artillery was the man-killer supreme, critically important to the success of attack or defence. It created the lunar landscape across which it was difficult to obtain a clean breakthrough because the enemy was always able to deploy his reserves quickly over the unbroken ground to his rear, and thus it was artillery which dominated tactics for much of the war. Because its application was mathematical, precise and impersonal it was, until the arrival of the tank, more feared than any other weapon system, and continued exposure to it deprived many of their last remaining shreds of sanity. Even during a 'quiet' day on the British sector, with no major offensive operations in progress, wastage caused by German harassing and interdiction fire was often responsible for more casualties than were incurred during the entire Falklands Campaign.

In this terrible war, into which the nations of Europe had entered with such naïve enthusiasm, there were numerous stands by isolated infantry brigades, battalions, companies and platoons which would in other circumstances have earned them immortality, but so broad was the conflict, so great the national effort involved and so horrendous the overall loss of life, their their details now lie submerged in official archives, half-forgotten folk-memories of a generation now all but gone. What that generation recalled with agonizing clarity were the Pals' battalions, raised on a local basis from groups of eager volunteers, scythed down as they advanced unflinchingly into the teeth of the enemy's defensive barrage and machine-gun fire. Yet, it was sensed instinctively that if the fight reached the guns themselves, it was around them that great issues would be decided.

In 1914 Germany intended adopting a defensive stance against Russia until she had destroyed the French armies. The latter was to be achieved by the Schlieffen Plan, conceived in 1905. This took account of the fact that in any war between Germany and France one flank of the contending armies would rest on the frontier of neutral Switzerland. Using this flank as a fixed pivot, it was intended that the German right wing would be flung forward, marching west, then south-west, then south and finally south-east, bending the French left back upon its centre, then upon its right until the entire French Army was pinned against its own frontier defences and the Swiss border, surrounded and cut off from its bases. The plan's major disadvantage was that it required space for the right wing to develop its enormous wheel, space which could only be obtained by invading Belgium, and it was this violation of neutrality which brought the United Kingdom into the war.

The outer edge of the great German wheel was formed by General Alexander von Kluck's First Army. Everything hinged on the ability of von Kluck's heavily laden infantry to march continuously, day after day, without rest. Timing was of the essence, there being little or no margin for such checks as might be encountered, and von Kluck had been selected for the task because he was known to be hard-driving and ruthless.

The German Army of 1914 was the most formidable in the world. Superbly equipped, it was led by a brilliant General Staff and its officer corps was professional and efficient, as were its long-service NCOs. It was, however, a conscript army whose soldiers were trained for a war of manoeuvre *en masse* which made few demands on the soldier's personal knowledge of fieldcraft or individual initiative; nor did such a war require an above-average standard of musketry.

There was, therefore, something of an historical irony in the fact that deploying directly in the path of von Kluck's troops was an army which excelled in these very qualities; the British Expeditionary Force. The British Army as a whole had learned some very sharp lessons during the South African War of 1899–1901, and it had taken them to heart. In size it was dwarfed by the conscript armies of the great continental land powers, but at the tactical level it was unequalled. In particular its infantry, using clip-loaded bolt-action Lee Enfield magazine rifles, had developed the technique of firing sixteen *aimed* rounds a minute, creating a fearful fire-storm against which no troops on earth could stand. Moreover, during its first battles the BEF consisted solely of regular soldiers and recalled reservists with years of experience to their credit, many of them having seen active service in India, South Africa or elsewhere in the British Empire. Their first encounters with the men in *Pickelhauben* and field grey left them unimpressed, since it was immediately apparent that they were not professionals. 'Oh, we don't give a **** for old von Kluck, And all his ****ing great army!' they sang to the tune of *The Girl I Left Behind Me*, and they meant it.

At Mons on 23 August, von Kluck's attacking columns were shot flat by the BEF. The British felt capable of holding their positions indefinitely but, to the annoyance of the BEF's commander, Field Marshal Sir John French, were compelled to conform to the withdrawal of the French Fifth Army on their right. Von Kluck, angry at the day's delay which had been imposed, pressed hard behind and at Le Cateau on 26 August almost succeeded in encircling the British II Corps, commanded by General Sir Horace Smith-Dorrien, whom we last met at Isandhlwana. Sheer hard fighting enabled II Corps to break free and resume its retreat, although the cost had been heavy. Three of the German First Army's seven corps had been employed in the battle and von Kluck, whose march had been delayed by a further day, believed that he had beaten no less than nine divisions; in fact, Smith-Dorrien had only three.

The Allies continued their retreat to the Marne. Von Kluck, intent on destroying the BEF, which was in far better shape then he imagined, caught up with the British rearguards on 1 September at Crépy-en-Vallois, Villiers-Cotterets and Néry, and was again vigorously shaken off. The last of these engagements, while small in scale, was to have totally unexpected anf far-reaching consequences which would ultimately be disastrous for the commander of the German First Army.

Néry, a small village near Compiègne, lies approximately 50 miles to the north-east of Paris. During the evening of 31 August Brigadier-

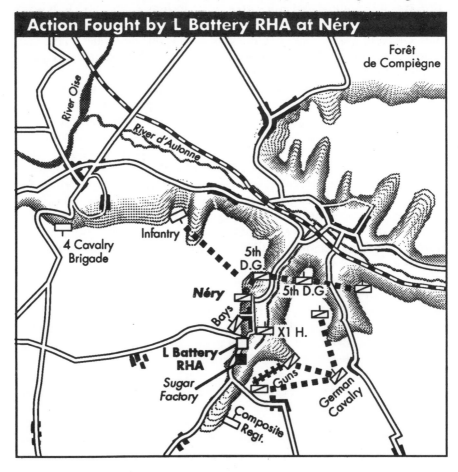

General C. J. Briggs' 1st Cavalry Brigade, which was screening the exposed western flank of the BEF's line of retreat, rode in from the north. There had been no contact with the enemy and Briggs' units (The Queen's Bays, 5th Dragoon Guards, 11th Hussars and 'L' Battery Royal Horse Artillery), picketed their horses and settled down for the night.

The days of this fine summer were still unbearably hot, although they were coming to an end and were now followed by chillier nights. Briggs had intended moving off at 0430, but the landscape was covered by a dense mist and the move was postponed for an hour. 'L' Battery used the interval to water and feed its teams, which were then hooked into their vehicles, the poles of which were lowered to the ground to ease the weight on the wheelers' shoulders while they were standing. The mist was clearing slightly, revealing a deep ravine to the east of the village, beyond which lay a plateau dominating the entire area.

Leaving his officers talking by some haystacks in a corner of 'L' Battery's field, the Battery Commander, Major Sclater-Booth, made his way to Briggs' headquarters in the village, which he reached at 0505. Hardly had he arrived when a shell burst overhead and an 11th Hussar patrol galloped in with a report that German cavalry had been encountered on the high ground to the north of Néry. Within minutes, heavy and sustained artillery, machine-gun and rifle fire from the plateau to the east, delivered from a range of between 600 and 800 yards, was sweeping through the village and its surrounding bivouacs. The 1st Cavalry Brigade had been taken completely by surprise and Briggs' only hope was to hold his ground until help arrived. Sclater-Booth attempted to return to his battery but found the Bays' horses stampeding down the main street of the village; a shell burst among them, blocking the road with screaming, kicking carcasses. He cut through to the rear of the houses, saw that three of his six 13-pounders were going into action amid the wreckage of the battery, and noted the position of the enemy's artillery, whose gun flashes could be seen on the plateau through the slowly dispersing mist. Then a shell burst in front of him and he lost consciousness.

The enemy were the 4th Cavalry Division, who were screening the right flank of von Kluck's advance. The division's establishment included three 4-gun horse artillery batteries, and for the German gunners the sight of 'L' Battery, lined up in close order ready to move off, and the open cavalry bivouacs with their tethered horse lines, was an artillery-man's dream come true. Four of the guns immediately concentrated their fire on 'L' Battery while the remaining eight engaged other targets in and around the village. Simultaneously, the German cavalry squadrons dismounted and opened fire with rifles and machine-guns on the British position.

Within minutes 'L' Battery had become a shambles as the shells and rifle fire tore into the packed mass of men and animals, cutting them down where they stood. Plunging with terror, the horses tried to bolt but could not because the dropped limber poles were driven into the ground by their forward movement, holding them fast. Soon, the battery's field was strewn with dead gunners, dismembered horses, overturned limbers and apparently abandoned guns. Yet, despite the apparent hopelessness of the situation, the moment produced the men. With a shout of 'Come on! Who's for the guns?' Captain E. K. Bradbury, the Battery Captain, ran from the haystacks and, with his three subalterns and those gunners still on their feet, managed to unlimber three guns and swing them round against the enemy. Bradbury and Sergeant D. Nelson manned one, Lieutenants Campbell and Mundy the second and Lieutenant Giffard and some gunners the third. More than twenty yards of bullet-swept ground separated the guns from the ammunition wagons and, although every round had to be brought across this, there was never a shortage of volunteers.

At first, 'L' Battery's three guns against the German four seemed reasonable odds. However, shortly after Campbell's gun came into action it was wrecked by a direct hit. The two subalterns ran to assist Bradbury, but Campbell was killed immediately. After Giffard had fired a few rounds some of his crew were killed and he and the remainder were seriously wounded. Bradbury now faced odds of four to one but he kept firing, ammunition for the gun being supplied by Gunner Darbyshire and Driver Osborn. He must have hurt his opponents, for after a while the eight German guns which had been engaging targets in the village switched their fire to 'L' Battery.

For an hour the lone 13-pounder fought on, one gun against twelve. Somehow, despite the fact that it formed the eye of a hurricane of bursting high-explosives, it survived. One by one, however, the ammunition carriers were hit and the rate of fire fell away. Mundy was seriously wounded and by 0715 only Bradbury and Sergeant Nelson, who had also been hit, remained at the gun. Battery Sergeant-Major G. T. Dorrell ran forward to join them. Bradbury left the gun to fetch ammunition and immediately sustained mortal wounds from a shell burst. Carefully, Dorrell and Nelson fired the few remaining rounds and then, at last, the 13-pounder fell silent.

For a moment, it seemed as though it had all been for nothing. Then, the tables were turned on the enemy in a manner as sudden as it was dramatic. Deprived of the support of their artillery, which had vainly been trying to suppress 'L' Battery, the German cavalrymen had been prevented from developing their attack by the rapid, accurate rifle fire of Briggs' troopers. Indeed, the initiative was already passing to the British, for two squadrons of the 5th Dragoon Guards had moved forward and were making a dismounted attack on the enemy's right flank. Concurrently, the sun was burning off the last of the dawn mist, revealing the reinforcements which Briggs had requested approaching the battlefield.

They consisted of the 4th Cavalry Brigade, with 'I' Battery RHA, followed by several infantry battalions from the 4th Division. 'I' Battery went into action at once, blanketing the German gun positions. The only rational explanation for what followed is that the enemy divisional commander, believing that his troops were about to be trapped between the hammer of the advancing relief force and the anvil of 1st Cavalry Brigade, ordered a hasty withdrawal. This induced a panic which quickly became a rout and ended in headlong flight. Eight of his guns were left where they stood on the plateau, and the four which were got away were later found abandoned in a wood. Eagerly, the 11th Hussars swung into their saddles and set off in pursuit, returning with 78 prisoners. The German 4th Cavalry Division, dispersed across many miles of wooded country, had ceased to exist as a fighting formation. Not until 4 September did it reassemble and even then it was considered unfit for duty.

British casualties during the engagement amounted to 135 officers and men, of whom five officers and 49 men belonged to 'L' Battery. The Victoria Cross was awarded to Captain Bradbury, posthumously, and to Sergeant Nelson and Battery Sergeant-Major Dorrell. In recognition of its critical part in the battle the battery was granted the Honour Title 'Néry'. At the time of writing one of its 13-pounder guns is on display at the Imperial War Museum in London.

The outcome of the action at Néry was one of a number of telling factors which resulted in the failure of the Schlieffen Plan. Von Kluck, obsessed with his mission, obstinately ignored important battlefield intelligence because it did not conform with his own thoughts. In his eyes, the BEF's resumed withdrawal meant that it had been roundly beaten and therefore ceased to count. Even if this had been true, there were still naggingly persistent reports of unexpected clashes with French troops to the west of his line of march, but these he dismissed as involving nothing more than local Territorial units. The truth was that the French were assembling a new army, the Sixth under General Joseph Maunoury, on the left of the BEF, and this posed a most serious threat to the German flank. If the 4th Cavalry Division, which formed the eyes and ears of von Kluck's right wing, had not been destroyed at Néry, he would doubtless have been informed of the fact. As it was, he commenced his all-important wheel to the east lacking vital intelligence. To make matters worse, on 2 September French troops ambushed a staff officer's car containing maps which showed the routes along which First Army's corps were moving, these details being confirmed by air reconnaissance the following day.

On 7 September Maunoury struck, initiating what became known as the Battle of the Marne. Once again, von Kluck under-estimated the threat and sent back a single corps to contain the French. As the pressure grew, he was forced to commit most of his army. This, in turn, opened a gap between himself and General von Bülow's Second Army, and into this moved the BEF. Suddenly, the Germans lost heart. Von Kluck's infantry had been marching and fighting continuously for four weeks, sometimes covering 24 miles a day. Weary and hollow-eyed, their boots worn out and uniforms in rags, latterly they had staggered along, kept going by promises that they were on the verge of a decisive victory. Now, forced to retreat by an enemy who showed no signs of being beaten, they knew that the plan had failed and many simply gave up.

Von Kluck and von Bülow, their flanks turned, executed a skilful withdrawal behind the Aisne and there both sides, utterly exhausted, dug in as the weather broke. Each attempted unsuccessfully to restore mobility with outflanking moves to the west. Soon the lines stretched from the sea to Switzerland and the era of trench warfare had begun. Both sides attempted to break through with concentrated artillery fire, which merely aggravated the problem. The Germans tried poison gas, but because of shifts in the wind, this proved to be a two-edged weapon. The British resorted to tunnelling and exploded huge mines beneath the enemy trenches, but the immense effort involved produced only limited gains. The tank, developed concurrently by the British and French, seemed to offer the best prospects for success, although, because of the limited technology of the time, it was painfully slow and so lacking in stamina that it required a complete overhaul after covering a very few miles.

The British first employed tanks, in small numbers, during their 1916 offensive on the Somme, and were criticized for forfeiting the element of surprise by not waiting until sufficient were available for a mass attack. There was, however, another side to that particular coin. Senior German officers who examined captured examples regarded them as rickety mechanical curiosities and, for the moment, decided against developing their own tank arm. This opinion seemed to be justified by tank losses in the shell-torn mud wallow of the Ypres Salient, but it was not a view shared by the average German soldier who had experienced at first hand the shock and fear generated by a successful tank attack, and some divisions trained their field artillery regiments in anti-tank tactics.

For its part, the Tank Corps, commanded by Brigadier-General Hugh Elles, demanded the chance to demonstrate its true potential with a mass attack over good going. After some prompting from General Sir Julian Byng, whose Third Army front contained the most promising ground for such an attack, Field Marshal Sir Douglas Haig, commanding the BEF, sanctioned what was described officially as a 'tank raid' against the enemy's communications centre of Cambrai, to be delivered over rolling chalk downland as yet little spoiled by shellfire. For the attack the Tank Corps assembled 376 gun tanks, plus a further 32 fitted with grapnels for clearing wire, eighteen supply tanks and a handful of communications and bridging vehicles. In their path lay the formidable defences of the Hindenburg Line, consisting of trenches dug so wide and deep that they were considered tank-proof by the Germans, and to counter this many tanks carried huge brushwood fascines which could be released into the trenches, so forming causeways across.

During the morning of 20 November 1917 the Tank Corps achieved complete surprise and overran the Hindenburg trenches without difficulty. A gap six miles wide was torn in the enemy's defences and in celebration of the victory church bells were rung throughout the United Kingdom. The jubilation, however, proved to be premature, for while the tanks had demonstrated their ability to overcome prepared defence systems, as yet they lacked the speed and stamina to extend their success into a clean breakthrough and, for various reasons, the cavalry were not released to exploit the gap. Once again, the enemy was able to rush in reinforcements to seal off the penetration and the moment passed without decisive result.

It was, perhaps, on the Flesquières sector that the most important opportunities of the day were lost, and for this much of the responsibility is shared by two men, one a British divisional commander and the other a German artilleryman whose identity has never been firmly established.

Flesquières village and the nearby ridge were among the objectives of the 51st (Highland) Division, the advance of which was led by 'D' and the major part of 'E' Battalions of the Tank Corps. For sheer fighting ability, the division ranked with the best in the British army and was always respected and feared by its opponents. It was commanded by Major-General G. M. Harper, a leader of immense personal courage who was fiercely proud of his Highlanders and protective of their lives. To his officers and men he was known unofficially as Uncle and, despite the unfavourable criticism he attracted, they remained staunchly loyal to him, stoutly defending his actions into their last years. The problem was that Harper was a commander of the old school in both senses; his qualities as a leader were undoubted, but he was quite unable to adapt to the changes on the battlefield which had taken place since his youth. He was, for example, opposed to the development of the machine-gun on the grounds that too much reliance on such weapons would be detrimental to the overall standard of musketry, refusing to accept that the two were complementary. Needless to say, he disapproved of tanks and described the entire concept of the great attack at Cambrai as 'a fantastic and most unmilitary scheme'.

Much careful thought had gone into the detailed planning of the attack. It was appreciated that there must be the closest possible co-operation between tanks and infantry if the attack was to succeed, since each could solve some of the other's problems. If machine-gun posts pinned down the infantry, the tanks would deal with them; if, on the other hand, the tanks were faced with field artillery firing in the anti-tank role, it would be the infantry who attacked the gunners. The tanks were to work in sections of three, with the infantry following in *files* some

25 yards behind so that they could pass quickly through the gaps which would be crushed in the enemy's barbed wire entanglements. The leading tank would turn left to rake the fire trench, into which the second tank would drop its fascine, then cross and turn left to rake the support trench, into which the third tank would drop its fascine, cross and turn left to engage the defenders from the rear. Finally, while the captured trenches were cleaned out and consolidated, the remaining infantry and tanks would rally on the objective and resume the advance.

Naturally, divisional commanders were permitted to vary this drill to suit local circumstances, but Harper chose to ignore it altogether and substituted one of his own devising. He decided that the tanks would work in two sections of three, the second reaching the enemy position four minutes after the first. The first wave would drop its fascines in the fire trench, cross, and proceed directly to the support trench, where they would turn right and take its occupants. When the second wave arrived it was to cross the fire trench using the fascines already laid, then, while the tank in the centre went on to drop its fascine in the support trench, the two outer tanks would turn right to rake the fire trench. It is immediately apparent that Harper's variations of the official plan, as well as being needlessly complicated, required twice the number of tanks to achieve the same effect. Worse, however, was to follow. Knowing that the tanks would draw fire, and wishing to save his men casualties, Harper insisted that they should advance a minimum of 100 yards behind the second wave, not in files, but in *extended order*. This was counter-productive in two ways. First, the extended lines would naturally contract as they approached the gaps in the wire crushed by the tanks, and secondly, contact between tanks and infantry, already tenuous, would quickly be broken if the gap between them opened further, to their mutual detriment.

Nevertheless, at first all went well. Led by the two tank battalions, the division attacked promptly at 0620 and within two hours had overrun the enemy's main line defences. There had been little serious fighting, for the Germans had either fled, panic-stricken, or surrendered in large numbers. Everywhere along the front divisions were securing their objectives well ahead of schedule and their commanders were taking advantage of the fact by continuing the advance. Not so Harper, who decided to stick to the official timetable and allowed his men to rest before tackling the next objective, Flesquières Ridge and the village just beyond. No such rest was needed, although the tank crews were grateful for it as the temperature within their vehicles, in which the atmosphere was already fouled by expended cordite and engine fumes, could reach 120 degrees. For many of them, the clean air they were breathing was their last.

Beyond the ridge, the Germans were recovering from their initial shock. No longer under pressure, they reinforced Flesquières village and deployed several field artillery batteries, which had been trained in anti-tank tactics, along the open reverse slopes to await the attack. The presence of these guns was not suspected for when detailed air reconnaissance of the area was made prior to the battle they were lying snug in the camouflaged gun pits in which they performed their usual role.

At 0930 Harper gave the order for the advance to be resumed. The tanks lumbered slowly forward up the shallow ridge, but by now the infantry were some 400 yards behind. As they ground their way slowly across the crest the tanks presented perfect targets to the waiting German gunners. A sudden and murderous duel ensued in which 'D' and 'E' Battalions lost a total of sixteen tanks; no survivors emerged from the blazing wrecks. Fire from the remaining tanks, some of which worked their way on to the flanks of the guns, shot down their crews and at length the anti-tank batteries were silenced. One gun remained obstinately in action until the end and is believed to have accounted for five tanks. It was served by a single gunner who could be seen frantically loading and firing behind the gunshield; then he too went down. Reflecting bitterly that if the infantry had been present the situation could have been resolved less bloodily, the remnants of 'D' and 'E' Battalions continued their advance. There was no time to discover the identity of the brave men who had done so much damage.

Contact between Harper's severely reduced tank element and his infantry had been effectively broken by the gap between the two. As the tanks passed Flesquières village, a strong position which included a well-constructed wall surrounding the grounds of its château, they suppressed fire coming from the defences. The defenders, however, had merely gone to ground and they surfaced again when the Highlanders appeared. For the rest of the day Harper's division, supported by a handful of tanks, became bogged down in a protracted struggle for the village. This, in turn, delayed the advance of the 6th Division on the right and the 62nd Division on the left, neither of which wished to continue their advance with an unsubdued enemy on their open flank. At length, the commander of the 62nd Division offered to assist by attacking Flesquières from the rear, but Harper declined, feeling that this would reflect badly on his own troops. As night fell, the village remained in German hands, although its garrison, consisting of 600 determined survivors of the 27th and 84th Infantry Regiments under a Major Krebs, was withdrawn shortly after.

The failure to capture Flesquières early on the first day of the battle had important consequences. The 1st Cavalry Division was to have advanced through the village and exploited as far as Bourlon, where a ridge overlooked Cambrai itself, but of course that was impossible in the circumstances. The irony was that Bourlon, which was to witness some of the heaviest fighting of the battle, was for the moment undefended.

The attack continued for a few days more, but its sharp cutting edge had been blunted. The element of surprise had gone and the number of tanks available dropped steadily; by the end of the first day alone 179 had been knocked out, were ditched awaiting recovery, or had broken down. There was no doubt that the enemy had been badly hurt. Much ground had been taken, many guns captured and thousands of prisoners were being escorted to the rear. But German reinforcements were converging rapidly on the area and, day by day, the gains became smaller. The last offensive operations took place on 27 November. Haig's dispatch on the battle contained the following paragraph: 'Many of the hits upon our tanks at Flesquières were obtained by a German artillery officer who, remaining alone at his battery, served a field gun single-handed until killed at his gun. The great bravery of this officer aroused the admiration of all ranks.' The basis of this was a batch of reports describing the incident, supplied by 51st Division. Of these, the most important was written by Captain G. Dugdale, an officer of the 6th Division with no axe to grind, who visited the scene of the action early the same afternoon: 'I came to a German field battery, every gun out of action with the exception of one. By this was lying a single German officer, quite dead. In front of him were five tanks, which he had evidently succeeded in knocking out single-handed with his gun. A brave man.'

Naturally, Harper and his staff, acutely conscious that their division alone had sustained a decisive check on the first day, were inclined to emphasize the importance of the German's action in the hope that it might divert criticism that they had planned and conducted a thoroughly bad battle, with the result that they had lost their tanks at the critical moment; after all, generous praise accorded to a worthy foe reflects admirably on the donor. The story tended to grow with the telling, and at one time the officer was credited with destroying all sixteen of the tanks knocked out at this point. To those who, like Harper, were opposed to the development of the tank, it was a gift.

Knowing nothing of the incident, the Germans were naturally intrigued to discover that one of their officers had earned favourable comment in an enemy Field Marshal's dispatch and, after the war, they asked for further details. Unfortunately, no one had bothered to record the man's identity. By careful checking and process of elimination among their own records, they were able to identify Lieutenant Karl Müller of the 108th Field Artillery Regiment as being the most probable candidate. A strong alternative claim, supported by a German eye-witness, was made for an *Unteroffizier* Kruger, but more recent research suggests that Kruger was not present during the engagement and that the honour should be accorded to another *Unteroffizier* named Greising, whose body was found beneath the breech-block of his gun by a British sniper. After so many years it seem improbable that firmer evidence is likely to be presented.

The fighting on the Cambrai sector was far from over. On 30 November the Germans counter-attacked with a totally unexpected speed and drive. Suddenly, whole units found themselves cut off while others sacrificed themselves to stem the tide. The few tanks remaining in the area helped blunt the attack but by 7 December much of the ground captured the previous month was again in German hands. Neither Haig nor Byng could offer an intelligible reason why the enemy infantry had managed to break through their defences so quickly, and the unacceptable fact was that the Germans had also developed a means of breaking the deadlock of trench warfare.

This was first seen when the Baltic port of Riga was captured from the Russians three months earlier. Here, the German attack had incorporated three new elements. First, instead of poison gas being released from cylinders in the front line, it had been fired directly on to the Russian positions in specially designed shells. Secondly, the infantry had deliberately avoided sectors which continued to hold out, by-passing them and working their way steadily into the Russian rear areas. Thirdly, the attack was directly supported by waves of ground-attack aircraft which raked the trenches with machine-gun fire.

The following month the same techniques routed the Italian Second Army at Caporetto. Special emphasis was laid on the assault spearheads penetrating the Italian artillery and administrative areas, leaving centres of resistance to be eliminated by follow-up troops. Again, whereas reserves had previously been thrown in against the toughest objectives, they were now used only to support successful advances.

Together, the results of Riga, Caporetto and the Cambrai counter-attack convinced the German High Command that it had a winning formula and it began to refine it with a view to mounting a series of decisive offensives on the Western Front the following spring. First, they formed *Sturmabteilungen* (Assault Battalions) which would form the spearhead of their respective divisions. These were recruited from young, fit men of proven initiative and were the cream of the army. Next, the artillery was reorganized so that on the sectors chosen for attack the *Sturmabteilungen* would enjoy overwhelming local support designed to crush the defenders and their own supporting artillery before the attack began. This involved the formation of a 'travelling circus' of medium and heavy guns under the command of a Colonel Bruchmüller, who insisted that batteries should register their targets by mathematical survey rather than by ranging shellfire, thus achieving complete surprise when they did open fire. The Imperial Air Service also formed *Schlachtstaffeln*, the function of which was the strafing of targets in the path of the Storm Troopers. Finally, compelled to revise its earlier opinion of tanks by the success of the British attack at Cambrai, the German Army began forming tank battalions of its own, using captured British machines and a hastily produced design of its own.

The first of the German offensives, codenamed 'Michael', lasted from 21 March until 5 April. It struck the British Third and Fifth Armies, forcing them back 40 miles. The line came close to breaking, but was held by the dogged defence of battalions and batteries which fought to the last round, by the local intervention of tanks and dismounted cavalry, by Royal Flying Corps aircraft which strafed at ground level, and by little groups of clerks, cooks, mess waiters, signallers, batmen and drivers who fought like veteran riflemen until they were overwhelmed. Hardly had 'Michael' ended than the second offensive, codenamed 'Georgette', began. It was mounted against the British First and Second Armies in Flanders and, although it made less spectacular progress, it all but eliminated the emotive Ypres salient in which so much blood had been shed.

Halting the two offensives had cost the British Army almost a quarter of a million casualties. Some divisions, notably the 8th, 21st, 25th and 50th, had been bled white and were so worn out that they were no longer considered capable of holding an active sector. Generously, Marshal Ferdinand Foch, the new Allied Supreme Commander, suggested that their place should be taken by fresh French divisions and that they should recuperate on a quiet sector of the French line. Haig agreed and at the end of April the four divisions, grouped together as IX Corps under Lieutenant-General Sir A. H. Gordon, joined General Duchesne's French Sixth Army and began moving into positions at the eastern end of the Chemin des Dames ridge.

Here they rested and absorbed replacements, most of whom had barely finished their basic training. What impressed them most was that the front was so peaceful; the trenches were dry and comfortable, the shelling was light, the countryside was pretty and the birds sang. Yet, by the cruellest of coincidences, they had been moved directly into the path of the next major German offensive, codenamed 'Blücher'. As the days passed, British survivors of the earlier attacks began to recognize the tell-tale signs of preparation across the lines. Duchesne, however, remained unimpressed until the interrogation of two prisoners on 26 May revealed that the offensive was to begin the following day. By then it was too late for effective counter-measures to be taken.

The story of 5th Field Battery Royal Artillery, which formed part of the 8th Division's artillery element, is representative of the many units which went down fighting to stem the tide of the German advance that spring. The battery, armed with six 18-pounder guns, took over a position at Bois des Buttes, a mile south of Ville au Bois, on 12 May. The guns were emplaced in two sections of three, each section being protected by a sandbag parapet to the front and sides. Ammunition was stored in wheeled caissons behind the parapet, and in pits dug behind the gun platforms. The Battery Commander, Major J. C. Griffiths, also had a system of trenches dug for local defence.

When, at 1620 on 26 May, the entire sector was warned that an enemy attack was imminent, the 5th Battery was commanded by its Battery Captain, Captain John Massey, Griffiths having gone back to the division's rear area for a few days' rest, and one gun had been sent to workshops for repair. At 2100 the five remaining guns opened harassing fire on the enemy's probable concentration areas and routes leading forward.

The Germans made no response until 0100, when their front suddenly erupted. This was the most meticulously prepared of Bruch-müller's artillery programmes, and it left nothing to chance. For ten minutes gas shells rained on the battery position but gas masks were quickly donned and they caused few casualties. This was followed by a concentrated bombardment with high-explosives, the intensity of which confirmed that several German batteries had concentrated their fire on Massey's guns. At 0115 the infantry in front of 5 Battery sent up an SOS rocket. It was a call for assistance which could not be refused, but for Massey to expose all his crews to the tempest of blast and flying steel was to invite disaster. While most of the gunners took cover in their dugouts, he organized a system of reliefs involving each gun being manned by an NCO and two men at any one time. After firing in support of the infantry for the prescribed period, Massey resumed harassing and interdiction fire under his own control, the telephone links to the observation posts having been cut earlier.

The next phase of Bruchmüller's programme called for the systematic destruction of those British artillery positions which were still capable of response. During this his field guns were joined by heavier weapons which had been engaging targets to the rear, their combined fire being concentrated on each battery in turn. Three of the 8th Division's eight field artillery batteries had already been battered into silence when, at 0335, the full weight of the bombardment hit Massey's battery. The ordeal lasted only five minutes but it inflicted heavy casualties and left men shocked, dazed and deafened. One gun was knocked out and the rest came close to being blown into oblivion when a shell burst on the edge of an ammunition pit. The same round severely wounded Lieutenant J. E. Large, one of the two section commanders, but he declined to leave the guns. Miraculously, neither Massey nor his second section commander, Second-Lieutenant C. A. Button, were hit.

The Storm Troopers were now massing for their attack and most of the German artillery shifted its fire to support them. First it fired gas shells at the infantry trenches, which were already under continuous fire from massed trench mortars. This was followed by a rolling barrage of high-explosives which lifted forward in 200-yard bounds and remained static for six minutes at a time, jumping from trench to trench when it reached the Allied front line. Those who lived through the experience described it as far worse than anything they had endured during 'Michael' and

'Georgette'. The infantry positions were reduced to a shambles of cut wire, caved-in trenches, wrecked machine-gun posts and smashed dugouts. Casualties were severe and all communication with the rear was lost.

At 0340 the Storm Troopers, aided by a dense mist, closed up to their barrage and began moving forward. They experienced no difficulty in effecting penetrations and isolating Allied units but the latter, shaken and depleted as they were, hit back hard and it sometimes took several hours of bitter fighting before they were subdued. The 7th Battalion Durham Light Infantry, for example, held up the entire 5th Guards Division for almost an hour, but were eventually surrounded and forced to surrender.

Meanwhile, 5 Battery, still under fire, continued to give what support it could, although its guns were firing blind. By 0600 it was apparent that the line had given way as the sounds of heavy infantry fighting could be heard coming from the immediate right. It was clear that the battery position would itself soon be under direct attack. At 0630 the enemy artillery fire lifted and, right on cue, several hundred Storm Troopers emerged from the mist, 200 yards distant, and immediately made for the guns. Massey ordered Direct Fire and the 18-pound shells, delivered at point-blank range, blew great gaps in the packed ranks, stopping the attack in its tracks. Then, seizing a Lewis gun, he led a small counter-attack group, formed from four now-unemployed telephonists armed with rifles, out of the right side of the battery, evidently intending to fall on the enemy's flank. The little party must have run into trouble shortly after, for they were never seen again. Writing in the April 1987 issue of the *British Army Review*, Captain G. Donaldson, RA, mentions unconfirmed reports that Massey died of multiple wounds in a German casualty clearing station.

It was soon apparent that the enemy had also broken through on the left and was beginning to close in on the battery's rear. Simultaneously, the Germans to the front mounted a fresh assault. In Massey's absence, Large assumed command and again ordered Direct Fire. Sending Button to burn the maps and codes, he snatched up a Lewis gun and, with those gunners armed with rifles, assisted in holding off the Storm Troopers. Clearly the position was about to fall and, as he ordered the gun crews to smash their breech-blocks and dial sights, he was shot dead. Running from the Command Post, Button was also killed in the brief but savage fight which ensued as the Germans swarmed over the parapet. Two men, Gunner Sowerbutts and the mortally wounded Sergeant Schofield, shot their way out, and four more, who were unarmed, somehow managed to evade capture.

When the story of 5 Battery's continuous fight against odds became known, Massey was posthumously awarded the Military Cross. The French were rather more generous, recording the event in an Order of the Day and posthumously awarding the Croix de Guerre to Massey,

Large and Button. The Battery as a whole was honoured by the award of the Croix de Guerre with Two Palms, the ribbon of which still adorns the uniform of its members.

By 4 June the German advance had been halted at the Marne by Allied reserve formations which included two American divisions. For Ludendorff, the effective commander of the German armies, the arrival of the latter had a sombre significance, for he had hoped to defeat the British and French before the United States Army could reach the battlefield. By mid-July his capacity to mount further offensives had gone.

It was then that the real effects of such stands as that made by 5 Battery became fully apparent. They had taken a fearful toll of the Storm Troopers, most of whom were now dead. The *Sturmabteilungen* were Germany's best troops and, once they had gone, the units from which they had been drawn were inevitably of a lesser quality. Even worse, perhaps, was the fact that the German Army as a whole had been promised that its supreme effort would be rewarded by final victory. Instead, despite the immense sacrifices which had been made, peace was no nearer and daily the Allies grew visibly stronger. Disillusion, war-weariness and defeatism began to spread. So apparent was the general demoralization that when the Tank Corps again smashed through the German lines at Amiens on 8 August, Ludendorff was forced to advise his reluctant Kaiser that victory was no longer possible.

CHAPTER 7
The Defence of Wake Atoll
8–23 DECEMBER 1941

Wake Atoll lies in the Central Pacific and consists of three small islands name Wake, Wilkes and Peale. The group is surrounded by a coral reef through which a channel between Wake and Wilkes Islands penetrates the central lagoon. It is a remote, desolate place, rising but a few feet above sea level, and is partially covered by trees stunted to the size of scrub. Its only indigenous inhabitants are sea birds and a unique species of rat. Lying as it does off the main shipping routes, in the past the atoll offered no incentive whatever for ships' captains to call since it lacked even a natural source of fresh water. Not surprisingly, history overlooked Wake until in 1899 the United States took possession of the islands as a by-product of the Spanish-American War.

It was the aircraft which changed the fate of Wake. Located between two other widely separated American possessions, Midway and Guam, the atoll offered a convenient stopover and refuelling point for the Trans-Pacific Clipper service operated by Pan American Airways with four-engined flying-boats, and in 1935 the corporation built a hotel there to provide overnight accommodation for its passengers. The US Navy was also interested in Wake, as it was already apparent that in any future war in the Pacific air power would be the dominant factor. By the beginning of 1941 it was clear that the enemy in that war would be Japan and a large civilian construction team and its heavy equipment was shipped to Wake and began work on an airfield and seaplane base. The construction superintendent was a tough, two-fisted Irishman named Dan Teters who had played football for the University of Washington in his youth and served as a sergeant in the Army during the First World War.

Under Teters' direction the work continued apace and in October the major part of the garrison arrived. This consisted of the US Marine Corps' 1st Defense Battalion, commanded by 38-year-old Major James Devereux, who had seen previous service in Nicaragua, China and the Philippines. The battalion's weapons included six 5-inch guns which had formerly been the secondary armament of First World War battleships and were now destined for use in the coast defence role, twelve 3-inch guns intended primarily for anti-aircraft defence, eighteen .50 calibre machine-guns, thirty .30 calibre machine-guns, a searchlight battery and supporting units. There was, however, a shortage of fire-control equipment, including rangefinders, and the radar sets needed for early warning were still awaiting shipment at Pearl Harbor.

Before he sailed for Wake Devereux had been informed that his function was to defend the atoll against attacks of the type made by the German cruiser *Emden* on British islands in the Pacific during the First World War. It was never intended that his 400 Marines should withstand a full-scale invasion attempt, but, in that event, they were naturally expected to offer the maximum possible resistance. Nevertheless, Devereux was an extremely thorough officer and he worked his men hard emplacing guns and digging weapon pits until he was satisfied that every approach was covered. Then they began excavating magazines, command posts, and air raid shelters. Finally, they camouflaged each emplacement, weapon pit and fortification to the highest possible standard. Devereux kept them busy from dawn to dusk, seven days a week, but because of this, and the fact that in addition to his specialist skills every Marine was a trained rifleman, Wake became a fortress.

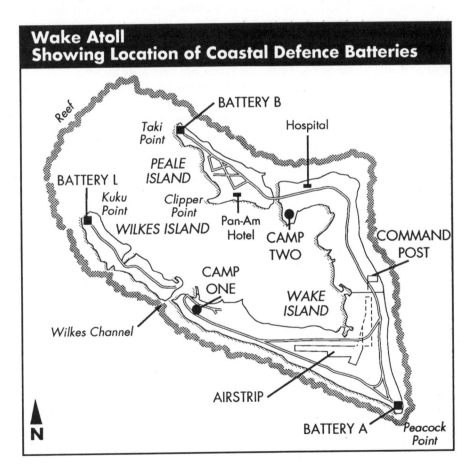

On 28 November Commander Winfield Scott Cunningham, an officer with wide experience of naval aviation, arrived to assume overall command of the atoll and Devereux reverted to his position as commander of the ground troops, as intended. By now there was little doubt that war with Japan was in the offing and this was apparently confirmed when B-17 heavy bombers, on passage from California to the Philippines, began touching down on the newly completed runway for refuelling. To their disgust, the garrison were forced to abandon their work on the fortifications and attend to the task themselves. This involved pumping 3,000 gallons from drums into each aircraft by hand, and if several bombers arrived at once the process could take up to twenty-four hours. Sadly, the additional effort was all for nothing, as most of the bombers were destroyed on the ground during the first Japanese air attack on the Philippines. On 4 December the atoll's own air element, twelve Grumman Wildcat fighters of Marine Fighter Squadron 211 (VMF-211), commanded by Major Paul Putnam, took off from the carrier USS *Enterprise* and flew 200 miles south-west to land on Wake. Putnam was pleased to renew his acquaintance with Devereux, with whom he had served in Nicaragua, but was alarmed to note that no revetments existed for his aircraft, which would have to park in the open and perforce be unprotected in the event of enemy air attack.

This apart, Wake was as ready for war as its officers could make it. On Saturday 6 December Devereux held a stand-to and was sufficiently pleased by the speed with which his men manned their positions that he allowed them the remainder of the weekend off. They spent the time swimming, fishing, writing letters or simply resting. On Sunday afternoon the west-bound Pan American Clipper *Philippine* landed in the lagoon, bringing mail for the garrison and the civilian workers.

On Monday 8 December reveille was sounded at 0600 and the garrison commenced its daily routine. The Clipper took off and banked away to the west, heading for Guam. At 0650 the small US Army Signal Corps team present prepared to open communications with the airbase at Hickam Field, where, because Hawaii lay east of the International Date Line, it was still Sunday 7 December. The Hickam operator, clearly distraught and using plain speech, informed them that the airfield was being attacked by Japanese aircraft. Devereux, anxious to obtain confirmation, telephoned the Naval radio station which advised him that a coded transmission had just been received; Pearl Harbor was also under attack. He ordered the bugler to sound the Call to Arms. At first the troops though it was just another stand-to drill, but they were quickly jerked into the realization that Wake was at war. Within forty-five minutes all positions were manned. On the airield Putnam dispatched the first flight of his standing combat air patrol (CAP). Shortly after, the Clipper, warned by Cunningham, reappeared and landed in the lagoon to await further instructions. At 0800 Morning Colours was sounded and the troops stood to attention as the flag climbed to the top of its pole; it was to fly throughout Wake's ordeal.

The 1,100-strong civilian workforce was not, of course, subject to military discipline, but some were ex-servicemen and they, with many others, volunteered their services. Technically, Cunningham could not permit them to take an active part in the fighting, although a large number did so, but under the direction of Teters they relieved the Marines of much hard physical work. Some, a pathetic few, regarded this as being outside the terms of their contract and took themselves off into the scrub to hide; they were no safer there than anywhere else, and their indiscriminate fouling of open ground exposed the garrison to tropical diseases.

The first Japanese attack was not long in coming. At 1158 thirty-six twin-engined bombers, flying from Roi-Namur 700 miles to the south, struck the atoll without warning, their approach being screened from the patrolling Wildcats by rain squalls. Extensive damage was caused and raging fuel fires were started everywhere as the Japanese bombed and strafed to their hearts' content, their progress unhindered by the startled anti-aircraft defences' patchy response. VMF-211 suffered severely. Of its 55 personnel on the airstrip, 23 were killed and eleven wounded. Seven of the eight parked Wildcats were wrecked and the surviving machine was damaged. In addition, the squadron's supply of spares, tools, machinery, manuals and ground-to-air radio link were all destroyed. The runway itself remained intact, confirming the obvious deduction that the enemy wished to preserve it for his own use, but when the four-strong Wildcat patrol returned to the totally unexpected scene of devastation one of them was damaged on landing by a piece of debris blown across its path. The Pan American facilities had also been hit hard and the corporation's local manager decided to evacuate his staff aboard the Clipper. That afternoon, while Marines and civilians worked to collect casualties and extinguish the fires, the heavily laden flying-boat, itself scarred with bullet holes, staggered into the air and headed north-east for Midway.

Round One had undoubtedly gone to the Japanese, but since they were a methodical race it was anticipated that they would attack again at the same time the following day. At 1100 on 9 December Lieutenant Kliewer and Sergeant Hamilton, flying the two Wildcats of VMF-211's CAP, spotted a formation of Nell bombers approaching the atoll. They dived on them, sending one down in flames into the sea, but were forced to break off their attack when the anti-aircraft guns opened up. This time the bombers' target was the contractors' Camp 2 and the hospital, which they all but obliterated, although in the process five aircraft were seriously hit and began trailing smoke, one of which blew up over the sea. The Japanese recorded damage to fourteen aircraft, but this may refer solely to those which actually returned and take no account of badly damaged aircraft forced to ditch on the long haul home. It was now painfully clear to the 24th Air Flotilla, which had delivered the attacks, that Wake had sharp teeth.

Devereux was concerned that the attacks would enable the Japanese to pinpoint the positions of his gun emplacements, which they could then reduce piecemeal. There was nothing he could do about the coast defence batteries which he had established at Peacock Point on Wake, Kuku Point on Wilkes and Toki Point on Peale, each with two heavy 5-inch guns, other than to keep them meticulously camouflaged. The 3-inch anti-aircraft guns, however, were moved from time to time, a back-breaking task which involved not only moving the weapons themselves but also their fire-control equipment, generators, ammunition and the construction of new sandbag emplacements. For good measure, dummy anti-aircraft guns and emplacements were built on the vacated sites to confuse the enemy.

The Japanese attack on Wednesday 10 December had obviously been planned with the previous day's losses in mind. The twenty-six bombers employed arrived at 1045, somewhat earlier than usual, and they approached the atoll from the east instead of from the south, flying at a higher altitude of 18,000 feet. Captain Hank Elrod, commanding the CAP, pounced and shot down two. Bombs from the leading wave destroyed a dummy anti-aircraft battery, thereby justifying Devereux's caution. A second wave headed for Peale, but ran into heavy anti-aircraft fire and dropped most of its bombs in the lagoon or the sea before it turned for home with one of its aircraft trailing smoke. Wilkes was the target of the third wave and here the Japanese had better luck, hitting a construction shed containing no less than 125 tons of dynamite. The mighty explosion triggered the sympathetic detonation of every round of ammunition on the island, with spectacular results. Debris was flung across the entire atoll, the scrub on Wilkes was stripped of its leaves and began to burn and a searchlight truck half-a-mile from the centre of the explosion was completely wrecked. The 5-inch guns at Kuku Point sustained dented barrels and other damage, as did a 3-inch anti-aircraft gun. Incredibly, the total casualties sustained in the raid amounted to two dead and six wounded.

An important element in the Japanese conduct of war was the question of face, and for this reason the reports submitted by the returning airmen tended to be optimistic in tone. After all, whatever the losses incurred, each raid had left heavy fires blazing and the damage inflicted was considerable. The defences, it seemed, had been written down to the extent that the invasion force, already at sea, would have no difficulty in securing the atoll when it effected its landings on 11 December. Guam had already fallen on 10 December, as had the British possession of Makin.

The invasion force, commanded by Rear-Admiral Sadamichi Kajioka, consisted of the light cruiser *Yubari*, two older cruisers, six destroyers, two destroyer transports, two transports and two submarines. Kajioka's understanding was that Wake's garrison consisted of 1,000 Marines, plus 600 construction workers, and although he later claimed that he was expecting a rough reception, his conduct of the operation was over-confident and amateurish. He had a 450-strong naval infantry detachment at his disposal, of which he proposed landing 150 men on Wilkes and the rest on Wake under cover of the warships' gunfire; if necessary, he was prepared to reinforce the landing force with seamen from his destroyers. By 0300 on 11 December the atoll was in sight and his ships began moving towards their bombardment and landing stations.

Ashore, a sharp-eyed lookout detected the Japanese presence at once. Devereux was roused and immediately telephoned each battery in turn with specific orders that fire would not be opened until he gave the word. He then spoke to Putnam, who had four Wildcats available, and gave instructions that the aircraft would not take off until the coast defence batteries went into action. By 0500 the light was strong enough to reveal that the cruisers' armament outranged his own 5-inch guns and that the enemy would have to be lulled into a false sense of security and drawn inshore if the latter's fire were to be effective.

Fortunately, Kajioka was in a mood to oblige. *Yubari* began running westward parallel with the southern shore of Wake and the rest of the task force conformed. At 0530 the Japanese opened fire, concentrating on the beach and the contractors' Camp 1, where diesel oil tanks were set ablaze. At the end of her run *Yubari* and two destroyer transports reversed course, turning inshore as they did so, while the two light cruisers, three destroyers and two transports headed for a position off the western end of Wilkes. To the Marines manning the guns their passive vigil under fire seemed interminable and some began to mutter angrily that Devereux was waiting too long. At the eastern end of her bombardment run *Yubari* again reversed course, once more turning inshore to do so. This brought her within 4,500 yards of Battery 'A' on Peacock Point, commanded by First Lieutenant Clarence A. Barninger, and at 0610 Devereux gave the order to commence firing.

The first salvo passed over the cruiser, which immediately turned away and took evasive action, returning the fire as she did so. Barninger dropped the range by 500 yards and was soon straddling the target. At 5,700 yards two 5-inch shells punched their way through *Yubari*'s side, bursting in the boiler room and machinery spaces. The cruiser staggered, belching smoke and clouds of steam. At 7,000 yards she was hit again just aft of the first strike, the quantity of fresh smoke issuing from her wounds indicating that serious internal fires were raging aboard. One of her destroyers attempted to lay a smoke-screen between the battery and the cruiser, but intercepted a shell intended for *Yubari* and was herself forced to turn away with a wrecked forecastle. As *Yubari* limped slowly seawards wreathed in smoke, Battery 'A' bade her farewell with a round which smashed into her forward turret. Only one Marine had been slightly injured in the exchange.

If Battery 'A''s performance was spectacular, that of Battery 'L' on Kuku Point was astonishing. The battery, commanded by Second Lieutenant John A. McAlister, was hardly in a condition to undertake a major engagement as both its 5-inch guns were barely serviceable after the previous day's explosion, and it lacked even a rangefinder. Nevertheless, it set to with a will. The destroyer *Hayate* was lying broadside 4,500 yards offshore and, estimating the range, McAlister engaged her as soon as he received permission to open fire. Both rounds from his third salvo hit her amidships and she was torn apart by a huge internal explosion. Her back broken, she went to the bottom in minutes. Suddenly, the invasion force seemed to scatter as destroyers weaved in and out laying smoke. Targets became difficult to spot, but Battery 'L' scored further hits on a second destroyer, a transport and the stern of a cruiser which made off with a fire burning aboard.

Battery 'B' on Toki Point, commanded by First Lieutenant Woodrow M. Kessler, went into action against three destroyers at a range of 10,000 yards. One gun quickly became inoperable because of problems with its recoil mechanism, but when the other scored a hit on the leading destroyer the Japanese retired under cover of smoke.

By 0700 Kajioka had had enough and he ordered his battered force to withdraw. This was easier for some than others, for the transports had begun lowering their invasion barges and disembarking troops in a heavy swell. Recovery and re-embarkation was extremely difficult, especially under fire, and the occupants of some barges were undoubtedly drowned when their craft capsized.

Cunningham's men, however, had not quite finished with Kajioka. Putnam's four Wildcats, piloted by himself and Captains Hank Elrod, Herbert Freuler and Frank Tharin, had taken off when the guns opened fire and, having satisfied themselves that the enemy lacked carrier support, proceeded to harry the retreating invasion force without mercy. Boring in through the flak, VMF-211 attacked with machine-guns and 100-pound bombs, returning to Wake to replenish their munitions as soon as they were expended. Altogether, the Wildcats flew ten sorties during which they scored hits on both of the older cruisers, a destroyer, a destroyer transport, and started a fierce petrol fire aboard a transport. The climax of the air attacks came at 0730 when Elrod selected the already damaged destroyer *Kisaragi* as his target. His bombs hit the vessel's loaded depth-charge racks and she was torn apart by an immense explosion which almost engulfed the aircraft as well. All the Wildcats sustained damage during the engagement and two were so badly hit that they barely succeeded in regaining the island.

The Japanese must have signalled news of their reverse for at 1000 a formation of thirty bombers was spotted approaching the atoll from the north-east at 18,000 feet. The CAP, flown by Lieutenants Davidson and Kinney, sliced through them, shooting down two and setting fire to a third, which peeled off and turned for home. The anti-aircraft guns accounted for a fourth, plus three more sent on their way trailing smoke. The bombers caused no casualties and only superficial damage. From start to finish, American casualties on 11 December amounted to four Marines slightly wounded. It had, to say the least, been a day of above average interest.

Kajioka's interview with his immediate superior, Vice-Admiral Nariyoshi Inouye, can hardly have been pleasant. Coming as it did in the immediate aftermath of the tremendous destruction wreaked on the US Pacific Fleet at Pearl Harbor, followed by the sinking of the British capital ships HMS *Repulse* and *Prince of Wales* off the east coast of Malaya on 10 December, the failure was a blot on a hitherto peerless record of victory. Its results included two destroyers sunk, the Imperial Navy's first losses of the war, the new cruiser *Yubari* docked for heavy repairs, six other vessels damaged, several bombers shot down and some 700 men killed. Kajioka's invasion force was to be re-formed, reinforced and, with aircraft carrier support, it would return to Wake and capture the atoll *regardless of cost*.

Cunningham's report on the action generated one of the great propaganda coups of the war. Standard security procedure demanded that the first and last sentences of a coded transmission should be irrelevant gibberish. Thus, Cunningham's dispatch began: 'SEND US STOP NOW IS THE TIME FOR ALL GOOD MEN TO COME TO THE AID OF THEIR PARTY STOP CUNNINGHAM MORE JAPS . . .' In Hawaii someone recognized the pyschological warfare benefits inherent in the first and last words of the preamble, SEND US . . . MORE JAPS, and these were broadcast with the details of Kajioka's devastating repulse. To a general public profoundly depressed by the news from the Pacific and Far East, Wake's terrific stand was inspiring and the garrison's tough, uncompromising attitude was in the finest traditions of the service. SEND US MORE JAPS was to take its place in national legend alongside John Paul Jones' comment aboard the sinking *Bonhomme Richard* that he had just begun to fight.

The men on Wake were actually a little fed up with the desk warriors at Pearl Harbor. Among the many useless memos dispatched to the embattled atoll was a gem sanctioning the use of a heavy grade of official stationery as a substitute for broken glazing; the problem was that there were no windows to glaze, the buildings which housed them having been flattened long since by the enemy. The SEND US MORE JAPS story was understandably incomprehensible and annoyed everyone. The general feeling was that there were already plenty of Japanese to go round and that, as Wake's resources were limited, the gentlemen at Pearl Harbor would be better employed arranging re-supply, reinforcement and relief rather than composing snappy slogans. In fact the ill-fated commander of the Pacific Fleet, Admiral Husband E. Kimmel, had begun to put together a relief force as early as 9 December. It consisted of the carrier *Saratoga*, the heavy cruisers *Astoria, Minneapolis* and *San Francisco*, nine destroyers, a troop transport and an oiler. There was no shortage of volunteers, but all that could be spared from immediate defence requirements were 200 Marines and VMF-221 with eighteen obsolete Brewster Buffaloes. The departure of the relief force, commanded by Rear Admiral Frank J. Fletcher, was delayed pending the arrival of *Saratoga* from San Diego, and it did not get under way from Pearl Harbor until the evening of 15 December. Its speed was then tied to that of its ancient oiler and did not exceed twelve knots.

After 11 December, life on Wake assumed a monotonous quality in which the enemy's air attacks became a matter of routine and the days drifted together. Teters' earth-moving equipment had been used to excavate a protected hangar space which, provided with head-cover and tarpaulin curtains, enabled work to continue around the clock on VMF-211's damaged aircraft. Working without proper tools, a team of service and civilian mechanics directed by Second Lieutenant John F. Kinney and Technical Sergeant William J. Hamilton, kept the squadron's two remaining Wildcats flying by cannibalizing parts, and at one stage even produced a third aircraft assembled from the wreckage of the rest. Latterly, the Wildcats had much in common with the 200-year-old axe which, in its lifetime, had received six new heads and seven new handles.

VMF-211 continued to take its toll of Japanese visitors to Wake. At 0500 on 12 December two four-engined Mavis long-range reconnaissance flying-boats made a hit-and-run attack. Captain Tharin bounced one and continued to hammer it with his guns until it fell apart and plunged into the sea. There was no bomber raid that day, but during the evening the CAP made an unexpected and valuable kill. The engine of Lieutenant David Kliewer's Wildcat refused to start at first and he took off after the other two aircraft in the patrol. Some twenty-five miles south-east of Wake he spotted a surfaced submarine in an area where he knew no American boats were operating. From 10,000 feet he dived out of the sun and released both his bombs at the last possible moment, strafing as he did so. He estimated that his bombs landed within fifteen feet of the hull and when he circled the submarine had vanished leaving a spreading oil slick. Japanese records later revealed the loss of two submarines in this position during the fight for Wake, one as a result of accident and the other from unknown causes, and it seems that Kliewer's victim was the latter.

Some believed that the submarines provided radio direction signals for the bombers flying from Roi-Namur, enabling them to home accurately on the tiny atoll in the vast expanse of ocean. This may have been speculation, but if so it was a coincidence that no bombers reached Wake on 13 December, although garbled signals were intercepted by the atoll's operators. The day was somewhat marred, however, when one of the three Wildcats was damaged beyond repair during a take-off accident, fortunately without loss of life.

On 14 December three Mavis flying-boats droned over the atoll at 0300, dropping bombs harmlessly around the airstrip, but at 1100 a formation of thirty bombers delivered a heavy attack, the weight of which fell on Camp 1 and the fortifications on the south shore, although the fuselage of one of VMF-211's aircraft was also destroyed. Two of the raiders fell victim to anti-aircraft fire. Early the following morning Major Putnam, patrolling south-west of the atoll, spotted a submarine. The boat submerged almost immediately but he did not attack as its markings suggested that it might be Dutch. Cunningham, however, believed that it was hostile and, significantly, there was no bomber attack that day, although during the evening an ineffective raid was made by up to six flying-boats. On the 16th the bombers returned, somewhat later than usual. Most of their payload went into the lagoon, one was shot down by the anti-aircraft batteries and four more were damaged. A solitary flying-boat arrived at 1800, strafed Peale and flew off.

And so it continued, day after day, until the point was reached at which the Japanese bombs were simply turning over the rubble created in earlier raids. On 17 December Cunningham dispatched a signal informing Pearl Harbor that all structures had been destroyed, together with half the vehicles, plant and machinery, and that his supply of fuel was almost exhausted. At 0700 on 20 December a signal was received from Midway informing the garrison that a Navy PBY Catalina flying-boat was on its way to them. It touched down in the lagoon at 1530 and taxied to the remains of the Pan American pier. A young, clean, crisp ensign stepped out and, doubtless with thoughts of a gently frosted glass in mind, asked the way to the Wake Island Hotel. He was politely directed to a pile of rubble. The PBY brought Cunningham news which could not be entrusted to insecure radio transmissions. The relief force was at sea and Wake was to be reinforced and re-supplied on 24 December. All but 350 of the construction workers were to be evacuated. When the flying-boat took off at 0700 next morning it carried dispatches from Cunningham, Devereux and Putnam, together with letters from the garrison and workforce. Those aboard were the last to see the Stars and Stripes flying above the battered atoll.

The Japanese were well aware that if Wake were reinforced it would present an even tougher nut to crack and they therefore assembled a formidable task force which was capable of swamping the defences. In overall command was Rear-Admiral Hiroaki Abe, while Kajioka remained responsible for the amphibious landing. The operation would have the support of the fleet carriers *Soryu* and *Hiryu*, six heavy cruisers and six destroyers. In place of the *Yubari* Kajioka was given a modern destroyer armed with six 5-inch guns, and the two destroyers which had been lost were replaced by sister ships. An additional transport and a seaplane tender were also made available to accommodate the enlarged naval infantry contingent, the strength of which had been increased to 1,000.

The operational plan demonstrated the intensity of Japanese feeling about Wake and also took due account of the lessons stemming from the previous failure. For two days prior to the invasion, carrier-based aircraft were to carry out the systematic destruction of the atoll's defences. The landings were to be made in the hours of darkness before dawn, thereby reducing the effectiveness of any coast-defence guns which still remained in action. To achieve surprise, no bombardment would be fired. The emphasis was on getting the troops ashore quickly and, with this in mind, the two destroyer transports were to be expended by running aground on the reef close to the airstrip. Simultaneously, infantry were to land from barges elsewhere on the south coast of Wake and on Wilkes. If the naval infantry were unable to make progress, they would be reinforced by a 500-strong reserve consisting of seamen. And if that still did not suffice, the two replacement destroyers were to be run aground so that their crews could join in the battle. Obviously, Kajioka dared not contemplate a second failure, yet the thought obsessed him. After a rehearsal, he sailed again for Wake on 21 December, joining Abe's covering force at sea. The fate of the atoll now depended entirely upon whether the invasion fleet or the relief force arrived first.

At 0850 on 21 December, less than two hours after the PBY had lifted off on its return flight to Midway, twenty-nine Val dive-bombers, escorted by eighteen Zero fighters, dropped out of cloud cover above Wake to bomb and strafe. They did little damage but Devereux's men instinctively recognized that the moment of truth had arrived, for the aircraft could only have flown from a carrier group, the close proximity of which clearly indicated that an invasion force was in the offing. At 1220 thirty-three bombers arrived. One sustained damage but they managed to destroy the fire-control equipment of the anti-aircraft battery on Peale. Wearily, the garrison began its daily routine of clearing up and moving guns.

The carrier aircraft returned at 1300 on 22 December, thirty-three dive-bombers flying at 18,000 feet, escorted by six Zeros. With supreme gallantry the CAP, flown by Captain Freuler and Lieutenant Davidson, dived on the formation, Freuler tackling the fighters while Davidson tore into the bombers. Freuler turned one Zero into a fireball and then a second latched on to his tail, wounding him and seriously damaging his aircraft. He managed to escape in a steep dive to effect a crash landing on the airstrip, but his Wildcat was written off. Davidson did not return; he was last seen hammering a Val while a Zero closed in on his tail.

Wake's little air force had ceased to exist, but Putnam immediately volunteered the services of his remaining pilots and ground crew as infantry.

That night flashing lights were observed far out to sea. At about 0100 a reported landing near Toki Point turned out to be a false alarm. Devereux remained uneasy, and his lookouts on the south shore kept reporting movement. At 0235 it was definitely established that the enemy was ashore on Wilkes. Devereux gave permission for one of the island's searchlights to be switched on. Seriously damaged by the dynamite explosion days earlier, it quickly cut out, but its glare revealed Japanese streaming across the beach from landing craft. Heavy firing broke out, but the enemy overran a 3-inch anti-aircraft battery. Then Devereux's telephone link with Wilkes went dead.

Off Wake, the two destroyer transports ground their way on to the reef and the troops aboard began tumbling into the water. The 5-inch guns at Peacock Point would not bear, but a 3-inch gun on a rise near the airstrip was quickly brought into action by Second Lieutenant Robert M. Hanna and a scratch crew of Marines and civilians, while the personnel of VMF-211 provided local protection. Hanna's first round burst on the bridge of the nearest transport, flaying seamen and soldiers with splinters. If the Japanese had intended recovering the vessel they were disappointed, for Hanna slammed fourteen more rounds into her, setting her ablaze. The flames illuminated the troops wading ashore through the shallows and machine-gun fire began to scythe through their ranks. Gradually, however, the numbers reaching the beach increased to the point at which they were able to mount a desperate charge against Putnam's men. Fierce hand-to-hand fighting forced the thin American line back until it was bent around the gun position, where Hanna was engaging and hitting the second transport.

One thousand yards to the west the occupants of two landing craft had reached the shore safely and had begun to push a small force of twenty Marines and fourteen civilians, commanded by Lieutenant Arthur R. Poindexter, back towards Camp 1. Elsewhere, Japanese were starting to fan out across the island and were bringing one position after another under mortar and machine-gun fire as well as launching suicidal attacks. By 0300 Devereux had lost contact with most of his units and the rain-laden darkness contained no hint as to the progress of the fighting. He called forward as many reinforcements as possible from Peale and with these established a defence line across the neck of Wake close to his command post.

At Pearl Harbor, where Kimmel had been relieved by Vice Admiral William St. Pye pending the arrival of the Pacific Fleet's new Commander-in-Chief, Admiral Chester A. Nimitz, a signal was received from Cunningham to the effect that enemy landings were in progress. In response, Pye could only supply cold comfort. 'NO FRIENDLY VESSELS

IN YOUR VICINITY NOR WILL BE WITHIN THE NEXT TWENTY-FOUR HOURS . . . KEEP ME INFORMED.' Cunningham's next message was timed at 0500: 'ENEMY ON ISLAND – ISSUE IN DOUBT .' The signal resolved a dilemma which had been troubling Pye and his staff. On 21 January the relief force was a little over 500 miles from Wake, but Fletcher, who was to be criticized for not displaying greater resolution, chose to spend the day refuelling his ships. Pye was already concerned by the presence of Japanese carriers within flying distance of the atoll and he was forced to consider whether the persevering with the relief attempt justified the risk of losing a major portion of the much reduced Pacific Fleet, including the most important element of all, the carrier *Saratoga*. Cunningham's signal that the outcome of the fighting was in doubt led to the inescapable conclusion that the task force was probably being committed to a lost cause, and in such a situation a gamble was not acceptable. Fletcher, having completed his refuelling, was once more on course for Wake and was 425 miles from the atoll when, at 0911 on 22 December (23 December on Wake), he received orders to return to Pearl Harbor. Pye's decision aroused bitter controversy, but, unpalatable as it was, in the circumstances it was undoubtedly correct. For the moment, the general public remained in ignorance of the aborted relief attempt.

Dawn revealed that Wake was ringed by Japanese ships, cruising slowly beyond the range of the 5-inch batteries. At 0645 three destroyers began closing in on Peale, but withdrew when Lieutenant Kessler's battery scored several hits on the leading ship. From his command post on Peale, Cunningham could see that the Stars and Stripes were still flying above Camp 1, but elsewhere on the southern half of Wake Japanese air recognition flags were fluttering. At 0700 the enemy's carrier aircraft arrived, bombing and strafing the American positions at will. Yet the Japanese were not having everything their own way. On Wilkes, Captain Wesley Platt and Lieutenant McAlister led a converging attack on the enemy who had captured the 3-inch battery, wiping them out.

When the shooting was over the only live Japanese left on Wilkes were two wounded prisoners; ninety-eight of their comrades lay dead, mostly sprawled in and around the gun positions. The American loss amounted to nine Marines and two civilians killed, plus four Marines and one civilian wounded. At Camp 1, stragglers had rallied to Poindexter, who now commanded fifty-five men. The Japanese advance was held and when, at 0800, their attacks ceased, he took the initiative, driving them steadily eastwards.

Devereux, his communications disrupted, knew nothing of these events. He believed that Wilkes and Camp 1 had fallen and the situation in his immediate vicinity was deteriorating rapidly as the Japanese by-passed VMF-211's position around Hanna's gun to reach the lagoon, isolated Battery 'A' on Peacock Point and began bringing pressure on his final defence line. He telephoned Cunningham to advise him of the situation and ask for news of the relief task force. Cunningham told him of Pye's earlier message. It was apparent that the defence could not last another twenty-four hours and neither man saw any point in spending further lives to no purpose. Cunningham gave the order to surrender. With a white flag and a Japanese escort Devereux toured the remaining defences and told his men to lay down their arms; it was 1330 before he reached Wilkes and the shooting stopped. Wake, the gallant defence of which had inspired the American people, had fallen at last.

The Japanese treated their captives with their usual mixture of cruelty and brutal indifference. In due course, the garrison was shipped to prison camps in China. On the way, a Lieutenant Toshio Saito had five enlisted men beheaded in revenge for the humiliation suffered by the Imperial Navy. After the war, four of the executioners were sentenced to life imprisonment, being paroled nine years later, but Saito, who is known to have survived, disappeared without trace. In China, and later Japan, the prisoners endured years of hard physical work on poor rations. Lieutenants Kinney and McAlister escaped in May 1945 and, assisted by Chinese guerrillas, reached friendly territory and were flown home. Cunningham and Teters escaped in March 1942 but were recaptured and sentenced to terms of imprisonment. Two years later, Cunningham escaped again but was recaptured and received a life sentence. Like the rest of the garrison's survivors, he was released and repatriated when Japan surrendered. For one hundred construction workers who had been retained on Wake by the Japanese there was, tragically, to be no release. On 7 October 1943 they were lined up and shot on suspicion of being in radio contact with American aircraft. The atoll commander, Rear-Admiral Shigematsu Sakaibara, and eleven of his officers were subsequently tried and sentenced to death for the murders.

The sixteen-day battle for Wake had cost the lives of forty-nine Marines, three seamen and seventy civilians. No accurate figures for Japanese casualties exist, but estimated losses of 900 killed and 1,100 wounded have been described as conservative. The airstrip which had been purchased at so heavy a price proved all but useless. It was cratered regularly by heavy bombers, carrier strikes and naval bombardments which claimed another 600 lives. Furthermore, the atoll was by-passed during the American drive westward against Japan and ceased to have any signficance. As the strength of the Imperial Navy and the Japanese merchant marine declined steadily its garrison rotted in isolation; latterly, only submarines dared to attempt the hazardous passage. Thus, a further 1,288 Japanese seamen and soldiers died from the effects of malnutrition and untreated disease. When, on 4 September 1945, Sakaibara surrendered, he had only seventeen days' meagre rations in hand and 400 of his men were bedridden.

Devereux's 1st Defense Battalion and Putnam's VMF-211 were honoured with Presidential Citations on 5 January 1942 and 'Remember Wake!' became a popular recruiting slogan. Taking formal possession of the atoll from Sakaibara, Commander William Masek, USN, described in a very few words the significance of Wake's defence to the American war effort. 'It was here,' he said, 'the Marines showed us how.'

Shortly after, an unusual but entirely fitting memorial was erected on Wake. It consisted of a battered Wildcat engine and propeller mounted on a plinth and was dedicated to Captain Henry T. Elrod, who had been killed in the savage fighting around Hanna's gun, and to all the gallant defenders of the atoll.

CHAPTER 8
The Defence of Outpost Snipe
27 OCTOBER 1942

The Second Battle of Alamein had been raging for almost three days when Lieutenant-Colonel Victor Turner, the commanding officer of the 2nd Battalion The Rifle Brigade, was informed that during the night of 26/27 October his battalion, which had hitherto been employed in support of sapper units clearing gaps through the extensive enemy minefields, was to take part in offensive operations on the Kidney Ridge sector. These would involve Major-General Raymond Briggs' 1st Armoured Division, and would attempt to sever the Rahman Track, the Axis army's principal means of lateral communication, lying two miles to the west.

The Eighth Army had opened the battle at 2140 on 23 October with a deafening bombardment fired by 592 guns. On the southern sector of the line diversionary attacks were mounted by Lieutenant-General B. G. Horrocks' XII Corps, while in the north Lieutenant-General Sir Oliver Leese's infantry-heavy XXX Corps delivered the main blow, capturing the minefields and clearing two lanes through them in the Meteiriya and Kidney Ridge areas. Progress was slower than had been expected, but by the morning of 26 October Lieutenant-General Bernard Montgomery, the army commander, felt that the moment had come when Lieutenant-General H. Lumsden's X Corps, which contained the 1st and 10th Armoured Divisions, should be pushed through the gaps in anticipation of a major counter-attack which would write down the Axis armour and force his opponent, Field Marshal Erwin Rommel, to exhaust his tiny and irreplaceable reserve of fuel. For his part, Rommel was holding his two German and two Italian armoured divisions in reserve for just such a counter-stroke, and was unlikely to ignore so obvious a threat to the Rahman Track. It was inevitable, therefore, that the operation would result in a major tank battle.

Turner's battalion, together with 7th Battalion The Rifle Brigade and 2nd Battalion King's Royal Rifle Corps, formed the 7th Motor Brigade, commanded by Brigadier T. J. B. Bosvile, the infantry element of 1st Armoured Division. Unlike the standard infantry battalions, the motor battalions were small in numbers but possessed high mobility and heavy firepower. Thus, although the motor battalion could deploy a mere 90 assault riflemen, its order of battle also contained an anti-tank company with sixteen recently issued 6-pounder anti-tank guns, scout platoons with a total of 33 tracked carriers, machine-gun platoons armed with the Vickers medium machine-gun, capable of sustained fire, and a platoon of 3-inch mortars. Casualties sustained by 2nd Battalion Rifle Brigade during the early phase of the battle had reduced the number of riflemen to 76 and there were now only 22 tracked carriers available, but in other respects the battalion was complete. Most of the men came from London and they were old desert hands, used both to working with tanks and to standing them off. In view of the nature of the operation, Turner was reinforced with a further eleven 6-pounder anti-tank guns manned by 239 Battery of 76th Anti-Tank Regiment, Royal Artillery, another experienced unit which had originally been raised in North Wales as a Territorial battalion of the Royal Welch Fusiliers before converting to the anti-tank role. Sixteen sappers of 7th Field Squadron, Royal Engineers, also arrived, bringing the total number of men under Turner's command to almost 300.

When Turner reported to Bosvile's headquarters at 1600, Briggs was already there and the general outlined the plan to him. It all sounded deceptively simple. 2nd Battalion Rifle Brigade was to advance west from Kidney Ridge and establish a firm base on a feature named Snipe; at first light, 24 Armoured Brigade would use Snipe as a pivot of manoeuvre during its advance towards the Rahman Track. To the north, 2nd KRRC were to establish a similar base at a location named Woodcock which would perform the same function for 2 Armoured Brigade.

The operation was to commence at 2300 and, leaving his second in command, Major Tom Pearson, to assemble the force, Turner went as far forward as possible to reconnoitre the ground it would have to cross. His binoculars revealed very little, for the terrain ahead was simply open, featureless desert with a sparse covering of camelthorn. Nor was he absolutely certain of his own position, as the staff of 1st Armoured Division had incorrectly calculated the location of its own units, and of the neighbouring 51st (Highland) Division, by a margin of approximately 1,000 yards. Uneasy, he returned to brief his officers, telling them, with prophetic insight, that the task ahead was likely to be a 'last man, last round' sort of job.

Nevertheless, the battalion crossed the start-line on time, led by the carriers with the rifle companies following behind; the anti-tank guns, carried on Chevrolet portees, remained at the start-line with the supply lorries until summoned forward. Turner had been told that his supporting barrage was to be fired on a bearing of 233 degrees, but if this varied he was to conform to it. In the event, it rolled forward on 270 degrees. It was a cold night and the going was sand so soft that it was little more than dust, enveloping the column in a dense fog through which the newly risen moon seemed orange. Turner kept a dead-reckoning check on progress with his jeep's milometer and after 3,000 yards had been covered asked his artillery Forward Observation Officer (FOO) to arrange for a smoke shell to be fired on to the objective. The round burst within 300 yards and Turner, satisfied that he had reached the objective, occupied an oval depression measuring 900 by 400 yards. This had formerly been used as a German engineer stores depot and contained a small dugout which became battalion headquarters. The previous occupants, some of whom were lying dead in the hollow, evidently belonged to a dirty unit which had fouled the ground with its excreta. The time was now 0015 and, while the companies dug in – no easy matter in sand which slid back into a hole as soon as it was removed – Turner signalled that the objective was secure. In fact, he was 900 yards south of the real objective, but the acquisition of the hollow proved to be providential.

Pearson now began moving forward from the start-line with the portees and ammunition lorries. Enemy shells had been landing around the column for about an hour and at 1130 an aircraft had released a stick of bombs, damaging several vehicles and causing personnel casualties which the battalion's medical officer remained behind to treat. Slowly, the heavily laden portees and supply lorries ground forward, sometimes colliding in the fog of dust, but more often than not having to extricate themselves from the soft going with spades, sand-mats and tow-ropes. Eventually, thirteen of the battalion's and six of '239' Battery's 6-pounders arrived and were off-loaded, together with water, rations and ammunition, by 0345. The battalion was now deployed around the perimeter, 'A' Company holding the north-east sector of the defences, 'B' Company the south-east and 'C' Company the west, the anti-tank guns being divided between them with '239' Battery under 'A' Company.

Meanwhile, the carriers of 'C' Company's Scout Platoon, commanded by Lieutenant Dick Flower, had set off westwards to reconnoitre. They took some prisoners, then came across the night laager of a mixed German/Italian battlegroup known as Gruppe Stiffelmayer, containing tanks, tank destroyers and other elements. With incredible cheek, Flower's men laid into them with Bren light machine-guns, setting fire to three supply lorries. The enraged tank crews manned their turrets and responded. The hulk of a derelict vehicle began to burn and the flames from this disclosed the carriers, which beat a judicious retreat when the tanks began moving against them.

Even without the news of Flower's contact, it was now apparent to Turner that his hollow lay just within the enemy's front line. There were camp fires twinkling to the west and, ominously, a greater concentration of them 1,000 yards to the north, where the bright moonlight revealed a larger tank laager; this, in fact, contained part of the 15th Panzer Division. At 0345 the sound of engines and tracks to the west indicated that the disturbed Gruppe Stiffelmayer was breaking laager. It was soon observed moving in two groups, one of which was heading towards 15th Panzer Division's laager and the other, in line ahead, towards the hollow.

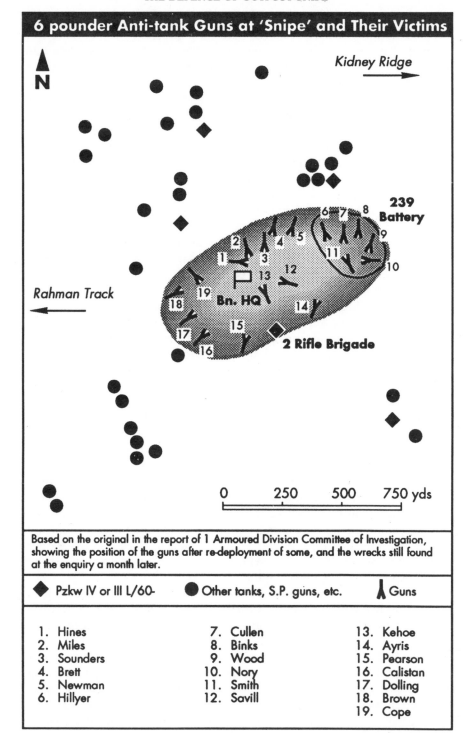

6 pounder Anti-tank Guns at 'Snipe' and Their Victims

Kidney Ridge

N

239 Battery

Rahman Track

Bn. HQ

2 Rifle Brigade

0   250   500   750 yds

Based on the original in the report of 1 Armoured Division Committee of Investigation, showing the position of the guns after re-deployment of some, and the wrecks still found at the enquiry a month later.

◆ Pzkw IV or III L/60-   ● Other tanks, S.P. guns, etc.   人 Guns

1. Hines	7. Cullen	13. Kehoe
2. Miles	8. Binks	14. Ayris
3. Sounders	9. Wood	15. Pearson
4. Brett	10. Nory	16. Calistan
5. Newman	11. Smith	17. Dolling
6. Hillyer	12. Savill	18. Brown
		19. Cope

The latter was led by a Pz Kpfw IVF2, known to the Eighth Army as the Mark IV Special; armed with a long 75mm gun, it was the most powerful tank fielded by either side at this phase of the desert war, and when the battle had begun the Afrika Korps had only thirty of them. It was clearly unaware of the British presence and 'C' Company allowed it to drive to within thirty yards of their position; then, it burst into flames as a single 6-pounder shot tore through its interior. Simultaneously, an 'A' Company gun knocked out a tracked tank destroyer. Alarmed, the remainder of the Axis group shied away and halted some distance to the west, there to await the coming of first light. The defence of Outpost Snipe had begun.

The performance of the new guns was so markedly superior to that of the old 2-pounders that the jubilant little garrison, having tasted blood, was now in the mood to take on all-comers. At 0400, however, the FOO left the dugout to look around and did not return. It was later learned that he had been captured by a German patrol. His absence was keenly felt, since Turner was left without adequate means to control his supporting artillery. Nevertheless, for the moment all remained quiet and at 0545 Pearson departed with the transport vehicles. At about 0615 the sky began to pale and as the light grew stronger both enemy tank groups began moving westwards. Neither seemed to suspect that their losses during the night stemmed from the insertion of a unit with a strong anti-tank capability, and for this the concealment afforded by the hollow and the intervening scrub was to be thanked. At ranges up to 800 yards the 6-pounder went into action, engaging targets which were presenting their vulnerable side and rear armour. Each enemy group lost eight vehicles before it drew clear, their crews sought and killed by the Vickers machine-guns as they attempted to escape.

Thus far, Snipe had destroyed eighteen enemy armoured vehicles at no cost, but now its secret was out. The outpost was subjected to sustained shelling and casualties began to mount. Turner was worried by the fact that, as yet, 24 Armoured Brigade had failed to put in an appearance. This stemmed partly from internal causes, and partly from uncertainty regarding the outcome of the parallel operation to the north in which 2 KRRC were to secure Woodcock. The battalion had, in fact, established itself in a position close to Woodcock, but first light revealed that this was untenable and a withdrawal had been made to a more secure location closer to the main British line. At about 0730 dust clouds to the east told Turner that the tanks were approaching, but he was quite unprepared for what happened next. On reaching the crest of the ridge the leading unit, 47th Royal Tank Regiment, opened fire on Snipe, mistakenly believing that the strongpoint, surrounded by a litter of Axis armour, was an enemy laager. Lieutenant Jack Wintour, 2nd Battalion Rifle Brigade's Intelligence Officer, sped off in his carrier to warn them of their error, but he was only partially successful. The unwarranted punishment continued until approximately 0800, when Turner noticed some 25 German tanks taking up hull-down positions 1,000 yards to the west. His own guns opened fire on them and set fire to three.

This revealed the true state of affairs to 47 RTR, who ceased firing and by 0830 had reached Snipe. The enemy reacted fiercely, lashing the outpost with the fire of tanks, anti-tank guns and medium artillery. Within fifteen minutes six Shermans were blazing within the perimeter and by 0900 47 RTR, reduced to five Shermans and six Crusaders, had been forced to retire behind the ridge. To their left, 41 RTR conformed to the move, having lost twelve tanks. Snipe's riflemen and gunners were glad to see them go, for neighbours who attracted that sort of attention were hardly welcome. None the less, the fact was that 24 Armoured Brigade's attack had been decisively halted and the outpost now stood alone.

Almost immediately, Italian infantry were observed forming up for an attack on the post from the south. Turner ordered Flower's scout platoon out and the carriers quickly put them to flight, inflicting heavy casualties and destroying two vehicles which were towing captured British 6-pounders. Not long afterwards, thirteen Italian M13 medium tanks launched an attack from the south-west. To meet this, Turner moved two guns to reinforce the threatened sector. This was no easy matter, as it involved manhandling the weapons through deep sand and several men were killed in the process. In the event, the attack was not pressed, for after four of their thin-skinned tanks had been penetrated the rest withdrew. These moves had been intended to neutralize Snipe while Gruppe Stiffelmayer counter-attacked 24 Armoured Brigade. As a result of their failure the Germans had to detach part of their main body against Snipe when they moved forward at approximately 1000. The counter-attack went in south of the outpost with the result that the side armour of the tanks attacking 24 Armoured Brigade was exposed to Snipe's guns at 1,000 yards, while those tanks attacking Snipe exposed their flanks to the British tanks on the ridge to the east. Thus caught in a crossfire, the Germans had eight of their tanks set ablaze and withdrew.

It was now about 1100 and the morning's events had not left the garrison unscathed. Casualties continued to mount, the interior of the outpost was strewn with wrecked and burning vehicles, and only thirteen guns remained in action; worst of all, continuous firing had seriously depleted the stock of 6-pounder ammunition, particularly on the south-western sector. Turner had already sent out the most seriously wounded in three of the remaining carriers, one of which was hit in the process. Back on the ridge, Pearson had assembled a re-supply convoy which he was hoping to bring up, but this attracted such a storm of fire every time it tried to cross the crest that it would have been suicidal to have persevered with the attempt. Thus, Outpost Snipe, short of ammunition, lacking its FOO and medical officer, battered by the enemy's artillery, would somehow have to fend for itself.

For a while, apart from shelling and mortaring, the garrison was left alone. Behind the lines, British radio intercept operators monitoring the enemy's frequencies were already aware that he was alarmed by 1st Armoured Division's attempted breakout towards the Rahman Track and that he intended mounting a major counter-attack to restore the situation; they were aware, too, that he regarded Snipe as a stumbling-block which must be removed from the path of the operation.

At 1300, believing that the outpost had been softened up sufficiently, the Italians launched a fresh attack against the south-western sector with eight tanks and an assault gun. Someone had injected iron into their souls, for this time they came on regardless of loss, machine-gunning the whole way. Only one 6-pounder, that of Sergeant Charles Calistan, would bear and Turner, acting as loader, told the sergeant to hold his fire until the range had closed to 600 yards. Six of the enemy vehicles were hit in succession and began to burn. The remainder, however, continued to advance. With the gun crew down to their last two rounds, Calistan himself takes up the story:

'Two of my crew crept out on their bellies – right into the open to get some ammo. They were under fire the whole time and their progress was terribly slow. Then our platoon officer, Lieutenant J. E. B. Toms, decided to reach his jeep, 100 yards distant, which had four boxes of ammo on board. God knows how he got to it – they were machine-gunning the whole way. He started coming towards us and then they hit the jeep and it caught fire, but he kept on coming. We got the ammo off, but the Colonel was wounded in the head and we put him behind some scrub. He called out that he wanted to know what was happening and my officer kept up a running commentary. We hit three tanks with three successive shots and the Colonel yelled out: "Good work – a hat trick!"'

The attack had been stopped within 200 yards of the perimeter. Coolly, Calistan placed a can of water on the burning jeep and brewed tea for three. Turner's helmet had been penetrated by a shell splinter and, after having the wound dressed, he continued to tour his guns. He was terribly weak, however, and when he began hallucinating he was restrained gently and led to the dugout. By now the majority of the battalion's officers had been killed or wounded and some sectors were commanded by senior NCOs.

Snipe, of course, was by now no longer serving its original purpose and in the normal course of events Briggs might have withdrawn its garrison under cover of an attack by his armoured brigades. However, his intercept operators informed him that 21st Panzer Division was driving north along the Rahman Track and would spearhead Rommel's counter-attack that afternoon. In the circumstances, therefore, he had little alternative than to preserve his own armour for the encounter, and hope that the outpost would continue to hold its own. At approximately 1600 the garrison observed the tanks of 2 Armoured Brigade moving into position on the ridge to the north-east. They were then subjected to vicious shelling by the brigade's supporting artillery regiment, 11th Royal Horse Artillery, for much the same reasons 47 RTR had opened fire earlier in the day. This was soon stopped, but 1,200 yards to the west the enemy could be seen forming up for his counter-attack in two groups, one deploying some forty German and Italian and the other thirty German tanks.

The larger group moved forward to attack 2 Armoured Brigade at about 1700. They were clearly new arrivals, for their route took them past the northern flank of Snipe, the presence of which they did not seem to suspect. This was the chance which '239' Battery, now reduced to four guns, had been waiting for. The gun commanders waited until the sides of their opponents were fully exposed at 200 yards, then opened a murderous fire. The enemy ranks staggered as tanks burst into flames, those that turned towards Snipe being caught in the crossfire from 2 Armoured Brigade on the ridge. Simultaneously, the 6-pounders were firing as rapidly as they could be loaded; the breech of one gun, fouled by grit, would not close and had to be knocked shut repeatedly by the battery commander, Lieutenant Alan Baer, using an expended shell-case as a hammer.

His attack stalled on a killing ground, the enemy battlegroup leader had no alternative other than to withdraw, but he had not quite finished with Snipe. He detached fifteen tanks from his second wave and these advanced steadily on 'A' Company's positions, covering one another's movements with machine-gun fire and taking advantage of every fold in the ground. Only three guns, those of Sergeant Hine, Sergeant Miles and Lieutenant Holt-Wilson, could be brought to bear and the ammunition remaining to these amounted to an average of ten rounds apiece. It was the most scientific and potentially the most dangerous attack of the day, so dangerous that Turner ordered his adjutant, Captain F. W. Marten, to burn the maps and codes. Tensely, the gun crews waited while machine-gun rounds beat on the gun-shields and kicked up sand around the pits. Miles was hit and Colour-Sergeant J. E. Swann, whose own gun had been knocked out, crawled thirty yards to take his place. At 200 yards the 6-pounders let fly and four tanks lurched to a standstill, belching fire and smoke. Two more shared the same fate, the last a mere 100 yards from Swann's muzzle. The remainder reversed out to a depression 800 yards distant, from which they continued to fire until last light, when they were seen moving off towards their laager. Their commanders never knew just how close to success they had come, for the guns which had repulsed their attack were down to three rounds each.

At 1740 Brigadier Bosville came through on the radio and informed Marten, now the senior unwounded officer, that the garrison would be relieved at 2100. For various reasons, the relief force did not arrive and at

2300 Bosville gave Marten permission to withdraw. The enemy were now out collecting their own wounded, but neither side interfered with the other. Snipe's dead would have to be left behind, but the worst of the garrison's wounded were placed aboard three jeeps and six carriers, all that remained of the battalion's transport, and sent off. The walking wounded were supported by their comrades in a small column, 200 strong, which trudged wearily towards its own lines. With the exception of one of '239' Battery's guns, which was driven out aboard a bullet-riddled portee, the 6-pounders had to be left where they were; before they left, their crews removed the breech-blocks and sights. Around the now silent, wreckage-strewn hollow lay the remains of nearly seventy tanks and self-propelled weapon systems, only seven of which were British.

In the wider context, the day's fighting had not succeeded in cutting the Rahman Track, but it had seriously written down the enemy's armour, and for this the epic stand at Snipe was largely responsible. Rommel, who had personally commented on the outpost's 'tremendously powerful anti-tank defence', could not afford to lose tanks at this rate, since few replacements were reaching him. He had also burned much priceless fuel to no purpose.

Word of the tremendous fight at Snipe spread through the Eighth Army like wildfire and a month later a Committee of Inquiry visited the site to record the details officially. Some of the less severely damaged vehicles had obviously been recovered by the enemy, although it is very doubtful whether these had been repaired when the battle ended on 4 November, and others had been towed away recently by British recovery teams. Nevertheless, by subjecting the performance of every gun to critical analysis, the Committee was able to establish that twenty-one German and eleven Italian tanks had been totally destroyed, plus five assault guns or tank destroyers, and that a further fifteen, possibly twenty tanks had been knocked out and recovered. This produced a grand total of fifty-seven, of which nineteen were claimed by '239' Battery. The enemy's personnel losses could not be assessed, but were far higher than the 72 casualties incurred by the riflemen and gunners.

For his outstanding leadership throughout the operation, Lieutenant-Colonel Victor Turner was awarded the Victoria Cross. Major Thomas Bird, commanding the Rifle Brigade's anti-tank company, received an immediate Distinguished Service Order; he already held the Military Cross with Bar. Sergeant Charles Calistan, already the holder of the Military Medal, was recommended for the Victoria Cross, but the strict rules governing this award had changed somewhat since it was established and he received the Distinguished Conduct Medal; subsequently commissioned, he was killed in Italy. The DCM was also awarded to Colour-Sergeant Swann and Rifleman D. A. Chard. There were, too, awards of the Military Cross and Military Medal for those selected from the many who earned them that day; among them was Lieutenant Toms, who received a Bar to his MC.

The defence of Outpost Snipe, like that of Rorke's Drift sixty-three years earlier, became a legend and the lessons arising from it were similarly self-evident.

CHAPTER 9
Sidi Nsir
26 FEBRUARY 1943

T he story of the 5th Battalion The Hampshire Regiment during the early years of the Second World War paralleled that of many Territorial infantry battalions. Together with 1/4th and 2/4th Battalions of the same regiment, also Territorials, the 5th formed part of 128 Brigade, 43rd (Wessex) Division. When, in 1939, it became clear that war was inevitable, its drill-halls had attracted so many recruits that it became possible to form another battalion, the 7th, from them. However, in the wake of mobilization came disappointment, for the long period of political neglect of the armed services had left the Army under-equipped, and priority was naturally given to units serving with the British Expeditionary Force in France. The situation began to improve slowly after Dunkirk, but in the meantime 5th Hampshires philosophically settled down to training and a long series of home defence duties. With regret, some of the older officers and men, who had served with the battalion throughout the inter-war years but were no longer fit enough for an infantryman's war, were posted elsewhere to less exacting duties, their places being taken by younger men. Nevertheless, despite the fact that many of the newcomers came from other parts of the country, the battalion retained the essentially local character which is the strength of the regimental system. In August 1942, now fully trained and equipped, 128 Brigade joined the 46th Division, with which it embarked for North Africa the following January.

The overall situation was that, following his defeat during the Second Battle of Alamein, Field Marshal Rommel was retreating with the remnants of his army towards the security of the Mareth Line, lying just within the Tunisian border with Libya. In the west the Allied First Army, which 46th Division was to join, had effected landings in French North Africa, but had failed to capture the ports of Tunis and Bizerte, through which the Axis powers were pouring reinforcements. These included an additional panzer division and a battalion of Tiger tanks, the latter armed with an 88mm gun capable of destroying any Allied tank in service and protected by frontal armour which was proof against tank and anti-tank guns alike. These troops were commanded by Colonel-General Hans-Jurgen von Arnim, who had succeeded in stabilizing a line in the mountains of western Tunisia while he waited the arrival of Rommel and his troops.

Meanwhile, 46th Division's convoy reached Algiers on 17 January. 128 Brigade, commanded by Brigadier M. A. James, VC, were transhipped along the coast to Bône, where they occupied a transit camp in which vehicle and equipment losses, incurred when one of the convoy's transports had been torpedoed, were made good. At the end of the month the brigade moved up to take its place in the line in an area known as Hunt's Gap. This sector was regarded as being particularly sensitive, as Hunt's Gap marked the exit from a valley running south-east from Mateur. Unlike the hills on either side, the valley offered good going for tanks and, if Hunt's Gap could be forced, the enemy armour could deploy on the open plain beyond and capture the vital road and rail junction at Béja. Through Béja flowed the supplies required to maintain the northern end of the Allied line, and its loss would mean that the line itself would have to be withdrawn many miles to the west, with serious strategic implications for the future conduct of the campaign.

At Hunt's Gap the 1/4th and 2/4th Hampshires took up defensive positions astride the road, but 5th Hampshires, commanded by Lieutenant-Colonel H. C. C. Newnham, were sent twelve miles up the valley to the hamlet of Sidi Nisir, where they relieved 1st East Surreys. There was little at Sidi Nsir save a few small, stone-built Arab huts and a railway station, but the hamlet did possess some tactical importance in that the road and railway connecting Béja with Mateur diverged at this point, the road swinging east into the hills while the railway continued to follow the easier north-easterly route. The tasks Newnham's battalion were to perform included patrolling, but more importantly it was to absorb the first shock of any enemy attack directed against Béja, imposing delay which would permit the defenders of Hunt's Gap to be reinforced.

Newnham, therefore, had been handed the somewhat grubby end of the stick, since he could not be supported directly by the rest of the brigade, nor could he receive effective fire support from the field artillery covering Hunt's Gap. Nevertheless, however dirty the job, it was undertaken willingly, but the difficulties were compounded by other factors closer to hand. Sidi Nsir lay in a hollow and could only be defended by positioning the rifle companies on different hill features surrounding the hamlet, where they would be unable to provide one another with mutual support and also difficult to reinforce and resupply with ammunition if they were attacked. Most difficult of all were the problems of anti-tank defence, for although a minefield had been laid across the Mateur road the battalion possessed only obsolete 2-pounder anti-tank guns, issue of the much superior but scarce 6-pounder being confined to the Royal Artillery's anti-tank regiments in First Army.

Some of these problems were partially solved by the arrival of 'E' and 'F' Troops of 155 Battery (172nd Field Regiment Royal Artillery) under Major J. S. Raworth during the evening of 5 February, with their

WATERLOO

Above: *La Garde Impériale à Waterloo*, by Bellangé (1850). General Pierre Cambronne rejects the British call to surrender, although not in the noble words generally ascribed to him. By the time this incident took place Napoleon, shown on the right, had already left the square. (Musée de l'Armée, Paris)

Right: *La Garde Meurt*, by Bellangé (1840). The end of the three Old Guard battalions destroyed near La Belle Alliance cannot have been very different, but the men were wearing their greatcoats and have been drawn as being much older than they were. Napoleon did not witness the event, as suggested. (Musée de l'Armée, Paris)

THE ALAMO

Above: The death of Colonel William Travis at the north-western corner of The Alamo's defences. Travis is known to have ordered a uniform, but is believed to have fought in a tail-coat. Most accounts say that he received a fatal head wound and fell back across the gun. However, one version has it that the wound was caused by a spent ball, that he rolled down the ramp, stunned, and that when he came to he and a Mexican officer ran each other through simultaneously. The artist seems to have allowed for both possibilities. At the foot of the ramp is Travis' servant Joe, who was spared by the Mexicans. (Daughters of the Republic of Texas, The Alamo)

Above: *The Fall of the Alamo* by Onderdonk. The figure with the clubbed rifle is undoubtedly intended to represent Davy Crockett, although it has been suggested that one of Crockett's arms was broken by a musket ball before he and his men were cut off as they retreated from the stockade. The man with pistol at the bottom-left corner may be John MacGregor, although other Scots were present. (Daughters of the Republic of Texas, The Alamo)

Bottom left: *The Battle of the Alamo* by Gentilz is widely believed to be the most accurate depiction of the assault. On the left the Mexicans are streaming through the breach in the north wall and are attacking the Long Barracks, having brought up a gun to batter down the sandbagged doors; above the roof of the building in the foreground a second column is advancing from the south-western corner to outflank the stockade and attack the church. On the right a third column in open order is charging the stockade; the Mexican tricolour with 1824 in the centre is flying above the church but, curiously, there is no sign of the Texan guns known to have been emplaced on a ramp in the apse. In the background are the Mexican cavalry, whose function was to cut down any Texans who attempted to escape, and also to prevent their comrades deserting. (Daughters of the Republic of Texas, The Alamo)

CAMERONE

Above: *Camerone 1863*, by Edouard Détaille (1880). The Legion's Third Company nears the end of its long fight. (Musée de l'Armée, Paris)

LITTLE BIG HORN

Left: Brigadier General George Armstrong Custer and Mrs Elizabeth Custer. (US Army Military History Institute)

Right: Edgar Paxson's reconstruction of Custer's final moments on Last Stand Hill is generally accepted to be accurate, save for the presence of the guidon. (USAMHI)

Right: Major Marcus A. Reno, photographed as a Brigadier General at the end of the Civil War. (USAMHI)

Far right: Captain Frederick W. Benteen was not promoted Major until 1882, more than six years after the Little Big Horn. His career prospects, already damaged by his antipathy to Custer, may have been further prejudiced by his association with Reno. (USAMHI)

ISANDHLWANA/ RORKE'S DRIFT

Left: C. E. Fripp's famous painting of the 24th Regiment (later the South Wales Borderers) at Isandhlwana, showing the scene shortly after the ammunition supply had failed. To the right of centre can be seen an example of two Zulus fighting as a team to kill an infantryman. (National Army Museum)

Left: Saving the Colour. Lieutenants Teignmouth Melville and Neville Coghill escape from Isandhlwana with the Queen's Colour of the 1st/24th. Both were killed when they had almost reached safety, but the Colour did not fall into Zulu hands and was later recovered from the Buffalo River. (National Army Museum)

Opposite page, top: *The Defence of Rorke's Drift*, by A. de Neuville (1880). On the left Surgeon-Major James Reynolds helps in the rescue of patients from the burning hospital; Lieutenant John Chard, Royal Engineers, in command of the post, is in the centre of the picture, pointing; to his right the Revd. George Smith, with beard, distributes ammunition; the commander of 'B' Company 2nd/24th,

Lieutenant Gonville Bromhead, is on the far right, bareheaded and fighting with rifle and bayonet. (National Army Museum)

ARTILLERY ACTIONS, 1914–18

Centre right: Rear view of the Néry Gun, preserved at the Imperial War Museum. Note the smashed spokes and rim on the left-hand wheel, also visible in the Matania print of the action, and scars left by shell splinters on the right-hand wheel. (Imperial War Museum)

Below: The last gun of 'L' Battery, Royal Horse Artillery, in action at Néry, 1 September 1914. From a print by Fortunino Matania. (National Army Museum)

Above: After the First World War, 'L' Battery was posted to Risalpur, India, but on each anniversary of the battle its members arranged for a wreath to be placed on the Néry Gun in memory of lost comrades. On this occasion the wreath was fittingly placed by ex-Driver Drane, a member of 'L' Battery at Néry. Note the heavy damage sustained by the muzzle of the weapon. (IWM)

Below: '5' Battery, Royal Field Artillery, at Bois des Buttes, 27 May 1918. The figure with the Lewis gun is Captain John Massey, the acting battery commander; the officer to his left is Lieutenant J. E. Large. A painting by Cuneo in the possession of '5' (Gibraltar 1779–83) Field Battery, RA. (Royal Artillery Institution)

WAKE ATOLL

Right: Albin Henning's painting of the final Japanese assault on Wake Atoll. The viewpoint is on Wilkes Island, where the attackers were wiped out. (US Marine Corps)

OUTPOST SNIPE

Right: Six-pounder anti-tank gun in action in the Western Desert. (IWM)

Below: The only gun to survive the action at 'Snipe' was this 6-pounder of 239 Anti-Tank Battery, RA, seen here being lowered from its portée. (IWM)

Left: Major Thomas Bird (hatless, with bandaged head) and the officers and senior NCOs of 2nd Rifle Brigade's Anti-Tank Company shortly after 'Snipe'. (IWM)

Left: Sergeant Charles Calistan (left) and other senior NCOs of the 2nd Rifle Brigade's Anti-Tank Company provide details of the action at 'Snipe' for the editor of the Eighth Army Newspaper *Crusader*. Calistan, who received the Distinguished Conduct Medal, was subsequently commissioned but was killed in Italy. (IWM)

SIDI NSIR

Left: The Battalion Headquarters of 5th Hampshire Regiment was located in the station at Sidi Nsir. The building was gutted by fire during the final stages of the battle. (IWM)

Above: Hill held by 'A' Company 5th Hampshires during the fighting at Sidi Nsir. (IWM)

Below: A sketch by Bryan de Grineau showing the last stand of 155 Battery at Sidi Nsir. The details are accurate save that the Royal Artillery numbers its guns from the right rather than as shown. (*Illustrated London News* Picture Library)

BETIO, TARAWA ATOLL

Top left: Tarawa. Marines cross the sea wall into the teeth of the Japanese fire. (US Marine Corps)

Bottom left: Tarawa. Even inland, the fighting was at close quarters. To the right is one of the Japanese concrete command bunkers, carefully camouflaged. (US Marine Corps)

Top right: Tarawa. Amtracs unload 75mm pack howitzers and stores on Red-2 during the final phases of Operation 'Galvanic'. Some details of Red-1 can be seen in the background. (US Marine Corps)

THE ADMIN BOX

Centre right: A parachute supply drop falls into the Admin Box close to Lee tanks and other vehicles. (IWM)

Bottom right: Vultures circling over the Blood Nullah sector of the Admin Box defences, Nature's way of disposing of the Japanese dead. (IWM)

ARNHEM BRIDGE

Left: Paratroopers moving into Arnhem from their drop zone to the west of the town. (IWM)

Left: An air reconnaissance photograph showing the wreckage of the failed panzergrenadier attack on the northern ramp of Arnhem bridge and part of the area held by 2nd Battalion The Parachute Regiment and other troops. The school is to the right of the bridge. (IWM)

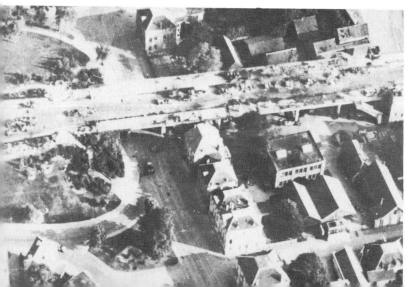

Left: The same area seen from another angle. The 2nd Battalion's mortars were sited on the island in the lower half of the picture, where trenches can be seen. The building to the right of the island was known as the White House. (IWM)

THE IMJIN

Above: Ken Howard's painting of Staff-Sergeant P. E. Buss, the Glosters' Drum-Major, sounding the Long Reveille during the last dawn on 'Gloster' Hill. (Courtesy The Gloucestershire Regiment)

Above: A sketch by Captain M. G. Harvey, commanding the Glosters' 'D' Company, showing Battalion Headquarters on the summit of 'Gloster' Hill. Naturally, many more men were present than those actually shown.

(Courtesy The Gloucestershire Regiment)

Below: A cartoon which appeared in the *Toronto Telegram* shortly after the Imjin battle.

eight 25-pounder gun/howitzers. The 25-pounder was one of the outstanding artillery weapons of the war, capable not only of supporting offensive or defensive operations of other arms with indirect fire controlled from observation posts by Forward Observation Officers, but also of engaging tanks with armour-piercing shot over open sights; indeed, during the desert phase of the war in North Africa the 25-pounder had on several occasions proved itself to be every bit as efficient a tank killer as the dreaded German Eighty-Eight. The one thing the batteries could not reasonably be expected to do was perform both functions simultaneously, even if they were mutually supporting, and in the awkward defences of Sidi Nsir this was impossible. None the less, after settling in the guns began registering the defensive fire (DF) tasks requested by the rifle companies.

Elsewhere, events were taking place which were to have a bearing on the fate of Sidi Nsir. By the time Rommel's rearguards finally left Libya the Axis tank strength in Tunisia had risen to 280 and both German commanders felt capable of taking the offensive. The blow struck the inexperienced US 1st Armored Division at Sidi Bou Zid on 14 February, forcing it into a disorderly retreat through Kasserine Pass. The commander of the US II Corps, 1st Armored Division's parent formation, did not distinguish himself and in due course was replaced by Major General George S. Patton, Jr, but in the meantime the situation was regarded so seriously that the British V Corps, holding the northern sector of the line, was forced to send its reserves south to support the rallied 1st Armored in containing the penetration. Having inflicted serious damage, Rommel withdrew so expertly during the night of 22 February that at first the Allies were unaware that he had gone.

It was now von Arnim's turn. While Rommel redeployed against Montgomery's Eighth Army in the south, he planned a spoiling offensive against the weakened British V Corps in the north. This was code-named 'Ochsenkopf' (bull's head) and, as its name suggests, involved two major thrust lines, one directed against the road junction at El Aroussa on the southern flank of the corps' front, and the other through Sidi Nsir and Hunt's Gap towards Béja. The latter was by far the more important and was to be spearheaded by an armoured battlegroup consisting of the fourteen Tigers of 1st Company 501 Heavy Tank Battalion and II/Panzer Regiment 7 (10th Panzer Division) with twelve new Pz Kpfw IVs (known to the British as Mark IV Specials), eight old Pz Kpfw IVs and forty Pz Kpfw IIIs, plus I/Panzergrenadier Regiment 86, Reconnaissance Battalion 190, II/Artillery Regiment 22, anti-aircraft and engineer detachments, under the command of Oberst Rudolph Lang. The troops already in the line opposite Sidi Nsir belonged to two scratch formations named after their commanders, Division von Manteuffel to the west of the railway, and Korpsgruppe Weber to the east. Patrol activity had already confirmed that the former contained a paratroop element, the members of which

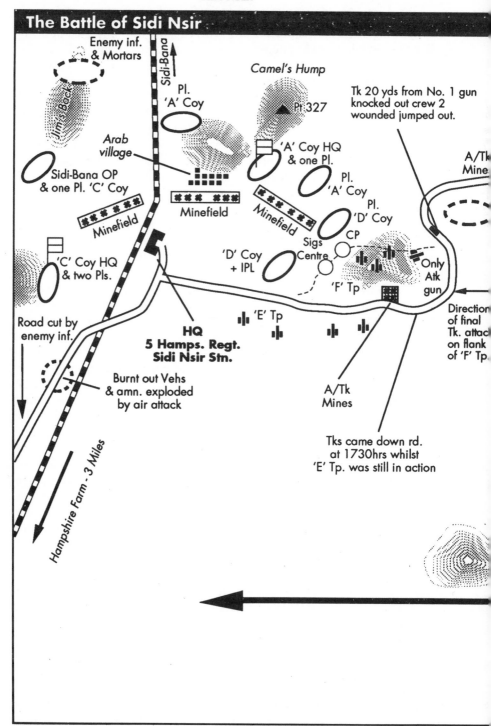

The Battle of Sidi Nsir

Enemy inf. & Mortars

Jim's Back

Sidi-Bana

Camel's Hump

Pt 327

Tk 20 yds from No. 1 gun knocked out crew 2 wounded jumped out.

A/Tk Mine

Pl. 'A' Coy

Arab village

'A' Coy HQ & one Pl.

Sidi-Bana OP & one Pl. 'C' Coy

Pl. 'A' Coy

Pl. 'D' Coy

Minefield

Minefield

Minefield

Sigs Centre

CP

Only Atk gun

'C' Coy HQ & two Pls.

'D' Coy + IPL

'F' Tp

Direction of final Tk. attack on flank of 'F' Tp.

Road cut by enemy inf.

'E' Tp

HQ
5 Hamps. Regt.
Sidi Nsir Stn.

A/Tk Mines

Burnt out Vehs & amn. exploded by air attack

Tks came down rd. at 1730hrs whilst 'E' Tp. was still in action

Hampshire Farm - 3 Miles

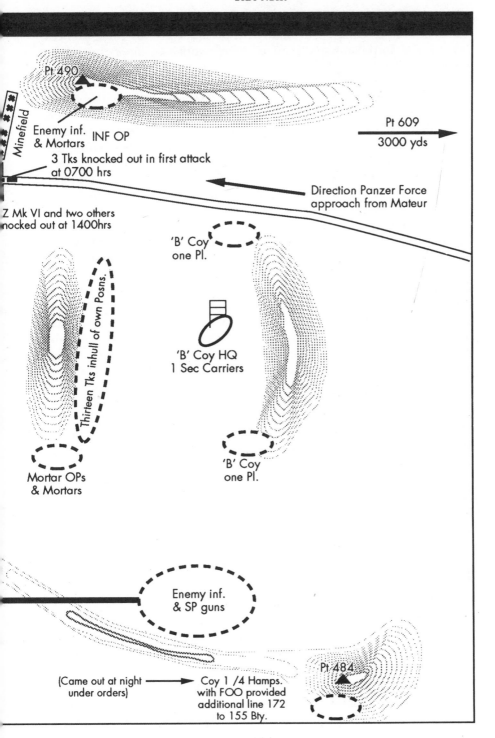

Pt 490

Enemy inf. & Mortars   INF OP

Minefield

Pt 609
3000 yds

3 Tks knocked out in first attack
at 0700 hrs

Z Mk VI and two others
knocked out at 1400hrs

Direction Panzer Force
approach from Mateur

'B' Coy
one Pl.

Thirteen Tks inhull of own Posns.

'B' Coy HQ
1 Sec Carriers

Mortar OPs
& Mortars

'B' Coy
one Pl.

Enemy inf.
& SP guns

Pt 484

(Came out at night
under orders)   Coy 1 /4 Hamps.
with FOO provided
additional line 172
to 155 Bty.

131

were young, tough and aggressive, while the latter included a penal unit which could be relied on to fight hard or suffer serious consequences. During the forthcoming offensive, Lang would be operating under Weber's control.

On the eve of 'Ochsenkopf', 5th Hampshires and their supporting artillery were deployed as follows: Battalion Headquarters in the station buildings with part of Headquarters Company in the station yard, defended by one 2-pounder anti-tank gun, one Vickers medium machine-gun and one section of the anti-aircraft platoon with light machine-guns; 'C' Company on the high ground immediately to the west of the railway, with one platoon supporting 'E' Troop's observation post two miles to the north at a group of huts known as Sidi Bana; 'A' Company, augmented by two 3-inch mortars and a Vickers MMG, on a hill half a mile north-east of the station, with a freshly laid minefield covering its rear; 'B' Company, plus two 3-inch mortars and one 2-pounder anti-tank gun, holding a long ridge one-and-a-half miles to the east, south of the Mateur road; 'D' Company, also with two 3-inch mortars and one 2-pounder, 800 yards east of the station, but north of the road; '155' Battery at an S-bend to the east of 'D' Company, with 'E' Troop south of the road and 'F' Troop to the north and echeloned forward beyond a low crest; 'F' Troop's observation post lying atop the towering Point 609, almost three miles north-east of the station, also supported by an infantry platoon; and a forward administrative area, housing the battalion's 'B' Echelon transport, located in a cluster of buildings called Hampshire Farm, three miles back along the road to Hunt's Gap. The area reminded many of the Scottish highlands, with the narrow road, having few passing places, winding along the empty valley between the hills, an illusion heightened by green vegetation and boggy tracks left by days of seasonal rain.

Since arriving at Sidi Nsir 5th Hampshires had been involved in nothing more serious than minor patrol clashes, during which two Germans had been killed and one captured. It was found that at night the enemy experienced no difficulty in working their way past the company positions to lay mines on the road to Hunt's Gap, and these had to be located and lifted at dawn each day. Ominously, the Luftwaffe demonstrated its local air superiority by strafing the road regularly, so that its use in daylight became hazardous.

Very few members of the battalion had seen active service previously and, despite having been in the line for more than three weeks, the unit was still painfully inexperienced, as was apparent from a number of minor but expensive mistakes made on 22 February. Before first light 'B' Company had sent out a patrol to occupy a hill south of the road to Mateur, there to lie up and observe until dark, when it was to return. On its way out the patrol captured two Germans and, instead of sending them back under escort and continuing with his task, its commander abandoned his mission and brought them in. Newnham, less than pleased, ordered 'B' Company to send out a full platoon to sweep through the area where the contact had occurred, then move on to the hill which had been the original objective, with the proviso that it should follow a route which remained in view from the company's position. This the platoon failed to do. It disappeared beyond a crest and at 0900 the sound of heavy and sustained firing was heard coming from the direction it had taken. After thirty minutes there was silence, but none of the platoon returned and the fate of its members remain unknown. At 1100 'B' Company's right was subjected to machine-gun and mortar fire and the enemy was observed in some numbers about 3,000 yards distant, apparently digging in. If the Hampshires had been more battle-wise they would have recognized that the Germans were probing to locate their positions, and thus the battalion's exposed flank, and would have remained silent. As it was, the company became involved in a long-range fire fight. Newnham sent up part of his carrier platoon to occupy the vacant positions of the platoon which had been ambushed, and towards evening a platoon from 'D' Company began working its way behind the enemy. The Germans, having got what they came for, broke contact and withdrew.

During the day Newnham had been told that his battalion was to be withdrawn to Hunt's Gap itself, leaving only one company and two 25-pounders at Sidi Nsir. His response was that if his entire command was considered inadequate to withstand a major assault, a smaller force would inevitably be squandered to no purpose. Brigadier James could but concur and the order was cancelled. Instead, as a result of the enemy's activity at Sidi Nsir, he decided that Newnham would be reinforced with 'A' Company 1/4th Hampshires, code-named 'Spitforce', which moved into a position intended to protect the battalion's open right flank against attack from the east. This was located at a track junction more than two miles south of 'B' Company and, unfortunately, the gap between the two could not be covered effectively, either physically or by fire. Nothing further of note occurred until 25 February, when the divisional commander, Major-General H. A. Freeman-Attwood, arrived at Sidi Nsir, accompanied by his senior artillery adviser, Brigadier Rigby, and the commanding officer of 172nd Field Regiment, Lieutenant-Colonel W. D. McNeil Graham. The party visited the observation post on Point 609 and remained there for two hours without seeing any sign of enemy activity or movement. That night, however, numerous flares were observed both from this OP and that at Sidi Bana. There were also prolonged bursts of machine-gun fire and aircraft droning overhead, the purpose of this noise being to mask the sound of Lang's tanks as they moved up the road from Mateur.

There were, too, other signs that a major attack was imminent, signs which older hands would have interpreted correctly at once. During the night the local herdsmen removed their numerous flocks, and themselves, far from the hills surrounding Sidi Nsir; and, long before dawn, the Arab stationmaster and his family scuttled into their cellar without explanation. There was nothing supernatural about it, for the Arabs' method of calling news from hill to hill was more reliable than the radio, and almost as quick. They had no interest in the foreigners' war, other than profit, and understandably had no intention of becoming involved.

At 0600 on 26 February the platoon commander covering the OP on Point 609 reported that his position was being heavily mortared. Thirty minutes later mortar fire began to fall on 'B' Company and 'F' Troop. The company reported that German tanks were advancing along the road from Mateur, but had halted when the leading vehicle ran into the minefield; its crew had been shot as they clambered out. 'F' Troop went into action over open sights, setting three tanks ablaze, but shortly after 0800 panzergrenadiers began scrambling from their lorries behind the tanks and they deployed quickly to bring 'B' Company and the gun positions under fire. Switching to high-explosive, the 25-pounders of both troops engaged the enemy continuously, but by 0930 were running short of ammunition. All the battery's available personnel turned to, carrying shells and charges to the guns by hand, despite the risks involved in crossing ground raked by machine-gun and mortar fire.

Newnham climbed 'D' Company's hill to obtain a better view of the battle. Thus far, the enemy had been held, notwithstanding the heavy and destructive fire being endured by 'B' Company and '155' Battery. This was gradually extended to 'A' and 'D' Companies and supplemented by strafing runs made by fighter aircraft. Two of the latter, which made the gun positions their particular target, were shot down as they flew through the hail of small-arms fire directed at them. Returning to his command post in the station, Newnham asked brigade to arrange an air reconnaissance of the Mateur road, which had been reported jammed with tanks and other vehicles, but his request could not be granted.

At 0940 the OP on Point 609 reported that it was under attack by infantry. The covering platoon held out until 1030 when its commander, Lieutenant Heath, signalled that his position had been overrun. At about the same time Lieutenant Amos, whose platoon was covering the OP at Sidi Bana, informed Newnham that he was under attack by two infantry companies. This fight against odds of six to one raged for an hour, when Amos came through again: 'Self and three men left. It can't be much longer. Good-bye and cheerio.' Thereafter, the link to Sidi Bana was silent. Next, 'A' Company reported that enemy infantry had seized the feature to their immediate front, known as the Camel's Hump, but for the moment had halted their advance.

The form of the battle was now apparent. The enemy had decided to attack Sidi Nsir with tanks and infantry along the road from the east, and simultaneously with infantry down the line of the railway from the north. His decision to eliminate the main OPs early in the engagement was sound, since it restricted the British artillery to engaging local targets, although the execution of this part of his plan was probably out of phase and completed much later than he had expected. Likewise, Sidi Nsir was proving a tougher nut to crack than he had anticipated and, instead of crashing its way through an apparently weak battalion position, the tank assault had stalled in front of the unexpectedly tough anti-tank defence offered by '155' Battery. Clearly, a major assault would be required to clear this obstacle on the road to Béja. For Newnham, the loss of the OPs was serious, although the defence was holding and he was fulfilling his mission by imposing delay on his opponents. In the gun-pits and slit trenches, gunners and riflemen recognized instinctively that each depended on the other for survival.

Meanwhile, Lieutenant-Colonel Graham had come forward to visit his gunners. The gun positions were being heavily and accurately mortared but the men were in good heart and were hitting back hard. Additional ammunition was being brought forward from Hampshire Farm in the battalion's carriers, some of which were hit and set on fire by enemy aircraft strafing the road from a height of 200 feet. Enough got through, however, to keep the guns firing, despite the difficulty involved in unloading the vehicles under fire.

For a while, the guns of 5th Medium Regiment Royal Artillery, firing from beyond Hunt's Gap, joined in the battle, controlled by Lieutenant G. S. Stavert of '155' Battery. They came into action at approximately 1145, when a group of eight tanks, supported by infantry, began moving forward. The War Diary of 172 Field Regiment describes the shoot as being unsuccessful, but this was compiled later from incomplete information, by which time Stavert was a prisoner. On the other hand, the Germans did not press their attack and it is possible that the eruptions of earth and rock when the heavy shells exploded around them may well have been a factor in this. Unfortunately, communications between Sidi Nsir and 5th Medium Regiment failed shortly after. By 1240 the enemy had assembled a force of thirty tanks and four self-propelled guns.

Simultaneously, 'E' and 'F' Troops were firing in support of the embattled Hampshire companies, engaging infantry, machine-gun and mortar positions in response to requests from the company OPs. The Germans were tightening their grip on the battalion and the ranges dropped slowly but steadily from 4,000 to 3,000, from 2,500 to 2,000 yards. At approximately 1400 one Tiger and two Pz Kpfw IVs began probing forward past the southern edge of the minefield; 'F' Troop promptly switched to armour-piercing shot and knocked out all three.

Meanwhile, enemy infantry had infiltrated the wide gap between the right flank of 'B' Company and 'Spitforce'. At 1500 they cut the road between Hampshire Farm and Sidi Nsir, preventing further supplies of ammunition reaching the guns. A comparative lull of almost two hours followed during which the Germans prepared for their final assault.

At 1700 Captain J. H. Lytle, the commander of 'B' Company, which had borne the brunt of the battle throughout the day, advised Newnham that his strength had been reduced to thirty men and that the position was under attack. Nothing further was heard from the company and none of its members returned. Thirteen tanks moved into hull down positions along an intermediate crest between 'B' Company's ridge and '155' Battery, engaging the gun positions with high-explosive and machine-gun fire while the rest ground slowly along the road and into the S-bend dividing the two troops. Newnham watched the attack and, some days later, described it to A. B. Austin of the *Daily Herald*. 'Thirty German tanks rolled down the road towards our 25-pounder battery. We had four guns on one side of the road, and four on the other. The tanks first took up a position from which they could fire at the guns on one side of the road. One after another the four guns were hit. Evert's gun fired till the last moment. Then the tanks turned against the guns on the other side of the road. The gunners kept firing, hitting tank after tank, but still the Germans came on. Three of our remaining guns were smashed. Only one gun crew left was still firing. When I last saw the German tanks they were bearing down on the crew, which was firing at ten yards' range. Seven tanks that battery had destroyed – seven tanks for eight guns! Those gunners, they were tremendous – every man was worth the Victoria Cross!'

Lieutenant Stavert, who had earlier controlled the fire of 5th Medium Regiment's guns, witnessed the end of 'F' Troop at close quarters.

'A row of turrets appeared along the crest and the world erupted in a jarring, shattering burst of noise as everything opened up at once. It was impossible to distinguish the noise of exploding shells from that of the 25-pounder firing back. The air was filled with horrid little red streaks of tracer. A row of little holes appeared across the top of the shield of No. 3 Gun. The sergeant yelled at his men to keep their heads down as they strove to break all records for reloading. They fired, and then he yelled again as the solid shot, its trajectory clearly revealed by its red spark of tracer, struck the front of a Tiger tank a glancing blow and went careering off into space. No. 4 Gun was already out of action, leaning untidily on a smashed trunnion in the middle of a pile of burning ammunition. Outside the pit a group of figures lay prone and still on the ground. A high-velocity shell hit the corner of the command post just by my ear. I saw the flash and heard the crack but didn't feel the blast at all. A gunner on No. 2 collapsed, shot through both ankles; another on No. 3 fell into the ditch, his face completely covered with blood. Yet still the covering tanks on the crest pounded at the weakening troop. Each gun-pit was now a circle of flames wherein Dante-esque figures ducked and lay, as one after another the open boxes of cordite charges burst like giant Roman candles, sending columns of black smoke upwards, tinged with red. A direct hit on No. 3 had folded up its shield like a piece of wet blotting-paper. The remainder of the detachment, incredibly still alive, tumbled into the ditch. I tumbled in after them. The last gun ceased firing, and a seemingly endless queue of Mark IVs, led by a Tiger, rolled slowly nose to tail across our front. If anything looked like moving, they shot it up.'

'E' Troop had a similar end, although at least one gun fired its last rounds at a range of between ten and twenty yards. The tanks smothered the position with machine-gun and high-explosive fire which focused on the smallest sign of movement. Some entered the position and crushed the slit trenches by neutral turning above them. At 1751 Gunner Edward Walsh, the battery's command post signaller, radioed 'Tanks are on us,' then grabbed his Morse key and defiantly transmitted ⋯ − ('V' for Victory). The sentiment was closer to the truth than Walsh or anyone else could possibly have imagined at that moment. In the failing light the leading tanks rolled slowly on down the hill through 'D' Company's position towards the station, leaving six in the battery position. Looking up from the ditch, Stavert noted the white palm-tree emblem stencilled on their sand-coloured sides. The shooting stopped and their commanders climbed out, beckoning the gunners to come forward. Major Raworth, infinitely weary but still in command, emerged from his command post and told his men to conform: 'Come along, everybody − there's nothing more we can do now.'

The battle was now effectively over. Of the fate of 'A' and 'D' Companies less is known save that, like 'B' Company, they fought their maiden action with a dogged tenacity that would have done credit to battle-hardened veterans, and they held their positions to the very end. The tank thrust penetrated as far as the rear of both companies, which were already engaged to the front with enemy infantry, and the probability is that their remnants were overrun at last light; certainly, the Arab hut which was 'D' Company's headquarters was blazing fiercely by then. Unable to contact either company by radio or field telephone, Newnham dispatched runners, but they were pinned down every time they attempted to get through.

By now, battalion headquarters had problems of its own. Shortly after 1800 two Pz Kpfw IVs made directly for the station buildings. The 2-pounder anti-tank gun in the yard banged once and was then blown apart. The tanks then opened fire on the buildings, but, probably deterred by a single strand of barbed wire which they suspected might indicate mines, declined to enter the yard. 'C' Company, despite losing a platoon at Sidi Bana, was still holding on the high ground west of the station and Newnham ordered its commander to withdraw, at his discretion, to Hampshire Farm, or to Hunt's Gap if the enemy were encountered. Within the station, the radios, telephone exchange, maps and codes were all destroyed, and small parties left by the rear of buildings, heading for

Hampshire Farm by way of 'C' Company's now vacant position. Finally, the last party to leave set fire to the station.

The majority reached Hampshire Farm safely, although some who strayed too close to the road were killed or captured. From the high ground flares could be seen rising from the positions occupied by 'A' and 'D' Companies, but firing had ceased. Newnham reached the farm at about 2130 and for a while was occupied with thoughts as to whether, using 'Spitforce', 'C' Company and the remnant of Headquarters and Support Companies, he could impose further delay on the enemy. Since he lacked heavy weapons and had no means of communicating with brigade, this was a forlorn hope, the more so when it became apparent that 'C' Company was long overdue. At midnight he decided to withdraw to Hunt's Gap. As enemy elements were believed to have infiltrated the intervening area, the route of the rain-drenched little column once more took them westwards into the hills before they turned south. At 0800 on 27 February Newnham reached the 2/4th Hampshires' position with about 100 men, including nine survivors of '155' Battery, and was relieved to learn that 'C' Company had arrived an hour earlier. 'Spitforce' came out by a similar route. During the day further small parties reached Hunt's Gap, including Lieutenant R. F. D. Pemberton and twenty-nine men of 'D' Company, who had made their way back through enemy lines in the darkness, and Captain S. T. Bormond, R.A., with nine gunners who had been in '155' Battery's wagon lines during the enemy's final assault.

Naturally, Newnham was deeply saddened by the loss of so many officers and men with whom he had served so long, and as soon as possible he wrote to the Colonel of the Regiment: 'I remember in the last war, when I was with our 1st Battalion in the "Stone Wall" Brigade, I thought they were tough, but these lads were tougher than anything I have ever served with or hope to serve with again. There was no suggestion of a waver; every man stood to his rifle, his Bren, his mortar, until the end. We are more than fortunate to have so many survivors and great credit is due to them for their providential escape."'

Colonel Newnham received the Distinguished Service Order and, because of the critical nature of the engagement, the US Army also awarded him its Distinguished Service Cross. Lieutenant Pemberton received the Military Cross. Private G. Minnigin was awarded the Military Medal for his gallantry in bringing up ammunition under fire; as a sergeant, he won the Distinguished Conduct Medal at Salerno and received a battlefield commission in November 1943. Many other men qualified for decorations, but they were either dead or prisoners in enemy hands and details of their actions remain unknown.

It is thought that, in addition to his tanks, the enemy employed the equivalent of three infantry battalions against Sidi Nsir. In the circumstances, it was impossible to estimate his personnel casualties and some disagreement exists concerning the number of tanks knocked out. In December 1977, Stavert, who had subsequently joined the Royal Navy and later became a lecturer at the Royal Military Academy, Sandhurst, published an interesting account of the battle in which he expressed doubts that the number of tanks actually destroyed had reached ten. On the other hand, the Official History of the campaign, produced with all the available facts to hand, states that '. . . about 40 of Lang's tanks were destroyed or crippled, although many were repaired because his troops held the field'. Despite the apparent disparity, the two figures are not incompatible, since for every tank completely destroyed two or three more would have been immobilized by damage of varying degrees of severity.

What is clear is that Lang's probes towards Hunt's Gap the following day were made with but a fraction of his original tank strength. The War Diary of 172 Field Regiment takes up the story:

'0700 – Tanks heard but not visible from OP. Rain started bogging the tracks and valleys off the main road.

0745 – 11 tanks, four armoured cars and lorried infantry moving down the road from Sidi Nsir. Engaged by '153' and '154' Batteries, '457' Light Battery (3.7-inch howitzers) and 5 Medium Regiment.

0945 – '154' Battery OP reported 18 tanks advancing from Sidi Nsir.

1000 – Column halted by terrific concentration from Regimental group; several tanks ablaze.

1135 – 5 Medium engage seven tanks concentrated on Sidi Nsir–Béja road. Two hit, no confirmation of destruction.

1237 – 13 enemy tanks observed facing south-west. A further ten enemy tanks on road engaged by '457' Light Battery; one set on fire by a direct hit.

1315 – '154' Battery engaged the 18 tanks previously reported.

1320 – Order from C.O. – "Engage and keep on engaging tanks on Sidi Nsir–Béja road; they appear to be stuck."

1445 – Another tank reported out of action. Reports from three sources confirm Mark VI [i.e., Tiger] tanks being used accompanied by four or five Mark III or IV. A panic was started by field artillery concentrations on the leading tanks. Six were abandoned and blown up later by our Royal Engineers, including Tiger.

1600 – Tanks started to withdraw, having been beaten off by the extremely heavy artillery concentration.

Heavy harassing fire tasks to prevent recovery of tanks were carried out throughout the night.'

Not until 0600 on 28 February was Lang able to mount a concentrated attack on Hunt's Gap. Thus, the twelve-hour ordeal of 5th Hampshires and '155' Battery had imposed a delay of 48 hours during which the defences had been strengthened and reinforcements rushed into the area. Brigadier James now had under command 1/4th and 2/4th

Hampshires, 2/5th Leicestershire Regiment, two Churchill tank squadrons of the North Irish Horse, 171 and 172 Field Regiments plus one battery of 102 Field Regiment RA, '457' Light Battery RA, 58 Anti-Tank Regiment RA and 5 Medium Regiment RA, while further reinforcements were on their way from 8th Argyll and Sutherland Highlanders and 2nd Parachute Regiment. Newnham's 'C' Company, back in the line with 2/4th Hampshires, were able to watch their old enemies batter themselves to destruction on the mile-wide killing ground as tank after tank fell victim to mines, artillery concentrations, anti-tank guns, hull-down Churchills and Hurricanes flying in the fighter-bomber role. Only on the hills were the German infantry able to make any impression, and their advance was soon halted.

On 1 March Lang attempted to renew the assault, but by the end of the day he had only five serviceable tanks left. Weber, recognizing that the chance of reaching Béja had gone forever, told him to withdraw his armour and go over to the defensive. 1st Company 501 Heavy Tank Battalion, having lost half its tanks, described the area as The Tiger Graveyard. Lang was scornfully dubbed Tank Killer by his own troops, a little unfairly since he could not have predicted the terrific defence put up by a handful of Territorial riflemen and gunners at Sidi Nsir, nor the boggy going which inhibited deployment off the road during the later phase of his advance, nor the shattering response of the concentrated British artillery. Operation 'Bull's Head' was over.

CHAPTER 10
Betio, Tarawa Atoll
20–23 NOVEMBER 1943

One of the reasons why the Japanese soldier was so formidable an opponent was the fact that he alone of all the combatants of the Second World War fought to the death, willingly, deliberately, without the slightest hesitation and as a matter of course. He did so because of a profound belief, instilled from birth, that the spirit of Japan was embodied in her Emperor, whom he regarded as a god. As a soldier, therefore, his life belong to the Emperor and it followed that to die in the Emperor's service was not only the greatest honour to which he could aspire, but also a religious duty the performance of which would ensure his place in the after-life. The concept of surrender was incomprehensible to him, and the greatest disgrace which could befall him was to fall alive into the hands of his enemies; rather than permit that, he would commit suicide or shoot his badly wounded comrades if capture seemed likely. Because of this, very few Japanese prisoners were taken during the early years of the war. Those that were taken frequently offered the fullest co-operation to their captors, the reason for this apparent perversity being that their capture in itself placed them beyond the pale of Japanese society. They had, in their own eyes, forfeited the right to return to their homeland because they had become untouchables. Long after the war ended, Japanese soldiers continued to emerge from their jungle hiding-places, incredulous that Japan had herself surrendered and that the Emperor had renounced his deified status.

It had always been acknowledged that the Japanese soldier possessed suicidal courage, but the fact that he would have to be exterminated in his positions only became clear once the Allies assumed the initiative. Nowhere was this more apparent than during the capture of Tarawa Atoll in the Gilbert Islands, between 20 and 23 November 1943. Of the entire Japanese garrison, a tiny handful survived, all of them dazed, shell-shocked or severely wounded. None possessed sufficient seniority to give a coherent account of the defences, although the course of the savage fighting tells its own story.

Tarawa Atoll forms part of the Gilbert Islands, then a British possession in the Central Pacific. The atoll consists of a series of small islands surrounding a central lagoon, which can be entered from the west. On both the seaward and lagoon sides the islands are protected by continuous coral reefs, lying between 400 and 1,100 yards off-shore. The most important of the islands was Betio at the south-western corner of the chain. Tadpole-shaped and palm-covered, Betio measured approximately 4,000 yards long by 500 yards at its widest point, and nowhere rose more than a few feet above sea level. On its lagoon side a pier, 500 yards long, had been built out to the edge of the reef, and 300 yards east of this was a shorter pier owned by the Burns-Philp Company, exporters of the copra which formed the atoll's staple produce.

When the Japanese landed on Betio in December 1941 the island's European population amounted to less than a dozen civilians. The small inter-island steamer *Niminoa* was deliberately run aground on the reef by her skipper to prevent her being used by the Japanese, and before they left the latter blew out her fuel tanks believing that this in itself would isolate the island. The Europeans, however, had concealed a small motorized cutter on one of the smaller islands and in this they made the difficult passage to Fiji, picking up six shipwrecked American sailors and a number of civil administrators from elsewhere in the Gilberts on the way.

In September 1942 a force of Japanese naval infantry arrived to form the basis of a permanent garrison. It had been decided that an all-weather bomber airfield would be built on Betio and in December a construction battalion was put ashore. By November 1943 the airfield had been completed and its defences were in position. The commander of the base,

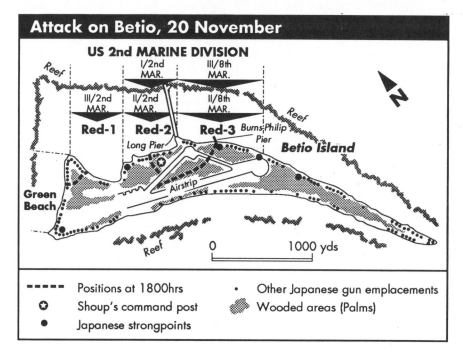

Rear-Admiral Keichi Shibasaki, had available 2,619 fighting troops of the Sasebo 7th Special Naval Landing Force and the 3rd Special Base Force, the former having seen active service at Guadalcanal, plus several hundred naval personnel, and a large (technically non-combatant) labour force recruited in Japan, Korea and Okinawa. His heavy weapons included four 8-inch naval guns captured during the Malayan campaign, four 140mm guns, six 80mm anti-boat guns, eight 75mm field guns, ten 75mm mountain guns, six 70mm battalion guns, nine 37mm anti-tank guns and a company of fourteen Type 95 light tanks, supported by dozens of light, medium and heavy automatic weapons and the fire of riflemen. The defences themselves consisted of a palm-long sea wall backed by numerous layered palm-log and sand weapon emplacements and bunkers with interlocking arcs of fire, connected by trenches, many of which were covered. In addition, large concrete bunkers had been built to house command posts, communication centres, ammunition dumps and the 8-inch naval guns.

In the shallows surrounding the island there were barbed wire aprons between 50 and 100 yards offshore, and lines of concrete tetrahedrons to disembowel landing craft. On the narrow beaches themselves were more barbed wire obstacles, intended to channel an assault force on to carefully prepared killing grounds. As there was so little room for tactical manoeuvre on the island, Shibasaki's plan was to defeat an enemy landing between the reef and the sea wall. Satisfied that he had left nothing to chance, he is said to have boasted that a million men could not take Betio from him in a thousand years of fighting. Certainly, he had made the island the toughest proposition any enemy could wish to face, but in essence he was relying on a cordon defence and had given little consideration to what might happen if that cordon were penetrated. In all fairness, however, he could not have foreseen that he would be faced by an enemy of quite exceptional courage and tenacity who had studied the problems of attacking a reef-girdled island and would employ radically new equipment to solve them.

During 1943 the keystone of the planned American drive towards Japan had been defined as land-based airpower which was capable of supporting offensive operations as well as protecting the lengthening line of communications. This meant capturing islands on which airstrips already existed or on which airstrips could be constructed quickly. Tarawa, lying at the outer limits of Japanese expansion in the Central Pacific, thus became an obvious target. Air reconnaissance revealed that there was little evidence of enemy activity on most of the atoll's islands, but that on Betio an airstrip and extensive defence works were being constructed. Once Betio had been secured, therefore, the next step forward across the Pacific could be set in motion.

The size of Shibasaki's force was calculated in a most ingenious way. With so many men crammed on to so small an island the Japanese had quickly realized that the accumulation of human waste would soon produce a crippling epidemic of one sort or another. Around the shoreline they constructed miniature piers which the garrison used as latrines, the faeces being dispersed by the tidal scour. The purpose of these piers was soon clear to the American photo reconnaissance interpreters and, by calculating their number and multiplying by the number of men they estimated would use each one, they concluded that there were 4,840 Japanese on the island. In fact, there were 4,836.

The overall responsibility for capturing Tarawa rested with Vice Admiral Raymond Spruance, the victor at the Battle of Midway the previous year, when the pride of Japan's carrier fleet had been sent to the bottom. In tactical command of the operation, code-named 'Galvanic', was Rear Admiral Richmond Kelly Turner, who had already led the amphibious landings on Guadalcanal and New Georgia. The troops that would make the landing on Betio were drawn from V Amphibious Corps, commanded by Major General Holland MacTyre Smith, nicknamed 'Howlin' Mad' because of his ferocious temper, and consisted of Major General Julian Smith's 2nd Marine Division.

Julian Smith's command contained many veterans of the fighting on Guadalcanal and had recently been brought up to strength with fresh drafts. Because the casualties incurred in the Solomons had inevitably meant promotions, there was some concern that much of the junior leadership was green. In the event, this was to prove academic, for, despite the hard training which the division had undergone in New Zealand, the conditions encountered on Betio were beyond anyone's experience. Including attachments, the strength of 2nd Marine Division amounted to approximately 20,000 men. The bulk of this consisted of three infantry regiments, the 2nd, 6th and 8th Marines, each containing three 1,000-strong rifle battalions, a heavy weapons company and supporting services. Artillery support ashore was to be provided by the 10th Marines, nominally capable of placing a 75mm pack howitzer battery at the disposal of each rifle battalion, with heavier weapons available for regimental and divisional targets. The fifth major unit was the 18th Marines, which at Tarawa was administratively divided into a combat engineer battalion trained in the destruction of fortifications, and a pioneer battalion which provided beach parties for the handling of incoming stores but could also fight as riflemen; each of these battalions was sub-divided into three companies which could be allocated to rifle regiments as required. In addition there was the 2nd Light Tank Battalion, consisting of three companies of Stuarts, supplemented by 'C' Company I Marine Amphibious Corps Medium Tank Battalion, equipped with Shermans. And, perhaps most important of all, there was the 2nd Amphibian Tractor Battalion, equipped with 125 Landing Vehicles Tracked (LVTs), otherwise known as amtracs.

Naturally, while 'Galvanic' was in the planning stage, much thought had been given to the problems of getting ashore. The basic plan was that the bombarding warships would stand off the atoll while the Marines were transferred from the transports into their landing craft; these would then enter the lagoon to launch their assault against the northern shore of Betio, accompanied by destroyers which would provide close-range gunfire support. The major problem lay in anticipating the state of the tide on D-Day, 20 November. Tidal variations at Tarawa were notoriously difficult to predict, but the Navy believed that there would be sufficient water covering the reef to permit the passage of their shallow-draught landing craft. Major Frank Holland, formerly Resident Commissioner of the Gilberts, where he had lived for fifteen years, did not agree. He was adamant that there would not be sufficient depth of water, nor would there be until the end of December. The Navy, however, had no intention of waiting that long. Fortunately, Holland had also communicated his grave reservations to senior Marine officers and, since they would pay the price of such mistakes, they were more prepared to listen.

In particular, Holland succeeded in convincing Julian Smith's operations officer, Lieutenant Colonel David Shoup, of the risks involved. Shoup first asked for a new type of shallow-water assault boat which was under development, but was told that none was available. He then suggested using amtracs, which would enable the assault waves to cross the reef and press on to the beach beyond, whatever the depth of water. The amtrac, a tracked amphibian originally developed as rescue vehicle in the Florida Everglades, had performed sterling service at Guadalcanal ferrying stores from transports to the beach. It had not been used in combat, but, given light armour, it could resolve the present difficulty. Julian Smith agreed, and so did Holland Smith, who went to see Admiral Turner. A furious row ensued in which Turner emphasized the view that there would be sufficient depth of water and wrote off the amtrac as being unseaworthy, while the corps commander virtually accused him of callous indifference to potential Marine casualties, concluding with the remark, 'No amtracs, no operation!' Turner gave way. Seventy-five LVT-1s, veterans of Guadalcanal, close to the end of their operational lives, were refitted and armoured with boiler plate, while the fifty LVT-2s available, which incorporated integral armour, were shipped direct from the United States to Samoa, where they were picked up by the invasion fleet on its way from New Zealand to Tarawa. Finally, it was agreed that the three leading waves of the assault would be delivered in amtracs, and the remainder in landing craft.

Some naval officers wondered what all the fuss was about. Confident that the landing craft could pass over the reef, they were also going to subject the tiny island to the combined fire of three battleships, six cruisers and nine destroyers, alternating with precision dive-bomber strikes delivered by carrier aircraft. The collective opinion of the Navy was that if any Japanese survived the supporting bombardment, they would be too stunned to offer serious resistance when the Marines hit the beach.

It was the Japanese who fired the first round in the battle for Betio. At approximately 0355 on 20 November the Marines began clambering aboard their amtracs and landing craft, the transports slowly drifting south on a two-knot current until they were in danger of masking the fire of the bombardment group. At 0431 they were ordered to cease disembarking until they had returned to their proper station, with the result that there was a delay in forming the assault waves. By now the suspicions of the garrison had been aroused. A red star shell burst over the eastern end of the island, illuminating the scene. Minutes later the Japanese coast defence guns opened fire. The bombardment group replied and after several salvoes there was a heavy explosion ashore. Following this, the enemy guns fell silent, but the warships continued to batter the island until 0542. Taking advantage of the pause and the strengthening light which enabled them to identify their targets, the Japanese opened fire again shortly after. Significantly, their 8-inch guns were no longer in action, but near misses fountained dangerously close to the transports, which withdrew northwards out of range when they had disembarked the fourth assault wave. At 0605 the bombardment group resumed firing until the first of the carrier air strikes arrived a few minutes later. The result was superficially impressive, leaving Betio smothered under a pall of dust and smoke in which flames glowed sullenly; in fact, very little serious damage was done.

Meanwhile, escorted by minesweepers and destroyers, the amtracs and landing craft were making their three-and-a-half mile passage from the open sea through the lagoon entrance. Within the lagoon, they began forming their assault waves on the line of departure while the destroyers silenced the nearest coast defence batteries. The preparatory bombardment was now in full swing, combing the island from end to end. From the sea, Betio appeared to be an inferno of continuous explosions, its riven palms barely visible amid the drifting clouds of smoke and sand. It began to look as though the Navy had been right after all, for ostensibly nothing could survive such an ordeal, but again, reality fell far short of the impression received. The layered log and sand pillboxes and bunkers were incredibly resilient and could withstand enormous punishment, as could the heavy concrete command structures. The majority of the warships' shells burst harmlessly on the surface, without penetrating, while others richocheted off the island to explode in the sea. A large number of heavy calibre rounds exploded between the reef and the landing beaches, creating submerged craters that were to hinder the attackers.

At 0855 a second carrier aircraft strike went in, strafing the length of the landing beaches. Most of the pilots, observing the nature of the defences below, believed that they were wasting their ammunition. By now, the landing was behind schedule, partly because of the delays which had arisen during disembarkation, and partly because the amtracs had been forging their way against the same current which had pushed the transports off-station. H-Hour, the moment the Marines' leading wave was to touch down on the shore, had initially been set for 0830, but had been postponed until 0900. Even so, the assault waves had not crossed the line of departure until 0823 and they still had some distance to travel when the last of the aircraft banked away. A moment of comparative calm ensued, for the warships had also ceased firing, with the exception of the destroyers *Dashiell* and *Ringgold*, which were providing direct support within the lagoon.

Shells began to explode among the amtracs or burst above them. At the head of the long pier Lieutenant William Hawkins and his 2nd Scout-Sniper Platoon swarmed from their landing craft in a dashing attack which eliminated the Japanese defenders and thereby prevented them from firing into the flanks of the assault waves as they swept past. Hawkins then transferred his men into passing amtracs and reached the shore. For his capture of the pier and the inspired leadership he continued to demonstrate until he died of wounds the following day, he received the posthumous award of the Congressional Medal of Honor.

Hawkins' action at the pier was, in fact, the only part of the landing which went according to plan. When the leading amtracs reached the reef those aboard felt their craft lurch as the steel tracks bit into the coral, indicating that the tide was lower than had been anticipated. Then, the amphibians were over and ploughing their way through the shallows towards the shore. This was clearly the moment Shibasaki's machine-gunners, mortar teams and anti-boat gun crews had been ordered to wait for. As the water round the craft was lashed into foam by the concentrated fire of automatic weapons, the amtrac gunners attempted to direct their heavy machine-guns against the flickering red weapon flashes behind the rapidly closing shoreline, but the majority of them fell back on those below, dead or seriously wounded.

The assault was being delivered on a three-battalion front. On the right, III/2nd Marines were approaching Beach Red-1, running 700 yards eastwards from the point at the north-western extremity of the island; in the centre II/2nd Marines were closing on Beach Red-2, running 600 yards from Red-1 to the long pier; on the left, II/8th Marines were due to touch down on Beach Red-3, stretching 800 yards eastwards from the long pier. From 0910 onwards the first wave of amtracs ground ashore, the Marines jumping over their sides into the teeth of the enemy fire. Red-1 ran round a shallow bay, dominated by a strong defensive complex located on the boundary with Red-2, and was thus a natural killing ground. The left hand company of the III/2nd was badly hit and the sheer volume of fire forced the amtracs carrying a company of II/2nd, destined for Red-2, to veer sharply to the right so that it was landed on

147

the right flank of Red-1. On Red-2 itself II/2nd incurred crippling casualties as it attempted to fight its way over the sea wall. Fortunately for II/8th a destroyer was lying directly off Red-3 and pounded it to such good effect that most of the battalion got ashore safely; two amtracs even found a breach in the sea wall and pressed inland almost 200 yards to disembark their passengers close to the airstrip's runway. Very quickly, however, Japanese resistance hardened and the penetration was contained.

Only eight of the amtracs had been sunk during the assault, but others, their armour proof against small arms but not heavy machine-gun or artillery fire, had been riddled and foundered on their way out to reload. Others, disabled by shellfire or with dead crews aboard, wallowed helplessly in the swell. Ashore, several were burning on the beach. Every surviving amtrac was now worth its weight in gold, for suddenly the overall situation had taken a dramatic turn for the worse.

The landing craft of the fourth assault wave had grounded on the reef, as Major Holland had feared they would. For their occupants, there was no alternative other than to wade towards the shore, up to 700 yards distant, through the withering Japanese fire. At first, the water was chest-high and offered a little protection, but for the last 200 yards the ocean floor sloped gently upwards and the men sloshed forward through knee-high shallows completely exposed. It was exactly the situation Shibasaki had envisaged, and his men took full advantage of it. In addition to the fire they were directing at the wading riflemen from the shore, the Japanese also had a further unpleasant surprise to offer, for they had put machine-gun teams aboard the stranded steamer *Niminoa*, lying beside the reef. These were not eliminated until late the following day and in the meantime they fired at will into the backs of the Americans. Those who were killed vanished at once, those who were wounded, heavily burdened, sank into the bloodied water and drowned unless their comrades came to their assistance. But there was no turning back, because there was no point in it. Units reached the beach decimated and seriously disorganized, their men shaken and, for the moment, exhausted both physically and mentally.

It had been decided that the Shermans would be landed immediately behind the assault waves, but because of the low tide they had to leave their landing craft at the reef and drive ashore. As the sea bed was an unknown quantity to their drivers, they had to be led in by guides wading ahead of the vehicles. Many of the guides were shot down, but there was never a shortage of volunteers to take their place. At Red-1 the five tanks of 1st Platoon, plus one tank of Company Headquarters, reached the shoreline safely but found their exit from the beach blocked by severely wounded casualties. They swung right to drive through the surf in search of an alternative exit, but in the process four of the Shermans ran into submerged shell craters and water flooded their engines. The two survivors, *Chicago* and *China Gal*, found a way off the beach and began moving inland, their arrival giving much encouragement to the pinned-down infantrymen. After they had penetrated some 400 yards they were engaged by a much smaller Type 95. The first enemy round jammed *China Gal*'s turret, but her commander ordered his driver to ram. The impact caused irreparable damage to the Sherman's 75mm gun and the vehicle reversed towards the beach with only her hull machine-gun in action. Undoubtedly shaken, the plucky Japanese crew then turned their attention to *Chicago*, which they set ablaze with their first round. To the hundreds of Marines watching the duel, its outcome was as depressing as it was unexpected.

Of the ten tanks of 2nd and 3rd Platoons, destined respectively for Red-2 and Red-3, two were sunk in their landing craft close to the reef. One of 2nd Platoon's tanks then ran into a deep crater beside the pier and the crew were drowned. The platoon's three remaining Shermans moved inland to support the infantry. One ran into a deep shellhole from which it could not extricate itself, the second was knocked out by a Japanese who was killed in the act of fixing a magnetic charge to the hull, and the third withdrew behind the sea wall. Four tanks of 3rd Platoon reached Red-3 safely and attempted to fight their way across the island. Three were hit by Japanese anti-tank gunners; of these, one was knocked out and another careered into a pit full of fuel drums, but the third, afire, quenched its flames by driving into the sea and returned to attack fortifications near the Burns-Philp pier. The platoon's fourth tank was knocked out by carrier dive-bombers whose pilots were unaware that American armour was ashore, but had been warned that Japanese tanks were active in the area of the Marines' forward positions. The same bombers hit the fuel dump, engulfing the stranded Sherman in an inferno. Surprisingly, all the crews survived their ordeal and managed to return to the beach. Thus, within a comparatively short period, the strength of 'C' Company I Marine Amphibious Corps Medium Tank Battalion had been reduced to one seriously damaged tank on Red-1, one tank on Red-2 and one tank on Red-3. The loss of so many Shermans was keenly felt, for their 75mm guns had a formidable bunker-busting capacity. Nor did the smaller Stuarts of 2nd Light Tank Battalion fare any better. One six-tank platoon of 'C' Company had originally been assigned to Red-1 but was then re-allocated to Red-3; four of its tanks were lost when their landing craft were sunk by gunfire off the reef, and the remaining two were not landed.

The need for armour had now become critical and it was decided to commit the 2nd Battalion's 'B' Company. Unfortunately, so confident were the planners that no one had envisaged a situation in which the company would be employed. Its Stuarts, in fact, lay at the bottom of their transports' holds with tons of equipment above them, an immense amount of time-consuming work being required before they could be loaded into their landing craft. As this continued, it became apparent that the company could not be landed before the early hours of 22 November, D+2. In the meantime, the Sherman crews would have to recover such tanks as they could, and a further attempt would be made to land 'C' Company's Stuarts on D+1.

Because of the bitter resistance encountered, the commanders of the assault regiments ordered their reserve battalions to land. There were just sufficient amtracs remaining for I/2nd Marines' rifle companies, but the rest of the battalion had to wade ashore. The I/2nd had been ordered to make for Red-2, but again the heavy fire from the complex of strongpoints at the western end of the beach broke up the landing formation and forced part of the battalion to join III/2nd in their toe-hold on Red-1. When, shortly after 1100, approximately an hour later, III/8th Marines were ordered to land on Red-3, no amtracs were available. So badly cut to pieces was the battalion as it waded in, using the scant cover of the pier, that its third wave was almost wiped out and those who reached the shore were in a worse state than those who had made the initial landings. The fourth wave disembarked a few men near the head of the pier, but its landing craft, now the focus of concentrated Japanese fire, had become disorganized and withdrew out of range to regroup. The carnage had been witnessed by the assistant divisional commander, Brigadier General Leo Hermle, who gave instructions that no further troops were to be landed until ordered.

The situation ashore was one of bloody chaos. Most of the landing force, dead, wounded and living, was confined to the narrow strip of sand between the sea wall and the water line. Any attempt to cross the sea wall into the sleet of machine-gun fire was tantamount to suicide. Some men had succeeded, and a few had even worked their way inland to the edge of the airstrip, but unless they could find refuge in a crater, where they were soon pinned down, they had little chance of survival. Together, the heavy casualties incurred and the disordered landings had combined to produce a horrific confusion in which officers sought their men and men sought officers to command them, in which communications were lost because signallers were dead or their sets ruined by salt water, and in which carefully rehearsed tactical plans disintegrated. As the day wore on, the beach became yet more congested as amtracs and carrying parties dumped supplies into the confined area, dispatched by well-meaning officers aboard the transports who were sticking to the operational timetable without any knowledge of the conditions ashore.

Shortly before noon, Colonel David Shoup, now commanding the 2nd Marines, managed to establish his regimental command post in the lee of a concrete bunker on Red-2. He was pestered by snipers, out of contact with his units on Red-1, and nowhere in the immediate vicinity had his Marines been able to advance further than 75 yards from the sea wall. In his opinion the outcome of the battle was in very serious doubt, but he sent Lieutenant Colonel Evans Carlson, a former Raider officer, with a personal message to the divisional commander aboard the battleship *Maryland* that those ashore were going to 'stick and fight it out'.

Carlson was able to provide Julian Smith with the first reliable news of the fighting on the island. Such fanatical resistance had not been anticipated when 'Galvanic' was planned, and because of this the 6th Marines had been placed in corps reserve, so that of the infantry remaining under divisional control only one battalion, the I/8th, had not been committed. The possibility that the Japanese would take the offensive could not be ruled out, and in such circumstances a single battalion would not make much difference. Large-scale reinforcement and re-planning might, however, carry the day. At 1330 Smith requested corps to return the 6th Marines to his command. He had no intention of abandoning the operation, but in case corps were unsympathetic he gave orders that the division's specialist troops – the clerks, drivers, signallers, engineers and artillerymen – should be formed into provisional infantry battalions; this, of course, was not quite the desperate measure it seems, as every Marine was trained in the basic skills of the rifleman. He need not have worried, for at 1400 Holland Smith released the 6th Marines, with Admiral Turner's blessing.

Meanwhile, the fighting ashore had become a rifleman's battle in which small groups of men, having recovered from their initial shock, slowly began to subdue the enemy's strongpoints with grenades, demolition charges and flame-throwers. On Red-3 a demolition team flung a charge over the sea wall into a large building, a store for torpedo warheads, near the base of the pier, and were rewarded with a tremendous explosion which blew everyone flat within a wide radius. On Red-2 Staff Sergeant William Bordelon, a combat engineer of 18th Marines attached to the II/2nd, arranged for the nearest riflemen to cover him while he went over the wall and used his charges to destroy two pillboxes. Wounded by machine-gun fire while attacking a third, he returned to the beach, where he refused medical attention and, under heavy fire, rescued two wounded comrades who were in danger of drowning in the surf. He then made up another charge and was crossing the wall again when he was shot dead. His gallantry earned him a posthumous Medal of Honor.

Such acts created the first cracks in the Japanese defence and as the afternoon wore on they steadily widened. By last light the Marines had been able to consolidate their small gains and establish perimeters. These were not continuous, for the III/2nd was still isolated on the north-western tip of the island and a gap existed between the defensive shoulder on the right flank of Red-2 and those troops who had been able to cross the airstrip's runway. From this point, however, a line of sorts was carried through on to Red-3, bending back to the beach just short of the Burns-Philp pier. The line was held by scratch units, consisting of men from different battalions who, in many cases, had rallied to officers and senior NCOs unfamiliar to them. On the other hand, heavy weapons including mortars, medium machine-guns and 37mm anti-tank guns were arriving and could be integrated into a defensive fire pattern. After dark, it was also possible to land some of 10th Marines' 75mm pack howitzers. At last the battle possessed some form and it became possible for Shoup, who remained in tactical command on the island, to plan for the morrow.

Victory, however, still hung in the balance. What might have happened if Admiral Shibasaki had chosen to launch a counter-attack must remain a matter for speculation, as must his reasons for not doing so. Certainly, it was within his power, and as his enemies were still disorganized and shaken by their ordeal the moment could not have been better. He could not have been unduly worried by the Marines' naval gunfire support, which, because of the close nature of the fighting, was being directed well beyond the immediate front, for obvious safety reasons. Quite possibly he believed that his men would achieve better results by fighting from their prepared positions than attacking across open ground. Whatever his thoughts, by the dawn of 21 November, D+ 1, the initiative had returned irrevocably to the Americans.

Shoup requested that the I/8th Marines, who had spent a day and a night afloat in their landing craft, should be landed on Red-2. The first of the battalion's four waves reached the reef at 0615 and began the long, murderous trudge to the shore. This time, the nightmare was less intense, for some of the Japanese bunkers had been captured, the fire of others was masked by wrecked amtracs, and some had been neutralized by delayed-action high-explosive howitzer shells which penetrated the log walls before bursting in the interior. Nevertheless, I/8th was severely cut up and lost much of its equipment, although it was able to take over the right flank of Red-2 and even make a little ground before the day was out.

This enabled Shoup to direct the remnants of I/2nd and II/2nd to advance the few hundred yards across the airstrip to the south shore of the island, assisted by an air strike, Had the enemy defences inland matched those covering the beaches the advance would have made very little headway. As it was, the two battalions, with a total strength of about two companies, sustained comparatively light casualties as they charged across the runway and into the belt of shattered trees beyond. Taking cover in abandoned trenches, they occupied a 200-yard-long stretch of coastline flanked by active enemy strongpoints. For the moment, it seemed as though they had jumped straight out of the frying-pan and into the fire, as they were immediately forced to beat off a counter-attack from the east. This left them with some 30 wounded to attend to, dangerously short of ammunition, and with very little food and water in hand. On being advised of the situation Shoup sent additional supplies across the island in amtracs, which also lifted out the wounded. The thrust had not quite succeeded in cutting the Japanese defences in two, but communication between the eastern and western parts of the island was now restricted to a narrow corridor.

On Red-3 the II/8th and III/8th also strove to expand their perimeter but made little progress against the interlocked fire of the enemy strongpoints. On the other hand, the rifle companies of both battalions had been joined by numerous stragglers and they now had the support, not only of the destroyers in the lagoon, but of 10th Marines' howitzers firing from Red-2 and other heavy weapons which had come ashore, including armoured half-tracks mounting a 75mm gun. Red-3 could now be regarded as secure.

Overall, the tank strength had not improved. On Red-2 the 2nd Platoon had begun the day with two Shermans, but one of these was lost in a submerged crater while approaching an objective through the shallows, and the other was disabled by 'friendly' mortar fire. At 1700 two Stuarts of 'C' Company 2nd Light Tank Battalion arrived and went into action in support of I/8th on the right flank. On Red-1 the 1st Platoon managed to recover one of its Shermans from the water and, together with the damaged *China Gal*, this remained in action throughout the day.

It was, in fact, on Red-1 that the Marines made their most decisive gains of the day. Here, the III/2nd, under the command of Major Michael Ryan, had sustained heavy casualties during the landing, although its strength had been augmented by elements of I/2nd and II/2nd who had been driven westward by enemy fire during their approach to Red-2. Ryan had been joined by a naval gunfire support officer, Second Lieutenant Thomas Greene of the 10th Marines, whose radio was functioning. Under Greene's direction first one destroyer, then another, arrived to administer a close-quarter battering to a strong defensive complex lying south of the III/2nd's toehold. Shortly after 1100 the fire was lifted and Ryan mounted an attack on a 100-yard frontage, led by the two Shermans *China Gal* and *Cecilia*. It was completely successful, breaking through to the island's south coast an hour later. Ryan then established a continuous defensive front facing east.

Julian Smith now knew where to commit the 6th Marines. Using rubber boats, the I/6th landed behind III/2nd on the island's western shore, designated Green Beach, at 1800, the first troops to reach Betio without coming under the direct fire of the enemy. Simultaneously, the II/6th was dispatched to the neighbouring island of Bairiki in response to an erroneous report that the enemy had begun withdrawing there, but encountered only light resistance which was soon eliminated. During the evening and throughout the night the Stuarts of 'B' Company 2nd Light Tank Battalion began landing, two on Green Beach and the remainder on Red-2, five being lost in submerged craters. Shoup, now confident that the battle could be won, was ready to take the offensive.

At 0800 on 22 November, D+2, I/6th passed through III/2nd and, with tanks leading, advanced on a one-company frontage along the south coast. On this sector the Japanese seemed to have lost heart, and by 1100 the attackers had broken through to the pocket held by I/2nd and II/2nd. Concurrently, III/6th began landing on Green Beach. Elsewhere, however, Shibasaki's men continued to offer the most determined resistance. I/8th made very slow progress against the complex situated at the boundary of Red-1 and Red-2, and II/8th remained stalled in front of a trio of defence works near the Burns-Philp pier. These consisted of a steel pillbox, a log emplacement and a large sand-covered concrete bunker, and as the approach to any one was covered by fire from the other two, they all had to be eliminated before the advance could continue. First to fall, at 0930, was the log emplacement, which blew up when a shell penetrated and exploded the ammunition within. Shortly afterwards the pillbox was silenced when a Sherman slammed several rounds into its interior. The bomb-proof bunker, however, continued to spit fire. At length, covered by every weapon that could be brought to bear, a small party of combat engineers led by First Lieutenant Alexander Bonnyman of 18th Marines managed to eliminate a machine-gun post on top of the bunker and then climb on to the roof. Here a flame-thrower was directed into the ventilation shafts while demolition charges were hurled against the entrances below. Suddenly, a party of Japanese burst from one of the doors to counter-attack those above. All were cut down by small-arms fire or blown apart by charges tossed among them, but not before Bonnyman was himself killed, winning a posthumous Medal of Honor. Conditions within the bunker had now become unbearable and, shortly after the failure of their sortie, large numbers of the enemy poured out of both main entrances in a desperate attempt to escape to the east; they ran straight into a hail of fire and 100 of them were killed in the first few yards. Nearby, Shibasaki's square headquarters bunker was next to be tackled, the heavy steel doors being blown in and the interior blasted with a flame-thrower.

II/8th and III/8th now advanced slowly and steadily eastwards. Many Japanese were found to have committed suicide in their positions, but against those who continued to resist the Marines deployed a new weapon: an armoured bulldozer which shovelled earth over the fireslits and then buried the defenders alive. If the Japanese emerged into the open to escape or launch self-destructive counter-attacks, they were shot down. In this context the Stuart's 37mm gun, while packing less punch than the Sherman's 75mm in the bunker-busting role, was extremely useful, as it fired a canister round which scythed down anything caught in its deadly spread.

During the day Major General Julian Smith came ashore to assume personal command. Shoup, who had not been off his feet for 50 hours, was exhausted but had the satisfaction of having turned a near-defeat into a victory, for which he also received the Medal of Honor. During the afternoon Smith arranged for the relief of II/8th and III/8th by halting them and ordering I/6th to resume its advance along the south coast and then extend its front across the island. Next, the fresh III/6th was brought forward from Green Beach and moved into position behind I/6th, ready to deliver the *coup-de-grâce* the following day. Finally, III/2nd also advanced from the western end of the island to form a continuous cordon with I/8th around the troublesome enemy strongpoint at the junction of Red-1 and Red-2.

By evening the majority of the Japanese survivors had been confined to the tail of the Betio tadpole. They knew that their last hour had come, but they were resolved to die fighting. After dusk a series of probing attacks were mounted against I/6th's line, but it was not until 0300 that the major assault was delivered by about 300 men, yelling and firing as they charged. A few reached the Marines' trenches before they were killed, but most were cut down by automatic weapons, mortars, artillery fire and naval gunfire support. Dawn revealed the area thickly strewn with bodies.

At 0800 on 23 November, in the wake of an airstrike and artillery support, III/6th passed through I/6th and advanced into the tail of the island with tank support. Little resistance was encountered amid the devastated terrain. Many Japanese had been killed by three days of bombardment, and most of the rest had died by their own hands in their bunkers. At 1310 the III/6th's leading company reached the tip of the island. Five minutes earlier the complex at the boundary of Red-1 and Red-2 had finally been overrun, having fought bitterly to the last and inflicted more casualties than any other sector of the defences. At last, after 76 hours, the concentrated slaughter had ended.

The rest of Tarawa Atoll was taken easily and at small cost. Of the entire garrison, only 146 were taken prisoner, and of these all but seventeen were Korean labourers. In performing their duty as they saw it, Admiral Shibasaki and his men had inflicted very severe casualties on the 2nd Marine Division. Fifty-one officers and 853 men were known to have been killed during the fighting, nine officers and 84 men subsequently died of wounds received, and the fate of a further 88 men was never established; 109 officers and 2,124 men were wounded. Naval casualties amounted to two officers and 28 men killed and two officers and 57 men wounded. Equipment losses were also heavy. The amtrac battalion, on which so much had depended, was particularly hard hit, having had 35 vehicles sunk and 26 disabled by gunfire; as a result of this, and other operational causes, including mines, damage ashore and mechanical failure, only 35 amtracs were still operational when Betio fell. The battalion commander, Major Drewes, was killed in the first assault wave on D-Day, and by the time the operation ended 323 of his 500 crewmen were dead or wounded.

When details of the action became known in the United States they created a sense of shock, deepened by war correspondents' accounts of the horrific scenes which had taken place in the lagoon during the early landing phases. Understandably, the public wondered whether so insignificant an objective was worth so terrible a price, and if killing on such a scale would accompany each stage of the Pacific War. In fact, the realization that the Japanese would willingly fight to the death meant that the lessons arising from Operation 'Galvanic' were quickly digested and acted upon. Every aspect of amphibious warfare was closely examined in the light of the experience. Operational mistakes were analysed and corrected, equipment was improved, new techniques were evolved, and in particular the vital importance of the amtrac was recognized. As Henry I. Shaw comments in his book on the operation, 'If there had been no assault on Tarawa, there would have been another island fortress where the painful lessons it taught would have been learned. The success of every subsequent operation in the Pacific owed a debt to the men who had died to take that tiny atoll and to the men who survived the battle to fight again.'

CHAPTER 11
The Defence of the Admin Box
ARAKAN, BURMA, 6–25 FEBRUARY 1944

By the beginning of 1944 the fact that the British could not claim to have defeated the Japanese in a single major engagement, let alone campaign, was beginning to cause serious concern to their American allies. The fault, in the opinion of many American officers, lay not in the fighting qualities of the British and Indian troops, whom they respected as being among the best in the world, but in their commanders' lack of aggression and seeming inability to solve the problems of jungle warfare. This was an over-simplification of a very complex problem, and largely ignored such crucially important factors as air power, but was apparently emphasized when aggressively handled Australian troops inflicted a series of telling defeats on the Japanese in New Guinea.

Certainly, the speed with which the Japanese had overrun the Malayan peninsula, followed immediately by the fall of Singapore, the worst military disaster in the history of the British Empire, had created profound psychological shockwaves. Hardly had these subsided than the army found itself conducting a long and painful retreat from Burma. Early in 1943 a limited offensive had been mounted in the coastal regions of the Arakan with a view to restoring morale. Unfortunately, the Japanese were very sensitive regarding this sector, from which access to Central Burma was possible, and they responded vigorously, working their way round the jungle flank to fall on the British lines of communication. Once again, the result was a difficult withdrawal and morale, far from being restored, was further damaged.

There was a sickening feeling that the Japanese always seemed to be one move ahead, and that they were always able to obtain local air superiority. Nevertheless, as the year 1943 drew to its close, it was decided to try again in the Arakan, in greater strength than before, and by then the situation had changed somewhat. The elderly Hurricanes which had been battling to contain the enemy's fighters and bombers had been joined by faster, more manoeuvrable Spitfires. On 31 December the hitherto cocky and complacent Japanese airmen were bounced by the new arrivals. Eight of their Sally heavy bombers went down, a further three were claimed as probable kills, and five more sustained serious damage. Of the escorting fighters, five Oscars were shot down, plus a further probable, and five were damaged. The RAF's loss amounted to one Spitfire damaged and another destroyed while crash-landing.

On 15 January 1944 the Japanese returned in force, determined to regain mastery of the air. A tremendous fighter dogfight raged over the Arakan, resulting in six Oscars and ten Zeroes being shot down, plus a further Oscar and four Zeroes probably destroyed, while nine Oscars and the same number of Zeroes were damaged. The British losses amounted to one Spitfire, plus two Spitfires and a Hurricane damaged. A further air battle took place on 20 January. This cost the Japanese one Oscar and six Zeroes shot down, two Oscars and six Zeroes probably destroyed, and three Oscars and five Zeroes sent home riddled and trailing smoke. Two Spitfires were lost and three were damaged.

These actions, particularly the massacre on 15 January, were witnessed by jubilant British and Indian troops on the ground, and in themselves did a great deal to dispel any idea that the enemy was invincible. Thereafter, the Japanese airmen were hard-pressed to hold their own and were unable to provide their ground troops with tactical support. The reverse was true of the Allied air forces and it was decided that, in future, units that had been by-passed by enemy counter-attacks would not retreat but would hold their ground and be supplied by air until they were relieved. This decision was also vitally important for a second reason. The explanation of the Japanese soldier's astonishing jungle mobility was really very simple. His primitive supply system was used almost exclusively for ammunition. He carried one or two days' marching rations but, beyond these, he was expected to feed himself from captured supplies. This was all very well while he was advancing continuously, as he had been in Malaya and Burma during the first year of the war, but if his opponents did not retreat he would go hungry unless he withdrew; and since withdrawal involved loss of face, the ultimate consequence would be starvation. Thus, what had once been a great source of strength against enemies who thought in terms of a conventional logistic system would become a fatal weakness if employed against those who stood fast and were supplied by air. It was, perhaps, too much to expect the Japanese commanders in the Arakan to interpret the results of the recent air battles in this way, for they were wedded to the offensive principles which had so far served them so well against the British, and few, if any, had given serious thought to the concept of air supply. On the other hand, they were foolish to imagine that the British had not learned some lessons from their defeats, and that these would be applied sooner than later.

The second Arakan offensive was mounted by Lieutenant-General A. F. P. Christison's XV Corps, consisting of the 5th Indian Division (Major-General H. R. Briggs), 7th Indian Division (Major-General F. W. Messervy), two brigades of 81st West African Division (Major-General C. G. Woolner), with 26th Indian Division (Major-General C. E. N. Lomax) in reserve. An armoured regiment equipped with Lee tanks, the 25th

Dragoons, commanded by Lieutenant-Colonel H. C. R. Frink, was also available.

The object of the offensive was to advance south and secure the line Maungdaw–Buthidaung, two towns on either side of the Mayu range, connected by the only good road in the area. This had been built on the trackbed of an old railway and, because it passed through two tunnels at its summit, was known as the Tunnels Road. The capture of the road, together with Maungdaw and Buthidaung, was essential for the supply of troops east of the Mayu range, who otherwise depended upon a fair-weather track which wound its way through the Ngakyedauk Pass some miles to the north. Once this objective had been taken, it would be possible to plan the next step forward. The 5th Indian Division was to advance on the coastal sector while 7th Indian Division conformed beyond the range, the left flank being guarded by the West African brigades.

Maungdaw was captured by the 5th Indian Division on 9 January, but further progress to the south was halted by an extremely strong defensive position at Razabil. The 25th Dragoons were called forward and quickly developed a technique for dealing with the enemy's bunkers. After some progress had been made, however, the tanks were held up by soft going and coastal *chaungs* which ran between banks twenty feet in height.

It was now becoming apparent that the Japanese were pouring reinforcements into the Arakan and that these would probably be employed in a counter-offensive east of the Mayu range. Christison therefore decided that the tanks should be re-deployed to support 7th Indian Division at Buthidaung and on 4 February the Dragoons began moving through the Ngakyedauk Pass, where engineers had improved the trail to the extent that it would support tanks and lorries. Simultaneously, the corps commander decided to break the impasse at Razabil by using part of 7th Indian Division to execute a wide turning movement down the River Kalapanzin, the effect of which would be to sever the enemy's communications. To free the troops involved, it was necessary that the 5th Division should take over some of 7th Division's front east of the Mayu range, and Brigadier G. C. Evans' 9 Indian Infantry Brigade, consisting of the 2nd Battalion West Yorkshire Regiment and 3/14th Punjabis, was also sent through the pass. Having relieved the right-hand brigade of 7th Division, Evans' men settled into their new positions with the Punjabis in the line and the West Yorkshire in immediate reserve with the additional task of providing security for 7th Division's Admin Box, containing the divisional services units, lying some three miles behind them at the eastern exit from the pass.

Meanwhile, the Japanese were preparing their own counter-stroke. They had available the crack 55th Division, heavily reinforced with troops of equal quality, and their commander, Lieutenant-General Hanaya, planned to repeat the tactics which had proved so successful against the British incursion of the previous year. This time, however, his counter-offensive, code-named '*Ha-Go*', was much larger in its overall concept and, after Christison's troops had been routed, envisaged capturing the vital port of Chittagong. The detailed execution of Hanaya's plan involved maintaining the defensive front between Razabil and Buthidaung while the major part of the 55th Division, under Major-General Sakurai, infiltrated the gap between the 7th Indian Division and the West Africans to capture the communications centre of Taung Bazaar. Following this advance, a force under Colonel Kubo was to cross the Mayu range and sever 5th Indian Division's supply line while a third column under Colonel Tanahashi captured the Ngakyedauk Pass and the Admin Box. If all went true to form – and Hanaya saw no reason why it should not – the two Indian divisions would instinctively try to fight their way out, being severely cut up in the process, and the West Africans, now isolated, would be forced to conform.

Whatever the faulty premises on which it was based, '*Ha-Go*' achieved complete surprise. Large-scale Japanese movement was apparent on 5 February and at 0600 the following morning a major attack was launched on 7th Division's headquarters. At about 1030 it was apparent that the area was untenable. Messervy and his staff, and such of the headquarters personnel as could, made their way in small parties through the jungle to the Admin Box, a mile distant, where 25th Dragoons supplied him with a radio set which enabled him to re-establish contact with his outlying brigades. Two of the regiment's squadrons performed invaluable work on the road between the Admin Box and the old divisional headquarters, providing cover for troops converging on the Box, recovering abandoned vehicles, escorting a mule train and recovering the heavy 5.5-inch howitzers of 6th Medium Regiment from the mud into which they had sunk.

The previous afternoon, Brigadier Evans had taken steps to ensure the security of the Box and ordered the 2nd West Yorkshires to move in, leaving their 'D' Company to reinforce 3/14th Punjabis in the line. The battalion commander, Lieutenant-Colonel G. H. Cree, was immediately aware of the difficulties his men would face when it came to defending the position.

'It was an area of flat, open ground roughly a mile square, surrounded on all sides by hills and jungle. It contained most of the first-line and all the second-line transport of the division, which was operating on an animal transport basis; the main dressing station (MDS); supply, ordnance, ammunition and engineer dumps stocked up with at least a month's reserves; spare mules, provost, artillery of several descriptions, and much else besides. These units and sub-units were in a rough defensive position and were supposed to be able to protect themselves against minor enemy enterprises using their own weapons and manpower. The manpower consisted very largely of Indians of the ancillary services. They were armed and had been basically trained in the use of their weapons. But the most that could be expected of them was purely static defence; they were untried in battle and untrained in anything but simply firing out of a trench.

'It would have been only too easy to have used up the battalion entirely for static defence; there were hills all round crying out to be occupied. But the Brigadier had said we were to keep the largest possible reserve. I therefore decided to use only 'C' Company under Captain Roche in a static role, to hold a vital position on high ground immediately

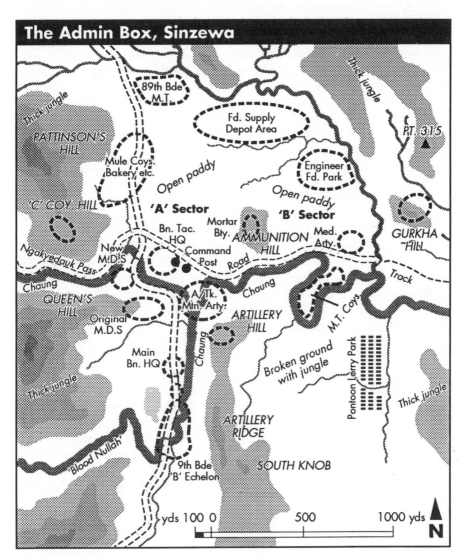

The Admin Box, Sinzewa

north of the entrance to the Ngakyedauk Pass, and to keep the others as a striking force to work with the tanks. 'A' Company, Major O'Hara, followed and were leaguered in the paddy north of the Command Post.

'The rest of the battalion, which consisted of HQ Company and Admin Company, were leaguered in jungle just outside the box, a position which they held until the end of the operation. They were joined there by the 12th Indian Mountain Battery and the 'B' Echelons of Brigade HQ, the 3/14th Punjabis and the 20th Field Company Indian Engineers. The whole composed 9 Brigade's 'B' Echelon and was placed under the operational command of Major Chaytor of the battalion.'

The West Yorkshires' 'B' Company arrived the following morning, taking up positions in the paddy on the eastern side of the Box. By now large numbers of non-combatants, sick and wounded were streaming past into the pass, hoping that they would get through before it was closed by the enemy. Messervy established his new divisional head-quarters within the perimeter and, although 9 Indian Infantry Brigade was placed under his command, he did not interfere with Evans' arrangements for the defence of the Box. From the outset, it was clear to Evans that he had an all but impossible task to perform. It was true that the Dragoons' Lees would prove a major factor in the defence, but tanks also had their limitations. They could, for example, capture ground, but they could not hold it on their own. Again, while they were capable of providing defensive fire support on fixed lines during the hours of darkness, they were completely blind after dusk and were most at risk then from the enemy's tank-hunting parties. Whichever way one looked at it, the integrity of the Box could only be preserved by infantry and, apart from the Dragoon's small close escort of Bombay Grenadiers, the only professional infantry present were the three West Yorkshire companies. In other respects, the outcome of the battle would depend entirely on whether Evans could inject some fighting spirit into his motley garrison, which also included a field bakery and an officers' shop. He made it perfectly clear from the outset that their immediate future consisted of only two alternatives: fighting hard to keep the Japanese at bay, or capture, with the prospect of being butchered, tortured or starved. He also instituted a daily competition in which a prize was awarded to the sector which killed the most Japanese during the previous 24 hours. At first, morale among his unwilling riflemen was poor, but with the first successes came confidence, and with confidence came aggression. Most of the rear-area personnel were probably more frightened of Evans than they were of the enemy, for he had a blunt, forthright manner and was described by some as a bully, which was just what was needed in the circumstances.

On the other hand, it was a mistake to address his more senior subordinates in this way. Even while the Box was being prepared for defence, Evans had a blazing row with Lieutenant-Colonel Frink, the

Dragoons' commanding officer. Both were too professional to permit a clash of personalities to influence them in so serious a situation, but to avoid misunderstandings which could result in dire consequences an accommodation was reached in which Frink continued to command his regiment while his second in command, Major Hugh Ley, was attached to Evans' staff as armoured liaison officer. Evans attached such importance to the tanks that he shared a slit trench with Ley, and there he met his Waterloo. Ley's soldier servant was a Lance-Corporal Evans who had been a gentleman's gentleman in civilian life. He disliked the army and saw no reason why it, nor the fact that vicious hand-to-hand fighting was taking place nearby, should result in lowered standards. Somehow, in the impeccable manner known only to the best servants, Lance-Corporal Evans informed Brigadier Evans that if he wanted a mug of hot tea after the first-light stand-to, he must remember that he was a guest in the Major's trench. So far as is known, the Brigadier gave the Lance-Corporal no cause for complaint.

Humour, however, was a rare commodity in the Admin Box. On 7 February it was apparent that the enemy had succeeded in cutting the Ngakyedauk Pass and the garrison was on its own. Shortly after dusk that night the Japanese launched their first attack. Approaching under cover of a ravine, they assaulted the MDS, guarded by a single infantry section and some twenty walking wounded. After a brief but fierce battle the defences were swamped and, in the comparative quiet which followed the firing, the screams of the patients and medical staff could be heard as they were shot and bayonetted. About forty were murdered in this way and others, tied together, were dragged off into the jungle and shot. Then, having sated themselves and wrecked the hospital, the Japanese dug themselves in amid the shambles. Some of the patients and one medical officer managed to make good their escape and from them the details of the massacre were learned. A carrier patrol sent by Cree to investigate confirmed the worst before it was driven off by grenades.

At 0800 on 8 February the West Yorkshires' 'A' Company, accompanied by a troop of Lees, attacked the MDS from two sides while a platoon of 'B' Company created a diversion on a third. No supporting fire from artillery or mortars could be provided as there were grounds for believing that some of the patients were still alive in enemy hands. The tough North Countrymen, seething with cold fury, fought their way steadily through the broken, brush-covered terrain, showing no mercy as they killed with machine-gun, grenade, rifle and bayonet. Some of the Japanese were difficult to locate as they had covered their positions with stretchers and it was not until early on the 9th that the last of them were killed. The surviving patients were rescued and evacuated to a new MDS which had been set up within the perimeter. 'A' Company, which sustained about fifteen casualties, returned to its reserve location when the operation ended.

For the Japanese, the cowardly and barbaric massacre at the MDS was counter-productive, generating as it did a profound revulsion throughout Burma. British and Indian troops retained few illusions about their opponents, but they had respected them as soldiers. Now, they saw them as merely dangerous animals, to be exterminated with every means at their disposal. In the shorter term, it put an edge on the determination of Evans' men to resist, and it proved that in close-quarter combat their enemies were not supermen at all.

The same was true of another action fought early that morning. At first light the 'B' Echelon area, at the southern end of the perimeter, was probed by a 60-strong party of Japanese who were driven off by the fire of a mule company. This was felt to be the precursor of a heavier attack and, shortly after, a column was observed making its way along a *nullah* which ran beneath the positions held by the West Yorkshires' Orderly Room staff, Sanitary Section and other personnel belonging to the battalion's Headquarters and Admin Companies, under the command of Regimental Sergeant-Major J. Maloney. His men had plenty of grenades and he detailed some as throwers while others were to pull pins for them. When the Japanese were below he gave the order to fire. Volleys of grenades burst around the startled column, followed by rapid rifle and automatic fire. In a slaughter lasting ten minutes 110 Japanese were killed, 45 of them in an area of forty yards, others as they tried to scramble up one or other banks of the *nullah*. A Japanese officer, frantic for revenge, slashed at the Orderly Room sergeant with his sword, but the latter caught the blow on his rifle and, with the assistance of his corporal, bayonetted the man. Maloney received the Distinguished Conduct Medal for his exemplary handling of the affair. The contents of the Japanese packs confirmed that many of the dead had taken part in the MDS massacre, and revenge in itself was satisfying. There were, too, other significant products of the engagement. First, a prisoner was captured, and, because he had allowed himself to be taken alive and had in consequence automatically become an outcast among his own people, he was willing to talk freely. Secondly, the detailed plans for Hanaya's '*Ha-Go*' offensive were found on an officer's body. The orders contained specific references to the Admin Box, which was to be attacked with 'fanatical fury' as a means of securing the accumulated supplies within. This windfall was immediately passed up the chain of command and put to good use.

By concidence, the orders also designated the point at which Maloney had staged his ambush as a rendezvous for infiltration parties. So bad were communications in the Japanese Army, and so slavish was obedience to orders despite conditions which differed wildly from those in which they had been issued, that groups continued to use the *nullah* daily, albeit in smaller numbers, and were wiped out as regularly. The area became known as Blood Nullah or Massacre Corner and at length

THE DEFENCE OF THE ADMIN BOX

the stench became so bad that a bulldozer was called in to deal with it.

The Japanese, nevertheless, obtained some limited successes on 8 February. Messervy had ordered 89 Indian Infantry Brigade to reinforce the Box, but its leading unit, a Gurkha battalion, was ambushed and split in two. One half resumed their march and arrived at a hill feature near the eastern exit from the Box where they again came under heavy pressure. Their situation was potentially dangerous and Evans ordered the West Yorkshires to go to their assistance. Cree reached them in a carrier to find that they had been unable to dig in and were already being pushed off the hill. While the Gurkhas rallied between the hill and the perimeter, Cree returned to the Box and organized a counter-attack force, consisting of Major A. C. Dunlop's 'B' Company and a troop of Lees. Supported by direct fire from the tanks' 75mm and 37mm guns, 'B' Company stormed the hill from the south and remained there until the Gurkhas had completed their reorganization and were able to resume possession.

The Japanese air force, while still unwilling to tangle with the Spitfires, put in an appearance and during the afternoon managed to land a bomb in the main ammunition dump on Ammunition Hill, starting a major conflagration. While shells exploded and small-arms ammunition cooked off with a rattle like Chinese crackers, working-parties fought desperately to move the dump and extinguish the inferno, which was eventually quenched by the heavy night dew.

The defenders of the Admin Box, however, had not been forgotten. A signal was received from Lord Louis Mountbatten, the Supreme Commander of Allied Forces in South-East Asia: 'Stand fast for fourteen days and you will make history.' Evans saw to it that everyone was aware of its content and to many who had not expected to survive the first day's fighting it was heartening.

After its hectic start, life in the Box settled gradually into a daily routine, described by Colonel Cree: 'At dusk we all stood-to for an hour, sometimes two, then followed the long night of double sentries, continual watchfulness and the expectation of a full-scale attack. No night ever passed without an affair of some sort on some part of the perimeter. The stand-to again before dawn, and the welcome daylight. By day there were innumerable patrols, escorts to working parties, the water convoy, work on the defences, besides the ever-present prospect of something brewing up. Nearly every day we got shelled by the Jap 105mm guns from Buthidaung, or from the infantry guns which they brought up to within point-blank range. Such was the congestion in the Box that almost every shell was bound to hit something and blazing ammunition dumps and vehicles were a common sight. The casualties were beginning to pile up in the MDS; the dust, the growing heat, the foul water and the abominable, eternal stench are memories which will long linger. Comfort, sleep and even rest were foreign to us.'

The Japanese also made good use of their mortars, and their snipers, who often tied themselves to the upper branches of trees, took a steady toll. As the firepower of the Lees made daylight attacks hazardous, most of their attempts to penetrate the perimeter took place at night. In the past, they had successfully played on the nerves of inexperienced troops after dusk, subjecting them to shouted orders or despairing screams for help in English or Urdu in the hope of provoking a reaction. This created tension, but the technique was now familiar and the enemy's difficulty with the letter 'L', which he pronounced as an 'R', was a certain give-away. In the same vein, some Japanese donned hoods or grotesque masks which they hoped would strike terror into their foes at close quarters; the effect, while eerie, was quickly dissipated when the wearers were shot dead. The principal Japanese failings, however, included an inability to co-ordinate their attacks around the perimeter, thereby permitting Evans to commit his reserve where it was most needed, and a predictability in repeating failed attacks over the same ground, which merely resulted in heavier casualties. Even if the Japanese succeeded in securing a lodgement, they were soon blasted out of it by the point-blank fire of the tanks. After the first few days it became clear that, having been forced into a stand-up fight, the soldiers of the 55th Division were actually poor battle practitioners. As confidence grew within the Box, its defenders began to patrol aggressively, especially on the 'B' Echelon sector, where the score of kills rose daily.

It was a sign of this confidence that, as early as 9 February, most of the Dragoons' 'A' Squadron was sent to join 33 Indian Infantry Brigade in its own box, which was reached safely. By 11 February Japanese air activity had tailed away sufficiently for the first parachute supply drop to be made. The sight of the chutes, coloured to indicate the nature of their burden, must have been galling in the extreme to the Japanese, who were even then consuming the last of their rations. That same day the enemy managed to establish themselves on the crest of Artillery Hill, in the southern sector of the defences. This feature, which provided a commanding view of the entire Box and directly overlooked the main headquarters area, water point and ammunition dump, had been visited regularly by patrols but was not held by a standing garrison. At 1140 a patrol provided by an anti-aircraft battery reached the summit to find the Japanese present. A fire fight developed and a platoon of the West Yorkshires' 'A' Company, commanded by Lieutenant C. H. Dean, was sent up to regain possession of the feature. Dean's attack succeeded but he was killed in its final moments. The Japanese counter-attacked and obtained possession of the entire hill.

The feature was kept under fire while plans were made to recapture it. At approximately 1720 two troops of Lees moved forward and began battering the reverse slopes. Simultaneously, two platoons of 'A' Company swarmed on to the crest and routed the Japanese. The hill was then put into a state of defence and was handed over next day to the remnant of 7/2nd Punjabis, one of the 89 Brigade units which had been ambushed and severely mauled while attempting to reinforce the Box.

Meanwhile, events elsewhere were also turning out badly for General Hanaya. Kubo's force had indeed reached the coast road, where it enjoyed mixed fortunes. To Kubo's chagrin, his presence had virtually no effect on Briggs' 5th Indian Division, which was being supplied by coastal craft through Maungdaw. Worse still, once the form of the batle became clear, Christison committed his reserve, 26th Indian Division, which began advancing southward. In the end it was Kubo, his flank threatened, who was forced into a disorderly retreat. Once this issue was resolved, Briggs was able to allocate some of his resources to re-opening the Ngakyedauk Pass and relieving the Admin Box.

The distant sounds of this battle could be heard in the Box on 12 February and the following morning Evans decided to mount a reconnaissance in force into the eastern end of the pass. Commanded by Major Dunlop and consisting of two 'B' Company platoons and a troop of Lees under Lieutenant Johnson, they penetrated three miles before being halted by a blown bridge, and rescued two Royal Engineer officers who had been forced to remain in hiding since they were cut off at the start of the enemy counter-offensive. The way home, however, was not so easy, as the Japanese had formed two road-blocks with felled trees, each of which was covered by machine-guns and snipers. The West Yorkshires sustained serious casualties, including the two platoon leaders, but those still on their feet, led by Company Sergeant-Major J. H. Shackleton, worked their way round through the jungle. The tanks had no alternative other than to fight their way through, but the Lee, while obsolete in other theatres of war, was in many ways an ideal vehicle for jungle warfare as its sponson-mounted 75mm could fire high-explosive ahead while the 37mm in the traversing top turret flayed the jungle on either side with man-killing canister. While the road-blocks were being blown apart some of the wounded infantrymen riding on the tanks' engine decks were hit for a second time.

The engagement proved that, for the present, the Japanese had no intention of relinquishing their grip on the Admin Box. That same day the main ammunition dump was again hit by bombs, and on 15 February it was struck by shellfire, resulting in yet more fires and explosions. The losses were made good by air drop, but the condition of the wounded gave grounds for serious concern since by the middle of the month the MDS contained almost 500 casualties, of whom very few could be evacuated, and these only by light aircraft from 114 Brigade Box, which could only be reached by a perilous journey through the jungle at night. Likewise, the incessant fighting had reduced the strength of the West Yorkshires to the equivalent of two platoons per company.

Despite deteriorating conditions in the Box, Tanahashi made no progress and began to lose face with his superiors. His excuse to Hanaya was that he had not expected to find tanks east of the Mayu range and from his unit commanders he demanded even greater sacrifice to overcome what he described as the 'hysterical' defence. The pressure on subordinate commanders to get on became so unbearable that on one occasion a suicide attack on the Dragoons' harbour area was mounted in broad daylight across open paddy. Needless to say, it foundered in a hail of machine-gun fire. On another, an attempt to destroy the tanks was made by setting fire to the grass around them with phosphorous shells, but this also failed. Turning the knife in the wound, the Dragoons' 'A' Squadron, working with 33 Brigade, performed a destructive twenty-minute shoot on Ngakyedauk village, suspected of being a Japanese supply depot, the site of which was then occupied.

One of the odder aspects of the siege was the survival of so much of the garrison's motor transport. This included a pontoon bridging train of more than 100 vehicles, and was parked outside the south-eastern edge of the perimeter. From start to finish, it remained in full view of the enemy but was neither shelled nor bombed, and some Japanese used the pontoons to sleep in. Hanaya had, in fact, given specific instructions that the transport should not be destroyed, as he intended using it during his drive on Chittagong.

On the morning of 15 February the Japanese mounted a determined attack on 'C' Company Hill. Because of demands elsewhere within the Box, the garrison amounted to little more than a single platoon. Two sections, plus the Forward Observation Officer and several men from the Indian Mountain Battery, held a position on the narrow crest, while a third section, with Company Headquarters, occupied a track junction just below on the reverse slope. Without warning, a machine-gun began to rake the area continuously from end to end. The source of the fire could not be located and was actually high in the branches of a tree. One of the two forward sections' light machine-guns was quickly put out of action. Lacking head cover, the occupants of the slit trenches were pinned down. This continued for some twenty minutes, when up to forty Japanese charged on to the crest and captured it. They then began consolidating their gains, ignoring 'C' Company Headquarters only twenty yards down the reverse slope.

Evans immediately ordered the recapture of the feature, using O'Hara's 'A' Company supported by a squadron of Lees. The slopes of the hill were extremely steep and covered with dense bamboo and tall trees. Only one practical route to the top existed, leading through the toe-hold still maintained by Roche and his handful, and for much of the way this was under enemy observation. At Major Ley's suggestion, the tanks were moved to a flank and employed the same fire technique which had proved successful against the bunkers at Maungdaw. Using high-explosives, they blasted the summit while 'A' Company climbed steadily upwards. When the latter had reached the safety limit a Very light was fired and the tanks switched to flat-trajectory armour-piercing shot and machine-gun fire to keep the enemy's heads down until the assault went in. The first attack was greeted with a shower of grenades and O'Hara fell back a little while the tanks renewed their fire. The second attack cleared the crest at the point of the bayonet, killing seventeen of the enemy. While this was in progress, the battalion mortars had been hitting the far slopes of the hill to prevent the enemy's escape and break up any counter-attack. Observing the effect of his fire, the mortar platoon commander saw a Japanese peering through the foliage in the area in which the enemy machine-gun was known to be situated. One mortar concentrated on this target to good effect; the gun and two dead Japanese were later found strapped to the tree.

That night, heavy firing was heard from the direction of the old divisional headquarters. This had nothing to do with the immediate defence of the Box, and Messervy knew that it did not involve troops from any of his equally embattled brigades, so the following morning the Dragoons' 'C' Squadron sent out a patrol under Captain Alexander to investigate. By 1000 contact had been made with the 1st Lincolnshire Regiment, the leading units of 26th Indian Division. The Lincolns' adjutant was brought in and was able to inform Messervy that their attack on Point 315, a feature covering the eastern approach to the Box, had been halted by determined resistance and that the battalion was having to pull back. While covering the Lincolns' withdrawal, one Lee was hit by mortar fire and burned out, and a second bogged down so badly that it had to be left where it was.

During the early hours of 16 February the 2nd King's Own Scottish Borderers entered the Box with Headquarters 89 Indian Infantry Brigade. The Borderers became responsible for all major infantry operations, taking some of the strain off the exhausted West Yorkshires, whose numbers had been seriously depleted by casualties and disease. The next few days were spent patrolling and cleaning out isolated enemy pockets around the perimeter.

For their part, the Japanese had reached the limit of their endurance. A prisoner, taken on 21 February, stated that he and his comrades had been existing on nothing but roots for ten days. That night, the survivors on the Blood Nullah sector mounted a suicide attack. Twenty-seven were killed by the divisional anti-tank gunners and the remainder vanished into the darkness. The orders for the attack, found on the body of the major who had led it, were as follows: '*2nd Battalion 122nd Regiment will attack and destroy the enemy in the nullah. Objects of the attack: (a) to procure food; (b) to destroy the enemy. Estimated enemy strength is one strong platoon. Our strength three officers and 73 men.*' As the historian of the West Yorkshire Regiment comments, when the Japanese counter-offensive began a fortnight earlier, this battalion must have numbered the better part of 1,000 men.

Meanwhile, 5th Indian Division was continuing to fight its way through the Ngakyedauk Pass, supported by a Lee squadron made up from the Dragoons' spare tanks and crews, which had been left west of the Mayu range. On 21 February a well-constructed bunker complex at the summit proved impervious to the tanks' fire and was not subdued until a 5.5-inch medium howitzer was brought forward the following day. Using two Lees for cover, the gun slammed twenty shells into the fire slits at short range, their explosions sending timbers, head cover, weapons and occupants flying through the air. This broke the back of the Japanese resistance and the advance was resumed. Simultaneously, 'C' Squadron and two companies of Borderers had left the Box to make contact. There were forced to deal with two road-blocks, but at 1120 on 22 February they met a company of 4/7th Rajputs, the leading battalion of 123 Indian Infantry Brigade, on the road. The siege had been broken, although the pass was not opened to motor traffic for a further two days. Major-General Briggs arrived in a Lee and distributed bottles of whisky and kegs of rum, but everyone was too tired to celebrate. While fresh troops took over the defences, a long convoy wound westwards through the pass carrying the 500 wounded from the MDS.

On 25 February Hanaya announced that the 'Ha-Go' counter-offensive was over. This was pure formality, for about 5,000 of his men lay dead around the Admin Box, in the Ngakyedauk Pass and among the hills of the Mayu range. The survivors, in rags, starving and riddled with disease, stumbled and crawled their way through the jungle towards imagined safety. XV Corps sustained 3,500 casualties during the same period but Christison immediately resumed his own interrupted offensive. Buthidaung and Razabil fell the following month, costing Hanaya a further 2,000 killed.

The long-term consequences were of even greater importance. In planning 'Ha-Go', Hanaya had hoped that the British would be forced to divert reserves from the Central Front, where the Japanese were on the point of mounting a major offensive against Imphal and Kohima. In the event, the reverse happened. 5th and 7th Indian Divisions were sent up to the Central Front and it was the Japanese who were forced to rush reinforcements into the Arakan, where fighting continued until the onset of the monsoon rendered further movement impossible. The following year XV Corps mounted a series of successful amphibious operations along the Arakan coast, culminating in the capture of Rangoon itself.

It can thus be seen that the Battle of the Admin Box was a major turning-point in the Burma Campaign. An assortment of butchers, bakers, clerks, drivers, muleteers and sanitary orderlies had handed out a fair beating to some of the best infantry in the Japanese Army and walked the taller because of it. The major share of the credit, however, must go to the two units upon whom so much depended, 25th Dragoons and 2nd West Yorkshire Regiment. Regarding the former, the history of the 5th Indian Division comments: 'The debt owed to these tanks and their crews cannot be over-emphasized. It was their accurate, high-velocity, close-range blasting which put our infantry back whenever the Japanese penetrated our defences or captured any vital position.'

The burden borne by the West Yorkshires was even heavier, given their small numbers. Of the 200 who fought in the Box, 142 became casualties, including forty-seven killed and eleven missing, fate unknown. The tribute paid by General Christison to the battalion was hard-earned and amply justified: 'I think that never has any regiment counter-attacked so successfully and so often as in that battle. The West Yorkshires were in that Box for 25 days. Every single hill overlooking it was captured by the Japanese and every single time the West Yorkshires, supported by tanks, drove them off.'

Major-General Messervy continued to command his division during the fighting at Kohima and was then appointed commander of IV Corps, capturing the vital Japanese communications centre of Meiktila almost exactly a year after the relief of the Admin Box. He was subsequently knighted and became the first Commander-in-Chief of the Pakistan Army. Brigadier Evans commanded 123 Indian Infantry Brigade with distinction at Imphal, and then the 7th Indian Division during IV Corps' drive on Meiktila. He, too, was knighted and retired from the Army in 1957 with the rank of Lieutenant-General.

CHAPTER 12
Arnhem Bridge
17–20 SEPTEMBER 1944

Victory, goes the saying, has many fathers, but defeat is an orphan. If Operation 'Market Garden', the Allied attempt to secure bridges over the Eindhoven canals, the Maas at Grave, the Waal at Nijmegen and the Lower Rhine at Arnhem, had succeeded, it would have been hailed as one of the most brilliant in military history, since it would almost certainly have shortened the war in Europe by many months. As it was, it is remembered principally as a very gallant failure.

The overall plan for 'Market Garden' required the dropping of the US 101st Airborne Division north of Eindhoven, the US 82nd Airborne Division between Grave and Nijmegen, and the British 1st Airborne Division at Arnhem, where they would be relieved in turn by the advance of Lieutenant-General Brian Horrocks' British XXX Corps. The initial drops took place on 17 December 1944. As planned, XXX Corps relieved the 101st Airborne on the 18th and the 82nd Airborne the following morning. The bridge at Nijmegen was captured after heavy fighting by a joint attack on the 20th, but XXX Corps' further progress towards Arnhem was barred by a strong defensive front at Elst, some miles beyond. At Arnhem, Major-General Roy Urquhart's 1st Airborne Division became the victims of bad planning compounded by ill-luck. It landed in an area where II SS Panzer Corps were refitting after its mauling in Normandy, and although one group succeeded in reaching the vital road bridge and holding its northern end against all comers for several days, the German reaction to the landing was so swift that the rest of the division was forced back into the suburb of Oosterbeek where, with ever-diminishing resources, it continued to fight a ferocious battle against steadily mounting odds.

On 22 September 1 Polish Parachute Brigade was dropped on the opposite bank of the river, where it was joined the following day by part of the 43rd (Wessex) Division, which had fought its way past the flank of the German defences at Elst. On the 25th Montgomery decided to withdraw the remnant of Urquhart's command and that night 2,163 men were ferried from Oosterbeek to the south bank; during the ensuing days and weeks several hundred more made their way to safety, many of them having been sheltered, at terrible risk, by Dutch families. But the fact remained that 1st Airborne Division, which had gone into action

172

10,000 strong, had sustained the loss of 1,130 killed, and 6,000 of its men, half of whom were wounded, were now captives. German losses during the fighting in and around Arnhem amounted to 3,300 killed and wounded.

Every unit of this fine division fought sturbbornly and well, but this story is concerned solely with the group which took and held the northern end of the great road bridge, for it alone performed the function set by the planners for the entire division, and it alone, by its presence in so sensitive an area, influenced the heavy fighting taking place at Nijmegen. The majority of the group belonged to the 2nd Battalion The Parachute Regiment, commanded by Lieutenant-Colonel (later Major-General Sir John) Frost, but also present were men from the divisional reconnaissance squadron, artillerymen, anti-tank gunners, engineers, signallers, drivers and most of the personnel of HQ 1 Parachute Brigade.

The planning errors and bad luck which troubled the entire division naturally affected Frost's group from the outset and it is, therefore, worth examining the more obvious of these. During the final briefing which Montgomery had given to his senior officers on 10 September, Lieutenant-General Frederick Browning, commanding I Airborne Corps was worried by the fact that the Arnhem bridge lay 64 miles behind the existing German front and asked how long XXX Corps' armoured spearhead would take to get there. Montgomery replied two days, Estimating the ability of his lightly armed paratroops to hang on, Browning commented that it could be held for four, adding as a cautionary afterthought: 'But, sir, I think we might be going a bridge too far.' Neither Montgomery nor his staff were impressed, for without Arnhem bridge the whole operation was pointless and, unless unforeseen factors intervened, they saw no reason why it could not be secured.

Another senior officer who disliked the idea was Major-General Stanislaw Sosabowski, commanding 1 Polish Parachute Brigade, who believed not only that the Germans were fully aware of the strategic significance of Arnhem and had already taken precautions against its capture, but also that the Allied forces were inadequate for the task. With Urquhart, Sosabowski took his reservations to Browning who, whatever his private thoughts might have been, dismissed them.

Urquhart had no reservations concerning the ability of his troops, but the division's landing and drop zones were not of his choosing. He had wanted to be dropped as close to the road and rail bridges as possible with a view to exploiting surprise and seizing these objectives before the enemy could react, and he was prepared to accept 10 per cent casualties in the process. The RAF, however, informed him that the enemy's anti-aircraft defences in these areas had been strengthened recently, pessimistically predicting aircraft losses in the region of 40 per cent, which was certainly not acceptable at the start of the operation. With some reluctance, therefore, he accepted alternative landing and drop zones on open heathland some seven miles west of Arnhem, although this meant forfeiting much of the initial surprise gained by the drop and thereby permitted the enemy time to react while the division marched towards its objectives.

This was compounded by a second unfortunate factor, namely that there were too few transport aircraft available to carry the division in one lift. Half the division was landed during the afternoon of 17 September, during which it was intended that the objectives would be taken by Brigadier Gerald Lathbury's 1 Parachute Brigade while Brigadier Philip Hicks' 1 Air Landing Brigade, which had come in by glider, secured the drop zones. The rest of the division, including Brigadier (later General Sir John) Hackett's 4 Parachute Brigade, was delayed by bad flying weather and did not arrive until late the following day, by which time the form of the battle was set and the enemy had recovered the initiative. In his book, *A Drop Too Many*, General Frost comments that if the two drops had been re-scheduled for early morning and late afternoon on 17 September, thus taking full advantage of good flying conditions, the division's capacity for offensive action would have been greatly enhanced when it was needed most. As it was, the task of capturing the bridges was the responsibility of a single, unsupported, brigade.

It therefore goes, almost without saying, that had Urquhart's wishes regarding drop zones been respected, and had all his division been landed on the same day, the nature, and perhaps the outcome, of the battle would have been very different. Yet, as if this were not enough, 1 Airborne Division's internal radio communications broke down almost as soon as it landed. The essence of the problem was that buildings tended to screen the No. 22 Wireless Set's transmissions, and as much of the fighting took place in built-up areas contact was quickly lost with sub-units. Unfortunately, even those parts of the radio net which were functioning properly were overlaid by a distant but more powerful British transmitter operating on the same frequency. It was as a direct consequence of this that Urquhart and Lathbury left their respective headquarters and went forward to find out what was going on. They were cut off and compelled to remain in hiding for thirty-six hours. Towards the end of this period Hicks assumed temporary command, but in the critical hours which intervened the division was effectively leaderless.

So, thanks to the over-optimism of the higher military planners and the undue pessimism of senior RAF officers, 1st Airborne Division found itself in an invidious position from the outset, even before serious thught had been given to the enemy's strength and likely reaction. It was the worst possible luck that Lieutenant-General Wilhelm Bittrich's II SS Panzer Corps, consisting 9th SS Panzer Division *Hohenstaufen* and 10th SS Panzer Division *Frundsberg* were stationed near Arnhem, for although neither had recovered anything like their full strength they were both formidable opponents still capable of deploying tanks, artillery and panzergrenadiers against the lightly equipped landing force. On the other hand, while it was appreciated that the enemy would waste no time in rushing reinforcements into the area, his capacity for instant reaction was under-estimated. For more than a year the German Army and Waffen SS had been in retreat on the Eastern Front, which had been shorn up time and again with inadequate resources, and they were well used to responding to emergencies. They excelled in the art of dragging soldiers out of every imaginable nook and cranny, forming them into *ad hoc* units and dispatching these at a minute's notice to fill some gap in the line. Field Marshal Walter Model, the commander of Army Group 'E', had earned his reputation in this manner. As luck would have it, he was having lunch at the Tafelberg Hotel in Oosterbeek when 1st Airborne's pathfinders began dropping. He drove at speed into the town to alert the area commandant, Major-General Kussin, and then continued to Bittrich's headquarters. By the time 1 Parachute Brigade began leaving its drop zone a cordon had been thrown across its path by Major Sepp Krafft's SS Panzergrenadier Training and Reserve Battalion, reinforced by elements of 9th SS and other troops as they came up. Bittrich, now fully aware of the implications of 'Market Garden', also ordered one squadron of 9th SS Armoured Reconnaissance Battalion to cross Arnhem bridge and drive to Nijmegen, to be followed by the whole of 10th SS once the division was concentrated.

In fact, 1 Parachute Brigade had three bridges to capture: the railway bridge, a military pontoon bridge and, of course, the road bridge. It was appreciated that there would be a considerable lapse in time between the landing and the battalions reaching the town and because of this it was decided to capture the road bridge by *coup de main*, using the divisional reconnaissance squadron, commanded by Major C. F. H. Gough, which consisted of four troops equipped with armed jeeps. Gough himself did not like the idea, which committed his men to a seize-and-hold role more suited to an armoured car squadron with heavy weapons in support. He had suggested that the squadron would be better employed scouting the three parallel axes which the marching battalions were to take, as this would reveal the least contested route to the bridge, but this was turned down. He then suggested that the squadron be supplemented by a troop of air-portable light tanks, which could be brought in by glider. These vehicles were no match for German tanks, but they were capable of dealing with the enemy's reconnaissance vehicles and anything else which the jeeps might encounter. This, too, was turned down.

The gliders containing one troop's vehicles were missing but at 1530 Gough drove off with the remaining three troops, taking the northern route into the town, which was also to be followed by Lieutenant-Colonel D. T. Dobie's 1st Battalion Parachute Regiment. At 1600 the leading troop was ambushed by armoured cars and simultaneously Gough received a message that Urquhart wanted to see him immediately. He had no alternative than to leave the action in the hands of his second in command and, with a small escort, drive back to the landing zone.

Inexplicably, when Urquhart landed he was told that none of the reconnaissance squadron's jeeps had arrived and he wished to discuss with Gough some other means of mounting the *coup de main*. Unfortunately, by the time Gough returned to the landing zone the General had left and was driving after Frost's 2nd Battalion along the southern route. Frost was up with his leading company and, leaving a message for him which impressed the urgency of the situation, Urquhart turned north to look for Brigadier Lathbury, who had left his own headquarters to visit Lieutenant-Colonel F. A. Fitch's 3rd Battalion, already engaged with Krafft's blocking force on the central route; it was during this phase of the fighting that Major-General Kussin, the German area commandant, was killed, although this had no effect on the conduct of operations. Meanwhile, Gough had decided to follow Urquhart, but on reaching brigade headquarters, which was following behind 2nd Battalion, he was told that the General and the Brigadier were together, but their whereabouts was unknown. Wondering what to do for the best, Gough set off after Frost's battalion towards the bridges.

Together, Frost and his battalion were a thoroughly experienced team. In February 1942 he had led the Second's 'C' Company during the raid on Bruneval, which had secured vital German radar equipment, and in Tunisia and Sicily he had commanded the battalion throughout a series of hard-fought actions which, more often than not, found 1 Parachute Brigade fighting as conventional infantry on hard-pressed sectors of the line. During this period the Second had made two operational drops, at Oudna in Tunisia and at Primosole Bridge in Sicily, the lessons of which were that nothing could be taken for granted in this new form of warfare. Such risks, however, were the reason why most men had volunteered. Nor did they regard themselves simply as riflemen who reached the battlefield by air, for by its very nature their role demanded the highest standards of fitness, battlecraft, initiative and endurance. Tunisian veterans, echoing the calls of the Arabs across the hills, already mentioned in the chapter on Sidi Nsir, continued to hail each other with 'Wahoo, Mohammed!' until it became the Brigade's battle cry, wildly inspiring in attack, defiantly contemptuous in defence. In the days to come such cries would become fewer, but they were never silenced.

Ironically, the Second's drop went almost as smoothly as an exercise. During the early years of the war Frost, a keen huntsman, had been stationed in Iraq, where he had formed a pack of hounds known as the 'Royal Exodus' which hunted jackals across the desert. When he left, the Hunt Committee had presented him with a suitably inscribed copper hunting-horn and he had subsequently used this to rally his battalion during its drops in North Africa and Italy. It was one of those small things which give a unit a distinctive identity and in itself served to emphasize the aggressive role of the paratrooper. Now, for the last time, the Second converged on the sound and at 1530 commenced its seven-mile march from the drop zone to the road bridge, accompanied by the four 6-pounder anti-tank guns which it had been allocated and a contingent from the divisional engineer squadron under the command of Captain Eric Mackay. It followed a secondary route which ran close to the river

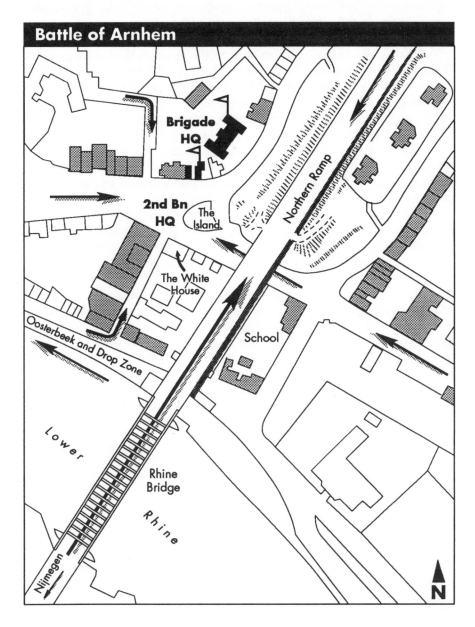

bank and this took it past the southern flank of the screen established by Krafft, although there was intermittent contact with isolated enemy units. Passing through Heaveadorp and Oosterbeek, the march was slightly delayed by welcoming Dutch civilians who pressed gifts of fruit and milk on the men. Beyond Oosterbeek Major Victor Dover's 'C' Company was detached to capture the railway bridge. They were engaged by Germans on the far bank of the Neder Rijn but, under cover of smoke and supporting fire, they reached the bridge and began fighting their way across. It began to look as though the structure might be captured intact when, with a roar, its southern span went up and collapsed into the river.

Leaving orders for Dover to capture the German Kommandantur in the town, Frost continued towards the second and third objectives. Just across the railway embankment, however, the way forward was denied by patrolling armoured cars and fire from a hill known as Den Brink. While an anti-tank gun was brought up Major Digby Tatham-Warter, commanding 'A' Company, which was leading the advance, decided to work his way into Arnhem through the back gardens of the houses. Assisted by the gathering dusk, the move succeeded. With the coming of darkness, the fire from Den Brink tailed off into sporadic, unaimed bursts and Frost led the rest of the column forward. He reached the northern end of the pontoon bridge to find that its central section had been removed, and, leaving Major Douglas Crawley's 'B' Company there for the moment, he continued towards the road bridge. Here he found that 'A' Company had secured the ramp which carried the road on to the bridge from the town.

At 2045 a platoon commanded by Lieutenant J. H. Grayburn attempted to cross the bridge and secure its southern end. The enemy were already in position there, but the attack was stopped by fire from a pillbox near the northern end, supported by an armoured car farther back, which inflicted eight casualties before the first fifty yards had been covered. Grayburn was among those hit, but despite this he continued to provide inspired leadership for his men until he was killed later in the battle, by which time he had sustained several more wounds. He received the posthumous award of the Victoria Cross.

The paratroopers rapidly moved into buildings on the waterfront and on each side of the ramp, establishing a firm hold on the northern approaches to the bridge. Frost's command now included his own 'A' and HQ Companies, the Brigade Headquarters personnel and defence platoon, Gough and several of his armed jeeps, Mackay and his engineers, and a Royal Army Service Corps platoon bringing with it a captured lorry filled with ammunition from the drop zone. Part of Frost's responsibilities included establishing a bridgehead at the southern end of the bridge in preparation for the planned drop of 1 Polish Parachute Brigade, and his intention was that his own 'B' Company should effect a crossing in river craft. Unfortunately, neither barges nor boats were available and communications with the company, which was still at the pontoon bridge, were lost until the following morning, when Frost ordered it to join him. With difficulty and some loss it managed to fight its way into the perimeter. 'C' Company, however, became pinned down during its attack on the Kommandantur and was unable to get forward, although the 3rd Battalion's 'C' Company, which had managed to work its way into the town along the railway, arrived unexpectedly at the bridge. Altogether, Frost had available between 500 and 700 men, the equivalent of a battalion, with which to stand off an enemy armoured division. Nevertheless, morale remained high and at this stage few doubted either that the remainder of 1st Airborne Division would break through from the west or that the armoured spearhead of XXX Corps would appear from the south.

The most pressing task during that first evening of 17 September was to destroy the enemy pillbox on the bridge. By tunnelling through the dividing walls of cellars, Lieutenant Robin Vlasto's platoon managed to approach the position, which was then neutralized by PIAT bombs and the engineers' flame-throwers. A wooden hut nearby caught fire, illuminating the whole area. Shortly after, a counter-attack was mounted from the south end of the bridge in four lorries, but as the upper storeys of the occupied buildings overlooked the ramp, this stood no chance at all. A hail of fire brought the vehicles slewing to a standstill near the blazing hut, where they in turn caught fire. Those enemy infantry that survived soon gave up, providing Frost with more prisoners than he wished to accommodate. The rest of the night pased without major incident, although each side probed the other's positions. Many of those around the bridge snatched what sleep they could. Most refilled their water-bottles from domestic sources, a wise precaution because the Germans cut off the supply.

The morning found the 1st and 3rd Battalions still trying to fight their way through to the bridge. They made some progress, but at terrible cost, and were finally halted in the area of St Elizabeth's Hospital. Later, Urquhart having been officially posted missing, Brigadier Hicks committed two more battalions to the attempt, but the German cordon was now solid and the airborne soldiers could neither match the enemy's firepower nor advance against his armoured cars and assault guns. Gradually the main body of the division was pushed back towards Oosterbeek and forced on to the defensive. While 9th SS had succeeded in containing the threat from the west, however, Frost's group at the bridge was strangling the principal axis of Major-General Heinz Harmel's 10th SS, which was desperately needed at Nijmegen. For the moment Harmel was forced to use the vehicle ferry at Pannerden, several miles upstream, but moving the entire division this way was an agonizingly slow process and only a trickle of reinforcements were reaching the embattled German garrison to the south. The recapture of the bridge was, therefore, a matter of critical importance. With typical German flexibility, the 9th and 10th SS exchanged their armoured reconnaissance battalions. That of the former, it will be remembered, had already crossed the bridge heading for Nijmegen the previous afternoon, and it was now ordered to return to Arnhem and break through Frost's defences with an attack from the south.

The unit's commander, Captain Paul Graber, decided to use surprise, speed and firepower to achieve his object, and he almost succeeded. His leading element, consisting of five armoured cars with guns blazing, tore on to the bridge at 0930. Expertly handled, the cars swerved past the still smouldering lorries, avoiding all but one of the Teller mines which had been laid during the night, and roared down the ramp into the town. Then came the main assault, consisting of half-tracks and more armoured cars, followed by infantry in lorries protected by grain sacks, then more infantry on foot, firing as they advanced. By now, the paratroopers had fully recovered from their initial surprise and, waiting until the leading vehicles were level with the houses overlooking the ramp, they opened fire from windows and slit trenches with every weapon at their disposal, including anti-tank guns, PIATs, automatic weapons and grenades. The two leading half-tracks ground to a standstill, their drivers dead, their occupants exposed to a murderous fire which none survived. The driver of the third vehicle, wounded, reversed blindly into the half-track behind. Locked together by the impact, the two vehicles careered across the road and caught fire. The rest of the column accelerated in the hope of battering its way through but failed and merely added to the tangle. One or two vehicles, completely out of control, smashed through the ramp wall at speed and crashed on to the road beneath. Pinned down by sustained fire from medium and light machine-guns, the SS attempted to fight on amidst the wreckage, but they were now taking additional punishment not only from the Second's mortar platoon, but also from 1st Airborne Division's 75mm pack howitzers, the latter firing from Oosterbeek under the control of Major Dennis Munford, who had managed to establish a radio link to the guns and was performing the role of Forward Observation Officer from an attic in the Brigade Headquarters building. It was more than flesh and blood could stand and, less than two hours after the attack had begun, the survivors broke and ran, pursued by derisive yells of 'Wahoo, Mohammed!' Graber, having led the attack with reckless bravery, now lay dead on the bridge.

Further attacks were mounted during the day against the Second's landward perimeter, sometimes with armoured car and half-track support, sometimes without, all being repulsed with heavy loss. Frost became concerned when the enemy brought up a 150mm howitzer which opened fire on his headquarters over open sights, each explosion causing the entire building to shudder, but this was towed away when his mortar platoon scored a direct hit, killing the gunners and damaging the gun itself. By careful spotting the mortar platoon also located a German mortar position and had the satisfaction of seeing the weapon and its crew being blown through the air when their rounds landed on target. In addition, the mortar and medium machine-gun platoons, together with the divisional artillery, continued to make life unpleasant for the enemy on the south bank of the river.

The SS panzergrenadiers were undoubtedly tough and, like Graber's reconnaissance unit, they relied on a combination of aggression and firepower to secure their objectives, believing that this reduced casualties in the long term. In the paratroopers, however, they had more than met their match, for although they managed to capture a number of buildings, the savage fighting for each room and staircase was beyond their previous experience, piling up dead and wounded at a horrific rate. Suddenly, an allegedly irresistible force had run into an apparently immovable object. The Germans decided to burn their opponents out by mortaring the roofs of the houses, but this proved to be a slow job as it took time for the fires to burn downwards and many of them were put out, at great risk, by the defenders.

Frost's men, too, suffered severely. Every building and street was raked by constant fire, rendering movement extremely difficult. Whenever possible, the dead were removed and the wounded taken to the comparative safety of the cellars. Ammunition expenditure had been prodigious, the water supply had been cut off and half of the rations issued had been eaten. Nevertheless, at this stage, Frost, while worried, still had some grounds of optimism, for although the remainder of the division had been unable to break through to him, during the afternoon 4 Parachute Brigade had been dropped successfully west of Arnhem and on the morrow the Poles were to drop south of the bridge. On the other hand, the interrogation of an officer prisoner confirmed that his opponents were II SS Panzer Corps rather than the poorer quality garrison troops he had been led to expect. It was one of the more shameful aspects of the planning of 'Market Garden' that the presence of Bittrich's corps was known to senior officers down to the level of I Airborne Corps, yet this vital intelligence was deliberately withheld from the field commanders on the spurious grounds that it might inhibit their actions.

With the coming of dusk the little perimeter became ringed with flames as each side set fire to buildings to provide illumination. During the hours of darkness many local initiatives passed to the British as men stalked armoured vehicles with their PIATs or sniped viciously to keep the enemy on edge. East of the ramp, the Germans mounted a major attack with flame-throwers and panzerfausts (bazookas) against the Van Limburg Stirumschool, held by Captain Eric Mackay's engineers and part of the Third's 'C' Company. The roof was set on fire and the south-west corner of the school blown down. Silence followed and, thinking the occupants were dead, the assault force began congregating outside. Suddenly, a shower of grenades exploded among them as Mackay's men stitched their ranks with the fire of six Brens and fourteen Stens, covering the ground with a writhing carpet of field grey.

Shortly after daybreak a German waving a white flag approached the school demanding surrender. Mackay told him to clear off, although only twenty-one of his fifty men remained on their feet. About the same time Harmel sent in a captured engineer sergeant to tell Frost that the British position was hopeless and that he was prepared to meet him under a flag of truce to discuss the terms of capitulation. Frost did not bother to reply and the battle continued.

German reinforcements were now converging on Arnhem from all directions. They included coast defence artillerymen, sailors, and a contingent of Dutch SS men. At least one of these *ad hoc* units, handed rifles at the railway station and packed off to the firing line without a proper briefing, was slaughtered before it got its bearings. The arrival of more tanks and assault guns enabled the Germans to stand off and batter the buildings within the perimeter, but still they made scant progress towards the bridge. Towards evening Tigers of Heavy Tank Battalion 506 joined the battle, but these monsters had not been designed for street fighting and their crews were none too willing to enter hostile territory without close infantry support; this, understandably, the badly mauled SS panzergrenadiers were less than keen to provide. Thus, two Tigers which crawled on to the ramp were content merely to blast several rounds through the already shattered walls of the school and then reverse out of trouble. The day, none the less, marked a turning-point in the battle for the bridge. The Poles, delayed by bad flying weather, remained on their airfields in England; there was no definite news of XXX Corps' battle at Nijmegen; and the rest of the division was barely holding its ground. As night fell all of Arnhem seemed to be burning and Frost accepted the fact that the prospect of relief was now remote.

In the meantime, Urquhart had evaded capture and returned to his headquarters in Oosterbeek. His division was now under pressure from every direction and, as the Second could not be expected to hold out much longer at the bridge, it had to be accepted that the Arnhem operation in its original form had failed. Nevertheless, he believed that it might be possible to salvage something of the concept by retaining his bridgehead on the northern bank of the river. With this in mind, he advised his superiors during the early hours of Wednesday 20 September that the Poles should be dropped, not at the southern end of the road bridge, but at Driel, across the river from Oosterbeek, thus forming a link between the division and the advance of XXX Corps. The decision was difficult and painful since it removed the last hope for those at the bridge, but it was correct as it continued to offer a slender prospect of success for 'Market Garden' as well as a withdrawal route if the worst happened.

At dawn on the 20th, Frost's men still held ten of the eighteen buildings they had occupied, the rest having been gutted by the flames or captured by the enemy. Harmel later admitted that the stand made by the incredible soldiers around the bridge was beginning to make him feel very foolish, but now he was determined to put an end to the matter. He supplemented his tanks with artillery weapons firing over open sights and ordered the systematic destruction of each building in turn, starting with the gables and then adjusting the aim floor by floor until the structure caved in. Yet, even this policy of total destruction absorbed priceless time, for as houses collapsed, sometimes with men still firing from the windows, more paratroopers took up positions in the rubble to exact their revenge.

During the morning Frost spoke with Urquhart, who congratulated him on the magnificent achievement of his battalion group. Frost described his position as satisfactory, although he stressed an immediate need for ammunition, food and a surgical team, but Urquhart was unable to help. At about the same time details of the casualties inflicted by the force at the bridge were passed back to Divisional Headquarters. These included:

tanks – one Tiger damaged and six Pz Kpfw IVs destroyed;
armoured cars and half-tracks – eight destroyed;
lorries – up to thirty destroyed or damaged;
personnel – up to 400 killed or wounded;
prisoners taken – 120.

Early that afternoon Frost was severely wounded in the legs. His second in command, Major David Wallis, had already been killed, so that when Urquhart came through again shortly afterwards he spoke to Gough, who told him that the Second were in good heart and could hold out for a further twenty-four hours.

In terms of morale this was undoubtedly true, for amid the continuous crash of explosions and rumble of falling masonry, the reek of burning timber and expended cordite, some men found a sense of complete release. One such was Major Digby Tatham-Warter, who discovered an umbrella and toured his company's positions with it, erecting it as a mock defence against mortar bombs as he sprinted between the houses. He was later seen waving it as he led a counter-attack, having supplemented his outfit with an old bowler hat. Most men, however, knew instinctively that the end was in sight and they accepted it quietly. James Sims, who served as a 19-year-old private with the Second, later wrote in his moving account *Arnhem Spearhead* that during the last hours bad language was rare and that in their concern for their neighbours rather than themselves his comrades seemed to grow in stature, ennobled in some way by their ordeal. Surrender, wrote Sims, was never mentioned and not considered.

By the end of the day, however, the physical means of resistance had dwindled. The perimeter had shrunk until it enclosed a few buildings around Battalion Headquarters. About 140 men were still on their feet, fighting with captured weapons and ammunition taken from the dead and wounded, which was all that was left. The 6 pounder anti-tank guns lay smashed in the streets, their crews sprawled around them. The last mortar rounds and PIAT bombs had long since been fired off. All that remained was the will to fight on.

The Second Battalion did not surrender, nor was it overrun. As the battle continued into the night, it was consideration for the wounded which brought the fighting to an end. At the school, a blazing ruin by late afternoon, Mackay's few unharmed survivors brought them up from the cellars under mortar fire and, having laid them in a garden nearby, those that could attempted to fight their way out; Mackay was captured but escaped soon afterwards and made his way to Nijmegen. The Battalion Headquarters building, still defiantly holding out, was also ablaze. In its basement the wounded, British and German, lay so tightly packed that there was barely room for the orderlies to move between them. The heat became intense and the cellar began filling with smoke. Since it was now simply a matter of time before the building caved in on top of them, a medical officer requested a ceasefire, which the enemy granted. Together, at great risk, both sides removed the wounded to safety. The task took about an hour and no sooner had it been completed than the structure collapsed into a heap of smoking rubble. The means no longer existed by which the small remnant of Frost's battalion could continue the battle.

Members of the Dutch Resistance who had joined the British were shot out of hand. So, too, was one paratrooper who resisted a body search. These incidents apart, the SS behaved correctly and even decently, many of them handing out cigarettes and portions of their own rations, as well as arranging transportation of the wounded to hospital. They had been deeply impressed by the tenacity of the defence and said so without animosity. A major told Gough that he had been at Stalingrad and it was clear that the paratroopers were very experienced in street fighting techniques. Gough replied that they had not tried it before and promised they would do much better next time.

At about the same time the fighting ended at Arnhem bridge, the bridge at Nijmegen was captured in a brilliant feat of arms by the Guards Armoured and US 82nd Airborne Divisions. The commander of the latter, Major General James Gavin, received the highest possible praise for the manner in which his 504th Parachute Regiment had crossed the Waal under fire in open assault boats to secure the northern end of the bridge. For his part, Gavin described the achievement of Frost's Second Battalion at Arnhem as the finest airborne battalion action of the entire war, for if Harmel's 10th SS had reached Nijmegen in strength the crossing of the

Waal might have been impossible, and in such circumstances the same was true of the partial evacuation of 1st Airborne Division, still fighting at Oosterbeek. Thus, the Second Battalion's sacrifice had not been in vain, for although 'Market Garden' did not end the war in 1944 and seven months were to pass before British troops returned to Arnhem, Nijmegen provided a pivot for Montgomery's drive through the Reichswald the following February, and this in turn cleared the ground for a full-scale crossing of the Rhine on the northern sector of the Allied front.

The people of Arnhem, who had suffered cruelly during the fighting, were the first to commemorate the stand made by Frost's Second Battalion group. Shortly after the war ended they took a stone column from the ruined Palace of Justice and erected it at the north end of the bridge with the simple inscription *17 September 1944*. Each year, a ceremony takes place in which wreaths are laid at its base, honouring those who fought there. Later, a plaque describing the battle was installed in a small building on the bridge. On 17 December 1977 the bridge itself was re-named the John Frost Bridge.

CHAPTER 13
The Imjin
22–25 APRIL 1951

In 1951 comparatively few families in the United Kingdom owned a television set and the majority of people still relied on the cinema for their visual news. During the late summer of that year the newsreels contained extensive footage of a parade held in Korea, showing detachments from all the units belonging to the British 29 Brigade Group, formed in a hollow square around senior American officers who were about to confer on some of those present the highest collective award their country could bestow, a Presidential Unit Citation. The essence of the document was contained in the following words:

'The 1st Battalion, Gloucestershire Regiment, British Army and Troop 'C'. 170th Independent Mortar Battery, Royal Artillery, attached, are cited for exceptionally outstanding performance of duty and extraordinary heroism in action against the armed enemy near Solma-Ri, Korea, on the 23rd, 24th and 25th of April 1951 . . . . The courageous soldiers of the battalion and attached unit were holding the critical route selected by the enemy for one column of the general offensive designed to encircle and destroy I Corps . . . . Completely surrounded by tremendous numbers, these indomitable, resolute and tenacious soldiers fought back with unsurpassed fortitude and courage . . . . Their heroic stand provided the critically needed time to regroup other I Corps units and block the southern advance of the enemy . . . . Without thought of defeat or surrender, this heroic force demonstrated superb battlefield courage and discipline. Their sustained brilliance in battle, their resoluteness and extraordinary heroism are in keeping with the finest traditions of the renowned military forces of the British Commonwealth, and reflect unsurpassed credit on those courageous soldiers and their homeland.'

As the news item ended audiences, drawn from a people normally stolid and undemonstrative, of whom one of their poets had written:

'God and the soldier we adore,
In time of danger, not before.'

rose spontaneously to their feet to cheer and applaud. They knew the story of the battle, they knew that many Glosters had died and that of the remainder all but a handful were enduring a cruel captivity, and this was as simple and obvious a way as any for them to reveal a pride deeply felt.

The battle, which took its name from the River Imjin rather than the

186

village of Solma-Ri mentioned in the Presidential Citation, captured the imagination of the entire world. In Washington, Dean Acheson, then Secretary of State, commented that, 'It was gallant. It was a superb thing . . .' The American press, notably the *New Yorker*, gave the event the widest possible coverage. The *Boston Daily Globe* of 4 June devoted a whole page to the story, headed, with very slight innacuracy:

'ONLY 5 OFFICERS AND 34 MEN LEFT OUT OF A BATTALION OF 622'

A Gripping, Factual Account of the Stand Made by Famous British Outfit which Allowed U.S. Units to Escape from Chinese Trap.'

In Paris the editor of *Le Figaro*, clearly moved, wrote that 'The courage and obstinacy of these Britons, together with the knowledge of their losses, is such that here one can speak of them only in hushed tones, with a mixture of admiration and a kind of reverent respect.' The Spanish Army's Director of Military Training, General Jose Ungria, wrote personally to the Regiment to say that the story of the battle had been read to the officer cadets of the Toledo Infantry Academy, who had then studied its tactical and moral implications in a series of theoretical and field exercises.

In London *The Times* took a broader view:

'The Glosters, for what they have now done and for what went before it, deserve to be singled out for honourable mention, but they did not stand alone. The Royal Northumberland Fusiliers, the Royal Ulster Rifles, and other Commonwealth units, each with a past to live up to, shared with the Glosters in this most testing of all hazards on the battlefield – attack by overwhelming numbers of the enemy.

'The "Fighting Fifth", wearing St George and the Dragon, and the "Irish Giants", with Harp and Crown, have histories that they would exchange with no one. As pride, sobered by mourning for the fallen, observes how well these young men have acquitted themselves in remotest Asia, the parts taken by the regiments may be seen as a whole. The motto of the Royal Ulster Rifles may have the last word – "*Quis Separabit?*" ' The Thunderer was right, of course; the murderous defensive battle fought by the Glosters could not be separated from that fought by the rest of the brigade group.

The war which took these men almost as far as it was possible to travel from the United Kingdom had begun on 25 June 1950 when the North Korean People's Army had attempted to overrun South Korea. The United Nations had reacted at once, forming an army under General Douglas MacArthur which was to defeat the invaders. Pending the arrival of their main body, the few UN troops present were penned in a perimeter around the port of Pusan, where they were hard pressed to hold their ground. On 15 September MacArthur effected an amphibious landing at Inchon on the west coast and a week later the UN troops at Pusan, suitably reinforced, broke out. Trapped between the two, the

NKPA was routed and fled north with the UN forces in hot pursuit.

Defeat, however, was not acceptable to the Communist world. In October Chinese troops began reaching the front and from this point the influence of the Chinese Communist Forces (CCF) in the conduct of operations became paramount. Meanwhile, the commander of the UN Eighth Army, Lieutenant General Walton H. Walker, was being urged by MacArthur to advance to the Yalu river, which formed the natural boundary between North Korea and Manchuria, although this danger-ously over-extended his front. The CCF took due note of the fact and on 25 November launched a massive counter-offensive with some 180,000 men. Now it was the turn of the Eighth Army to embark on a long and difficult retreat.

On 23 December Walker was killed in a traffic accident. His successor, Lieutenant General Matthew B. Ridgway, a tough paratrooper, reached Korea three days later but was unable to prevent Seoul, the South Korean capital, falling in the New Year. Nevertheless, it was apparent that the Communist offensive was running down and this provided time enough for Ridgway to prepare an appreciation of the situation. It could not be denied that his less experienced formations had been seriously shaken by the speed and nature of the Chinese offensive, in which infiltration played a major part. Position after position had fallen when they had been thus isolated, surrounded and then swamped by human-wave attacks. These tactics, while expensive, were suited to mountainous, scrub-covered terrain which formed much of the Korean landscape, and they enabled infantry carrying only personal weapons, mortars, machine-guns and a few days' marching rations to cover ground at great speed. There were, however, disadvantages inherent in this style of fighting. For example, because of UN air supremacy, the Chinese artillery had difficulty in keeping pace with the advance since it was compelled to move mainly by night; nor could the rickety supply system, which relied on coolie trains, bicycles, pack animals and a few lorries, cope with the lengthening distances over which it was required to operate.

In the final analysis Ridgway recognized that whereas the principal asset of the Chinese was manpower, that of the Eighth Army was firepower, and that the war must resolve itself into a contest between the two. He therefore devised what became known as The Meatgrinder, in which every available source of firepower, including aircraft, artillery, tanks and regimental weapons, was co-ordinated with the specific object of killing Chinese in large numbers. By the end of January the Eighth Army had gone over to the offensive, advancing slowly but steadily behind this terrible curtain of fire; on 15 March Seoul was recaptured and by mid-April the UN forces were firmly established on North Korean territory. On 11 April MacArthur, out of favour with his political masters, was relieved of his post as Supreme Commander and Ridgway took his place. The new commander of the Eighth Army, Lieutenant General James A. Van Fleet, thoroughly approved of the Meatgrinder and placed even greater emphasis on the artillery's participation, the extra physical burden on the logistical services and the labouring gunners becoming collectively known as the 'Van Fleet Load'.

The British 29th Brigade Group, commanded by Brigadier Tom Brodie, had reached Korea in November 1950 and joined Major General Frank W. Milburn's US I Corps. Brodie's command consisted of the 1st Battalion Royal Northumberland Fusiliers (Lieutenant-Colonel K. O. N. Foster), 1st Battalion The Gloucestershire Regiment (Lieutenant-Colonel J. P. Carne), 1st Battalion Royal Ulster Rifles (Lieutenant-Colonel R. J. H. Carson), 45 Field Regiment (Lieutenant-Colonel M. T. Young), with three batteries of 25-pounder gun-howitzers, 170 Independent Mortar Battery (Major Fisher Hoch), equipped with 4.2-inch heavy mortars, 11 (Sphinx) Light Anti-Aircraft Battery, armed with 40mm Bofors guns, and 55 Field Squadron Royal Engineers, armoured support being provided when required by the Centurion tanks of the 8th King's Royal Irish Hussars.

The three infantry battalions belonged to that long line of County regiments which provided the bulk of the United Kingdom's infantry, each of which was fiercely proud of its traditions and, while tolerant of the rest, was convinced that it was better at its job than anyone else, this being most obviously reflected in items of dress. Out of the line, for example, the Royal Northumberland Fusiliers wore a jaunty red-and-white hackle above their badge but, in the line or out, annually on 23rd April, St George's Day, roses were worn in their head-dress in honour of the Saint. These, having been flown in specially from Japan, were worn throughout the Imjin battle and were also conferred on the officers of the battery of 45 field Regiment firing in support. The Glosters wore a miniature version of their Sphinx badge at the back of their berets, awarded for an incident during the battle of Alexandria in 1801 when the Regiment, already engaged in a firefight with the French to its front, was simultaneously attacked from behind, the latter threat being dealt with when the rear rank faced about. The moral of the story, with which every Gloster was familiar, is obvious. The Royal Ulster Rifles, raised in 1793, wore the green Irish bonnet known as the corbean, pulled down over the right ear. Despite its title, which, much against its wishes, had been changed from the Royal Irish Rifles in 1922, the Regiment continued to recruit its officers and men from all over Ireland, reflecting the philosophy that while the Border might suit political aspirations, as far as service in the United Kingdom's Irish regiments was concerned it was no obstacle at all. Like all Riflemen, the RUR took pride in the fact that they thought, moved and shot faster than other infantrymen.

Each of the three battalions consisted of a Headquarters Company, four rifle companies each of three platoons and a company headquarters, and a support company, their weapons being the same as those used during the Second World War. The bolt-action Lee-Enfield rifle, with 10-round magazine and spike bayonet, was actually an improved version of the weapon which had torn von Kluck's columns apart at the beginning of the First World War, and the standard of musketry had not been lowered since. To drop ten targets at 400 yards in less than a minute was regarded as good but by no means exceptional. Each infantry section (squad) possessed a Bren light machine-gun and each infantry platoon a 2-inch mortar. For close-quarter work Sten machine-carbines were issued to section leaders and others, and most riflemen carried one or two grenades. The Support Company contained, for administration purposes, an anti-tank platoon armed with 17-pounder anti-tank guns, a 3-inch mortar platoon, a Vickers medium machine-gun platoon and an assault pioneer platoon, these elements being deployed at the battalion commander's discretion. By this phase of the Korean War the Communists had little armour in the field and the anti-tank guns, which took hours of work to emplace because of their size, were left with the rear echelon, their crews being employed as riflemen; RUR amalgamated the personnel of their anti-tank and assault pioneer platoons to form a Battle Patrol which specialized in forward reconnaissance. The only major change in equipment which had been made since 1945 was that the tracked Universal Carriers which transported the battalion's heavy weapons had been replaced by Oxford Carriers, which were simply turretless Stuart M5 light tanks. Because good roads were few and most positions were sited on hilltops, each unit was allocated a train of locally recruited porters who wore the unit number on a disc in their headbands. The task of the porters, who were capable of carrying astonishing weights on their simple A-frames, was to collect ammunition, radio batteries and rations from the unit's transport echelon at the nearest convenient track and then hump them up to the company positions, thereby ensuring that the maximum possible number of riflemen remained in the line.

The senior officers and NCOs of all three battalions had all seen active service during the Second World War, the remainder of their personnel being young Regulars or National Servicemen, supplemented by a large contingent of recalled reservists who were also veterans. It can thus be seen that while their average age was a year or two above the norm, they possessed a steadiness and a wealth of experience which was uniquely valuable to any commander fortunate enough to have them at his disposal. In January and February each battalion had been heavily engaged, either during the final phases of the Eighth Army's retreat or during the start of its counter-offensive, and this had given them the measure of their enemy. In an area known as Happy Valley the Rifles, their blood up, had fought the Chinese hand-to-hand, and beaten them. Long after the battle Rifleman Henry O'Kane, a thoughful young regular, was to write that he and his comrades had learned to respect the enemy, but man for man they were convinced they were the better soliders and were confident that in the straight fight the Chinese would always be the losers.

In the spring the brigade group was joined by a small Belgian battalion of three rifle companies, commanded by Lieutenant-Colonel B. E. M. Crahay. The Belgians, equipped with American arms, were all volunteers serving one-year tours in Korea and their ranks included paratroops, commandos, marines and sailors. They wore distinctive chocolate-brown berets with the Lion of Belgium, were obviously keen and possessed a tremendous *esprit de corps*.

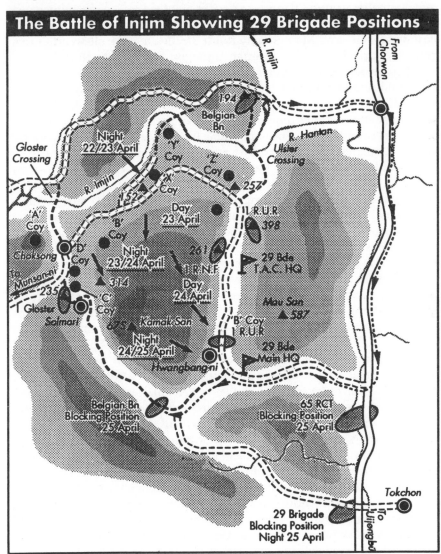

The Battle of Injim Showing 29 Brigade Positions

By 21 April Brodie's command had established itself on the River Imjin with the US 3rd Division on the right and the 1st South Korean (ROK) Division on the left. Altogether, the brigade group was responsible for some nine miles of front and was, therefore, somewhat over-extended. Furthermore, the position was itself awkward to defend since it was effectively cut in two by a towering feature named Kamak San, the foothills of which dropped sheer to the river's edge. The river itself offered some protection, being 300 yards wide, but was fordable in many places. Two tracks ran south from the Imjin, one being comparatively minor and running along the bottom of the valley between Kamak San and a smaller feature named Mau San, while the second, which was better, skirted the western slopes of Kamak San. Beyond Mau San to the east was US I Corps' Main Supply Route (MSR), a good, all-weather road running north from Seoul through Uijongbu and on into North Korea.

Brodie deployed the Belgians on a high feature across the river, their flank and rear being protected by the confluence of the Hantan; beyond this point the US 3rd Division's line swung away to the north, following the course of the upper Imjin. The centre of the position was held by the Royal Northumberland Fusiliers while two miles to the west were the Glosters, isolated from the rest by Kamak San, holding the left. One troop of 170 Independent Mortar Battery was attached to each of the forward infantry battalions. Some two miles behind the front and in reserve were the Royal Ulster Rifles, with Brigade Headquarters and the gun positions of 45 Field Regiment and 11 Light Anti-Aircraft Battery nearby. Many officers would have preferred to have consolidated their positions with wire, mines and trip flares, but the fact was that General Van Fleet regarded the Imjin not as a long-term defensive front, but rather as a line from which the next phase of his offensive would be launched. Extensive patrolling during the previous week had brought little contact with the enemy, whose main line was some ten to fifteen miles distant, and this in itself suggested that nothing was amiss, although rumours of the Chinese counter-offensive had been in the air since 15 April.

The rumours, unfortunately, were true, although the Chinese had displayed great ingenuity in concealing their intentions. Their *de facto* Commander-in-Chief was General Peng Teh-huai, who had once served Chiang Kai-shek. Peng, harsh and coarse-mouthed, had the reputation of caring little for the lives of his men, but he was no mere warlord; in fact, he possessed considerable ability, although he allowed his decisions to be influenced by a streak of obstinacy. He had lost face when Ridgway recovered Seoul and, determined to restore his reputation, had de-manded reinforcements to make good his heavy losses. These were forthcoming and he now had approximately 700,000 men under his command, half of whom were to be committed to the first phase of the general offensive he was planning. A great deal depended on the outcome of this. If it succeeded, the prestige of the Communist forces would be restored and the campaign would continue; if it failed or ended in stalemate the Korean adventure would have to be ended by face-saving negotiations.

Peng's principal thrust was, predictably, directed against Seoul and would therefore strike US I Corps. It was to be delivered by the 63rd Army, a shock formation brought down specially from China, consisting of the 187th, 188th and 189th Divisions, each about 9,000 strong and containing a high proportion of experienced, battle-hardened troops. Peng rejected the obvious axis of advance, along the good road which formed I Corps' MSR, since this would expose his troops to the full effects of The Meatgrinder and in particular to the overwhelming UN air superiority. Instead, he selected an axis slightly to the west, where the broken country favoured the Chinese style of fighting. Thus, the full weight of 63rd Army's attack would fall on 29th Brigade Group, the dispositions of which he was fully aware. The Glosters, he reasoned, would be quickly overwhelmed and his troops would be able to use the good track into the brigade's rear areas, destroying its artillery and surrounding its remaining battalions, which would already be heavily engaged to their front. Follow-through formations would maintain the advance to the south, capturing Uijongbu and thereby isolating the rest of I Corps, which would be routed in detail. The road to Seoul would then be open and Peng intended that 63rd Army's leading elements should reach the city only 36 hours after the first attack had been launched. Since speed was of the essence, his plan required 63rd Army to make a rolling start across no man's land, reaching 29 Brigade Group's positions after dusk, when his troops could take full advantage of the darkness to infiltrate the British line.

Sunday, 22 April, dawned crisp, cold and bright and was ostensibly no different from any other day on the Imjin. All seemed so quiet, in fact, that Lieutenant-Colonel Carson had left the previous day for a short period of leave in Japan, leaving Major G. P. Rickcord in command of the Rifles. The Glosters' chaplain, the Revd. S. J. Davies, visited the Royal Northumberland Fusiliers and held a Church Parade, taking as the theme of his sermon the endurance of St George, a soldier in the Roman Army, martyred for his Christian beliefs. In the days of severe trial which followed, many Fusiliers would be fortified by his words. The Belgians, the Fusiliers and the Glosters all sent out patrols and, as the hours passed, contact with the enemy became more frequent. During the afternoon, however, air reconnaissance revealed that all tracks leading southward to the Imjin were crowded with enemy infantry and vehicles. It was now apparent that the Chinese were indeed on the point of mounting a counter-offensive, but previous experience of their tactics suggested that prior to launching their assault they always probed for weak spots with strong fighting patrols, and in the light of this it was felt that, for the moment, they might simply be closing the gap between the two armies.

Nevertheless, as precautionary measures additional ammunition was brought up, weapons were cleaned in readiness and the artillery registered defensive fire tasks. 45 Field Regiment also shelled small parties of the enemy spotted north of Gloster Crossing, the ford fronting the Glosters' position. At about 1500 the Turks, serving with the US 25th Division, captured a Chinese artillery survey officer who revealed that the offensive was to commence that very night. By the time I Corps' senior headquarters had been informed, only hours remained before the blow fell.

In view of the enemy's intentions, the ensuing battle is best understood if the Glosters' part in it is described first. On 22 April the battalion was deployed as follows: 'A' Company (Major P. A. Angier), was on Hill 148, better known as Castle Hill because of a concrete observation bunker erected on the forward slope by American engineers, above the hamlet of Choksong and covering Gloster Crossing; 'D' Company (Captain M. G. Harvey) was on Hill 182, some 1,500 yards to the south-east and east of the track; 'B' Company (Major E. D. Harding) was on Hill 144, some distance to the north-east and covering the battalion's right flank; 'C' Company (Major P. B. Mitchell) was in reserve on a narrow ridge overlooking the defile through which the track passed southwards; in the defile and a little to the north of the village of Solma-Ri were Battalion Headquarters, the 3-inch mortar platoon and the 4.2-inch mortars of 'C' Troop 170 Battery, the last commanded by Captain F. Wisbey; above Battalion Headquarters and west of the track was Hill 235, held by the assault pioneer platoon; and dispersed where it would have the most telling effect was the Vickers medium machine-gun platoon. Excluding the battalion's 'A', 'B' and 'F' Echelons and the Left Out of Battle personnel who were sick or absent on leave or courses, there were 657 Glosters in the line, plus 46 members of 'C' Troop, the 32-strong Observation Post parties of 70 Field Battery (45 Medium Regiment), and 38 attached personnel from other arms, including armourers, signallers, members of the Royal Army Medical Corps and cooks, a total of 773 officers and men.

Among the intangible factors which were to influence the Glosters' defence there were, of course, their training, discipline and high morale, the back-to-back tradition retained in the sub-conscious and, most important of all, the personality of Lieutenant-Colonel James Power Carne, their Commanding Officer. Carne had been commissioned into the Regiment in 1925 and seconded to the King's African Rifles from 1930 until 1936. He returned to become the 1st Battalion's adjutant in 1937 and remained in this post until 1940. He then served in Madagascar and Burma with the KAR, commanding in succession their 2nd and 26th Battalions. From 1947 until 1950 he had commanded the Glosters' 5th (Territorial) Battalion and had then fulfilled the ambition of most regimental officers by being given command of his Regiment's 1st

Battalion. He had already been awarded the Distinguished Service Order for an earlier action in the campaign. He was thus a capable and very experienced battalion commander and was noted as a first-class infantry-man. In temperament James Carne was a quiet man who solved his problems with the aid of his pipe, and his pleasures included fishing. He used words as his riflemen used their ammunition, sparingly and to count. Above all, he possessed the great gift of leadership and by his presence, example and a few words of praise or encouragement, could inspire men to perform well beyond what they believed to be their own limits. Casualties among his West Countrymen hurt him deeply, and although he strove to conceal the fact it was apparent to those who knew him best. On 11 April he had celebrated his 45th birthday.

As dusk fell the air reconnaissance flights reported that the larger bodies of Chinese were still some ten miles distant, but Carne intended taking no chances. It was obvious that the enemy had designs on Gloster Crossing, for the previous night a 14-strong patrol had attempted to wade across; the Glosters' three-man listening post had opened a rapid fire, killing three of them outright, a further four being dragged back to the far bank by their comrades. Now, Carne sent down an ambush platoon under Second-Lieutenant G. F. B. Temple to provide early warning if the need arose.

Temple did not have long to wait. At 2230 the Chinese attempted to cross the ford in strength. Flares went up and by their light the platoon opened a sustained fire which sent numerous bodies in quilted uniforms drifting downstream. Simultaneously the artillery and mortars began landing concentrations on the far bank, causing carnage among the packed ranks waiting to cross. At midnight Temple was still holding, but, having expended his ammunition, broke contact under cover of an artillery strike and made his way back.

Meanwhile, the enemy, belonging to the 187th Division, had found an alternative ford one-and-a-half miles down river. Two battalions crossed and converged on 'A' Company's position. A savage six-hour struggle ensued as 'A' Company, supported by artillery and mortar fire, fought to hold its ground against odds of six to one. Time and again the defenders' fire, assisted by bright moonlight and parachute flares, ripped great gaps in the ranks of the advancing Chinese, but still the latter came on, spurred by a frenzied but unquestionable courage. By first light, having captured the bunker and established themselves in some numbers on the forward slope, they were well placed to overrun '2' and '3' Platoons and secure the crest. Major Angier ordered '1' Platoon, led by Lieutenant Philip Curtis, to counter-attack and neutralize the bunker. As the platoon crossed the crest it was confronted by hundreds of Chinese soldiers standing up to strip off their camouflage greenery in preparation for the final assault. A rain of grenades was sent bouncing down the slope among them and then Curtis's men opened up with every weapon at their disposal. Completely taken aback by this unexpected development, the enemy survivors ran for cover. Curtis then led an assault on the bunker but was seriously wounded by a grenade. His men dragged him to safety, but he refused to wait for a medical orderly and returned to the attack single-handed. As he threw his grenade he was killed by a burst of machine-gun fire, but the grenade rolled into the bunker entrance, where it blew the muzzle off the enemy weapon and killed its crew. His courage and self-sacrifice was recognized by the posthumous award of the Victoria Cross.

For the moment the steam had gone out of the Chinese attack. Angier, however, who was now on the crest with his FOO, Lieutenant A. B. S. Hudson, directing artillery and mortar fire on to the enemy below, recognized that 'A' Company's casualties had been so severe that it would be unable to contain another attack. He decided, therefore, that the company would withdraw while it still possessed the capacity to do so, but while the survivors were rallying on the rear platoon both he and Hudson were killed by machine-gun fire. Company Sergeant-Major H. Gallagher assumed temporary command and completed the withdrawal. 'A' Company, reduced to one officer and 53 men, took up fresh positions on Hill 235, subsequently known as 'Gloster' Hill. The Chinese, badly mauled and pinned down by bursting high-explosive and machine-gun fire, did not attempt to interfere with the move.

'D' and 'B' Companies had also been heavily engaged during the night and although both had held their ground Carne decided to contract the battalion's perimeter. At one point 'D' Company's '10' Platoon had been overrun with the loss of all but twelve of its men and at first light, in compliance with Carne's orders, the company had withdrawn to 'Gloster' Hill. 'B' Company, less heavily pressed, had all but annihilated the enemy units that had attacked it, although it had observed hundreds of Chinese streaming southward past their right flank and across the slopes of Kamak San. Carne ordered the company to withdraw 1,500 yards to Hill 314. This was found to be held by small parties of the enemy but by 1030 these had been disposed of. The effect of Carne's redeployment, therefore, was to concentrate the battalion with two rifle companies on either side of the vital track.

At dawn the battalion's 'F' Echelon arrived with additional food and ammunition. Some 40 wounded were evacuated in the Oxfords or lifted out by helicopter, the majority of the less severely injured deciding to remain with their companies. The departure of 'F' Echelon marked the Glosters' last physical contact with the outside world, for during the morning the Chinese established a strong road-block on the track leading to the rear. Later in the day Brigadier Brodie spoke to Carne and told him that an attempt to reinforce the battalion would be made the following day, the 24th, but that if this failed it was vital that the Glosters hold on.

It was now apparent to Major-General Robert H. Soule, commanding the US 3rd Division, that not only had the weight of the Chinese attack fallen on 29 Brigade Group, but also that the enemy was directing an increasing proportion of this effort against the Glosters. Peng's plan had demanded a clean breakthrough before the UN could react quickly enough to deploy blocking forces in the path of his advance, and with every hour's delay the prospects of success were diminishing. By the evening of the 23rd the plan was 24 hours out of phase. Under intense pressure to get on, the commander of the 63rd Army, his 187th Division disorganized and shot to pieces, decided to use elements of the 188th and 189th Divisions to eliminate the stubborn battalion once and for all.

It was soon evident that the Chinese attack would be delivered east of the track. At dusk they were spotted forming up in the valleys in front of 'B' and 'C' Companies and subjected to shellfire. When, at 2230, the Chinese advanced with mortars and machine-guns firing in support, the troops detailed to attack 'B' Company seemed uncertain of their objective and at first began moving obliquely across its front, being decimated in the process. Having discovered their mistake, they then found that the only approaches lay along spurs which had already been registered as killing grounds in the defenders' fire plan. Rank after rank was shot down in succession and, despite the fact that the FOO, Captain A. M. L. Newcombe, was forced to pull in the fire of the supporting 25-pounders to within 50 yards of the forward trenches, at first light the company was still holding. During the night, however, the enemy had reached the ridge connecting the two company positions, that of 'C' Company lying on somewhat lower ground. During the early hours of 24 April a mass attack rolled down the slope swamping, in turn, '8' and '9' Platoons. At 0400 Company HQ and '7' Platoon beat off a second attack, but it was now apparent that Battalion HQ and the mortar positions in the defile below were in serious danger. Carne moved them on to 'Gloster' Hill, where the remnant of 'C' Company joined them.

Shortly after 0800 Carne also ordered 'B' Company, now completely isolated, to break out under cover of an artillery strike and sustained fire from the Vickers medium machine-guns located on 'Gloster' Hill. This was no easy task, since '4' Platoon was still in close contact with the enemy and the 1,500-yard route westward to 'Gloster' Hill was under enemy observation and fire. To assist its withdrawal the company broke out in small parties, but only Major Harding and twenty men managed to rejoin the battalion; two more escaped southwards and reached the brigade lines. During the breakout Private Essex, wounded in the head and both legs, was captured and brutally interrogated by the Chinese. Dissatisfied with his answers, they flung a grenade at him, inflicting a further head wound, then left him for dead. Essex estimated that Hill 314 had been attacked by between three and four thousand of the enemy and, while he was unable to guess how many of them had been killed, he observed that it took them an hour to carry off their wounded.

During the day, as Brodie had promised, a relief force attempted to break through to the Glosters. Consisting of the Filipino 10th Battalion Combat Team, a troop of M24 Chaffee light tanks and part of 'C' Squadron 8th Hussars, this reached the old 'F' Echelon area but on entering the defile beyond, the leading M24 was hit by bazooka fire and burst into flames, completely blocking the track. In the circumstances, with the Chinese holding the hills on either side of the defile in strength, the attempt was abandoned at 1630 some four miles short of the objective.

Talking to Carne on the radio, Brodie said that a further attempt would be mounted next day, using a stronger force. In the meantime, he continued, the enemy, having been balked by the Glosters, was now bringing tremendous pressure on the rest of the brigade in hope of securing the secondary track. Carne, speaking calmly as though on a peacetime exercise, described the situation on 'Gloster' Hill. He had less than 400 men available, including numerous wounded; there was just sufficient ammunition for ten hours' fighting; there was a shortage of Brens, many of which had been lost during the two previous nights' fighting; the radio batteries, which sustained the lifeline to 45 Field Regiment's guns, would last between ten and fifteen hours if used sparingly; and, while there was a little food to be distributed, water was in desperately short supply, what there was being reserved for the wounded. There was, however, some encouraging news for Carne; ground attack aircraft, until now kept busy elsewhere, would become available for his immediate support next morning.

Meanwhile, Major Digby Grist, the Glosters' Second-in-Command and commander of 'F' Echelon, was aware of the situation on the hill. Unable to reach the battalion by road, he organized a supply drop using fifteen Sentinel light aircraft. Much of the drop fell beyond reach, but some small-arms ammunition and 3-inch mortar bombs were retrieved. Captain Wisbey's 'C' Troop, having fired the last of their 4.2-inch bombs, buried their barrels and baseplates and then turned to as an infantry platoon, while Wisbey assisted in directing the fire of 45 Field Regiment.

At dusk Carne pulled in his perimeter to the summit of the hill, partly to confuse the Chinese as to the companies' locations and partly to get them to expend their supporting fire on empty space. The feature was relatively easy to defend as its southern and western approaches were precipitous and its northern slopes steep. The best approaches lay along spurs to the north-west and south-east, which Carne was confident could be held. Few entrenching tools remained, so instead of digging in the majority of the men excavated scrapes with their bayonets and fronted these with low parapets made from rocks. 'A' Company, now commanded by Captain A. N. Wilson, held the north-western end of the feature; 'B' and 'C' Companies, combined under Major Harding, held the south-east ridge; 'D' Company, under Captain Harvey, was positioned on a smaller spur overlooking the defile; Support Company, under Major P. W. Weller with 'C' Troop under command, held the ridge-line between 'A' and 'B/C' Companies; and in the centre of the position was Battalion HQ and the Regimental Aid Post, and latter containing numerous stretcher cases.

At 2200, bugles blowing and whistles shrilling, the Chinese attacked up the north-western spur. They had, apparently, learned nothing from the experience of the previous two nights and their human-waves were shot flat by 'A' and 'B/C' Companies. The battle raged all night and twice Carne, armed with a rifle and grenades, personally led counter-attacks which routed parties of the enemy who had penetrated the defences. By first light the Chinese had established themselves in strength on the upper slopes. All round the position their bugles were braying and Captain Anthony Farrar-Hockley, Carne's Adjutant, imagining that he detected an irritatingly triumphant note, suggested that the Glosters' buglers should reply. Only Drummer Eagles' bugle remained, but with this the Drum Major, Staff-Sergeant P. E. Buss, disdaining the cover of his trench, sent the notes of the *Long Reveille*, and many other calls, echoing round the Korean hills. Later, rather than permit the Chinese to use it, Eagles blasted the bugle apart with a grenade.

Seven times during the next hour the Chinese, confident of victory, surged forward to capture the crest, and seven times the Glosters sent them reeling back down the slopes in bloody ruin. At 0605 Brodie gave the battalion permission to break out, but Carne replied that his men were too heavily engaged and requested air support. At 0755 the Glosters reported that only 30 minutes' life remained in their radio batteries; Brodie, sensing the end, wrote beneath this entry in the brigade signals log: '*No-one but the Glosters could have done it.*' By 0830 the batteries had died. The Glosters had never felt alone while the guns were firing in their support, but now the vital controlling link had gone. In the event, 45 Field Regiment could not have maintained its fire for much longer, partly because its gun positions were being attacked for the second time during the battle, and partly becaue it was having to limber up and conform to a limited UN withdrawal. Then, at the critical moment, the howl of jet engines was heard and a squadron of Lockheed F-80 Shooting Star fighters streaked at low level along the Imjin valley, their pilots searching for the enemy below. Spotting the smoke marker rising from the summit of 'Gloster' Hill, they delivered strikes in succession against its forward slopes, napalm drop-tanks curving through the air to burst in huge fireballs among the packed ranks of the Chinese concealed in the scrub. Six more passes they made across the burning hillside, hammering the enemy with rocket and machine-gun fire. Then a second F-80 squadron subjected the area between the hill and the river to similar heavy strafing, clearly indicating the presence of reinforcements which the enemy was bringing forward to deliver the *coup de grâce*. In effect, the remnant of the Chinese force detailed to capture 'Gloster' Hill had been wiped out.

A period of comparative peace descended on the smoking hill, disturbed only by sporadic machine-gun fire from the surrounding features. There was no more that could be done and at 1000 Carne assembled his company commanders for the last time, giving orders for them to lead their men independently back to the new UN line, taking a south-westerly direction towards the rearguard of 1st ROK Division. All weapons and equipment that could not be carried were to be destroyed. The hardest decision of all was to leave the wounded, but there was no alternative; the Medical Officer, Captain R. P. Hickey, elected to remain with them, as did his orderlies and Chaplain Davies. 'Take your own route,' said Carne as his officers prepared to leave. 'And may God see us through.'

With a heavy heart Captain Harvey watched the battalion disperse and then returned to his own company. Altogether his group contained three officers and 81 men of 'D' Company, joined by two officers and ten men from Support Company, and was the largest remaining on the hill. He decided that rather than follow the rest in a southerly direction he would strike north through the area devastated by the air strike, then swing west for a mile or two before turning south towards the South Korean positions. Everyone was warned that, exhausted as they were, they must travel fast and that there could be no stopping for any reason. At 1035 the group set off. For the first three miles there was no contact with the enemy and a Mosquito aircraft circled above, pointing the way forward. When they turned south a few Chinese were encountered but were dealt with. On entering a narrow valley, however, they came under machine-gun fire from the hills on either side and, sustaining casualties as they went, were forced to crawl along the bed of a stream. Emerging from the defile, they observed some Pershing tanks just north of the villaage of Taech'on, some 500 yards distant. These, belonging to the US 73rd Heavy Tank Battalion, opened fire on them in the belief that they were Chinese, but desisted when they were buzzed by the Mosquito and Harvey stood up to wave his cap. A final dash brought the party to the tanks, which then lifted them to safety under fire.

Harvey's party now numbered five officers and 41 men, of whom several were wounded. Of the rest of the battalion, very few got through, Carne being among the last to be captured. Surprisingly, only 58 Glosters had been killed in the three-day battle, although a further 30 would die in captivity. A total of 63 men escaped from the battle area and with these, plus the personnel of 'A', 'B' and 'F' Echelons and the Left Out of Battle party, Major Grist set about reconstructing the battalion at Yongdong-Po, a few miles from Seoul. By the evening of 26 April its strength had reached 203 officers and men and the Glosters, while in urgent need of reinforcement drafts, were back in business.

The battle fought by the rest of the brigade group was equally dramatic, and at times reached equal levels of ferocity. It had been intended to meet the anticipated Chinese offensive from a series of strong features designated the Kansas Line, between which and the Imjin the enemy's attack would be broken up by concentrated artillery fire and sweeps with armour. However, as mentioned previously, when the offensive opened during the evening of 22 April, it achieved a considerable measure of surprise and, instead of having withdrawn to their Kansas Line positions, Brodie's forward battalions were still occupying the foothills overlooking the river itself.

At 2240 that evening the Belgians' 'C' Company engaged a party of the enemy attempting to infiltrate the gap between them and the river, coming under increasingly heavy attack as the night progressed. The Royal Ulster Rifles' Battle Patrol was sent forward in Oxfords to secure the Belgians' bridges at Ulster Crossing, but the Chinese were there first and at 0200 the patrol was ambushed, sustaining serious casualties. Downstream, the Fusiliers' 'X' Company, commanded by Major R. M. Pratt, was holding a hill on the battalion's left flank and at 2030 a listening post reported that the enemy were crossing the ford to their front. Defensive fire was brought down on the crossing and maintained throughout the night. None the less, despite severe losses, by 2200 the Chinese were in position to mount probing attacks and at about midnight launched a major assault on the feature. This resulted in a fierce struggle at close quarters in which '4' Platoon was forced to pull back. By 0245 the situation had become critical, but as the position was simply an outpost Lieutenant-Colonel Foster gave Pratt permission to withdraw at his discretion. This operation was executed successfully, the company bringing out all its wounded, covered by '4' Platoon. It is said that the last man off the hill, enraged by the prospect of losing his traditional St George's Day turkey dinner, downed his opponent in a fist fight.

At about 0300 the Chinese achieved their major success of the night. By-passing 'Y' Company, which was also holding an outpost hill fronting the river, they advanced stealthily from Ulster Crossing against Hill 257, some 1,000 yards to the rear, held by Major H. J. Winn's 'Z' Company, and launched a sudden attack which drove '11' Platoon from twin peaks which not only overlooked Company HQ, but also Battalion HQ in the valley 700 feet below. The assault force was quickly reinforced and by first light on 23 April the hill was in enemy hands.

Foster was now faced with the simultaneous problems of extracting his isolated 'Y' Company and recovering Hill 257. The first was solved quickly with tank support from 'C' Squadron 8th Hussars, but the second was a much tougher nut to crack. 'Z' Company, reinforced with '1' Platoon of 'W' Company, mounted a daylight counter-attack which gained a footing on the summit but was forced back after a furious exchange of grenades. Later in the day Major General Soule made available the US 1/7th Regimental Combat Team, a black unit, which passed through the Fusiliers and attacked Hill 257 with the further object of re-opening communications with the embattled Belgians. The Americans advanced steadily, but after an hour they were pinned down by heavy mortar and machine-gun fire and were withdrawn at dusk. Last light found the Fusiliers deployed with 'Y' and 'W' Companies on the high ground to the west of the valley, and 'X' and 'Z' Companies on lower features within the valley near Battalion HQ. Support Company, at least, managed to salvage something of its celebration dinner, which was eaten cold; in the mortar platoon Captain R. E. Blenkinsop continued to carve birds while his own mortars, and those of 'A' Troop 170 Battery, were in action all around him.

At 0300 that morning, the Royal Ulster Rifles had been ordered forward by Brigadier Brodie. During the day 'A', 'C' and 'D' Companies established themselves on Hill 398 to the east of the valley, a feature crowned by the ruins of a castle from which spurs projected to the northwest, north and east. For the moment, contact with the enemy was light and, with minor adjustments, this position was held for the next two days. At Brodie's personal direction 'B' Company, commanded by Captain Richard Miller, was positioned at Hwangbang-Ni, where the track winding along the valley crossed a saddle. Major Rickcord set up his command post beside that of Lieutenant-Colonel Foster within a joint perimeter defence.

At one point during the day the enemy's inflitration parties had reached positions from which the gun lines of 45 Field Regiment and a nearby American 155m howitzer battery were brought under small-arms fire. Some of the 25-pounders switched to open-sights firing, but an even more impressive reply was made by 11 Light Anti-Aircraft Battery, which had earned its Honour Title of 'Sphinx' during the same campaign in which the Glosters won their back-badge. So complete was the UN command of the air that the battery, being under-employed, was given the task of providing local defence for 45 Field Regiment. Now, delighted to have some customers at last, it treated the Chinese to a rain of 40mm shells, each of which exploded with the effect of a mortar round. Finally, a large party of gunners snatched up their rifles and chased the enemy back into the hills. One Chinese soldier, found sitting quietly near 45 Regiment's command post, willingly identified himself as a member of 63rd Army's 187th Division. The affair gave grounds for satisfaction, but it was felt that the guns were too exposed and they were pulled back to a more secure area.

In general, by the afternoon of 23 April enemy pressure had slackened, save against Lieutenant-Colonel Crahay's Belgians and 'B' Troop 170 Battery, holding Hill 194 across the Imjin. Their entire perimeter was under such sustained attack that 45 Field Regiment's FOO, Lieutenant

Walsh, called in defensive fire so close that he was wounded by one of his own shell splinters. Nevertheless, their flanks rested securely on the river and they were holding their own. After dusk, Soule mounted a counter-attack on the Upper Imjin with the US 65th Regimental Combat Team, supported by tanks. This cleared the Belgians' right, enabling them to withdraw across a bridge into the American lines, bringing with them all their vehicles and equipment. They then drove down the MSR to re-enter 29 Brigade Group's sector from the east and were assigned a position at the southern exit of the Solma-Ri defile.

This easing of pressure was, however, only temporary, and by the early hours of 24 April the enemy's second echelon was beginning to enter the battle. At 0215 the Rifles' 'A' Company, commanded by Major Sir Christopher Nixon, was attacked in strength. The attack was beaten off but was repeated just before dawn, with similar results. Rickcord, worried that the enemy might work round the position to the east, asked Brodie to release 'B' Company from its blocking position on the saddle at Hwangbang-Ni, but his request was declined, wisely as it transpired. At 1025 an air strike was put in against the Chinese forming up on the slopes below 'A' Company, but this did not prevent them launching a further attack fifteen minutes later. Nixon calculated that, in all, the enemy made sixteen attempts to capture Hill 398, all of which were repulsed. A curious feature of the fighting was that the Chinese made little attempt to outflank 'A' Company, but instead continued to batter themselves against the position in a series of frontal assaults. Those of the enemy who attempted to snipe from the cover of rocks found these to be a very insecure refuge when they were blown apart by the company's bazooka.

Across the valley 'Y' Company had been attacked at 0330 and, having sustained four officer casualties, was forced from its positions, although a further advance against 'W' Company was checked. By dawn on the 24th it was known that the Glosters were surrounded and that large numbers of the enemy were moving south across the slopes of Kamak-San, which were well covered with trees, sharp ridges and steep valleys, and therefore entirely suited to their tactics of infiltration. To safeguard his left rear Foster dispatched 'Z' Company to a position some 800 yards to the south of 'W' Company, consisting of a rocky knife-edge with peaks at each end. It was now apparent that the Chinese intended isolating the entire brigade with a thrust across its rear towards the MSR. Throughout the day repeated air strikes blasted Kamak-San, but neither these, nor the gunfire of 'C' Squadron's Centurions directed against parties which showed themselves, nor a fighting patrol dispatched from the saddle into the hills by 'B' Company, could halt the flow, so that by evening the track leding to the rear was under sporadic fire.

'Z' Company came under attack at 2010. Each of its platoons was attacked in turn and shortly after 0100 the enemy obtained a foothold on the peak held by Lieutenant Sheppard's '10' Platoon. Major Winn ordered Sheppard to counter-attack, which he did successfully, and from this point onwards the Chinese redoubled their efforts. As his casualties began to mount Winn requested assistance as soon as possible. Foster ordered 'Y' Company, under fresh officers, to break through from the east while a platoon of 'W' Company closed in along the ridge from the north. 'Y' Company, still smarting from the previous night, were not to be denied and, after a brief action, chased off the Chinese from their side of the hill and broke through to 'Z'. The latter's casualties included five dead and 27 stretcher cases; Winn had himself been wounded three times, but he declined assistance and walked down the hill unaided when the relief had been completed.

Ominously, the saddle position, some miles to the rear, was also attacked during the night, coming under heavy mortar and machine-gun fire. Fortunately, in addition to 'B' Company, Miller had available 'A' Troop 170 Battery, a section of 3-inch mortars and a section of medium machine-guns, and, although casualties were sustained, the fire of these prevented the enemy from developing an assault.

On Hill 398, 'A' Company was unsuccessfully attacked from 0130 until 0300, when the weight of the assault was shifted to 'D' Company. Here the Chinese effected a small penetration but were thrown out at first light, dragging away most of their casualties but leaving behind nine dead, three badly wounded and a prisoner. Nevertheless, by dawn on the 25th the brigade was in serious danger of being encircled. However, Lieutenant-General Milburn, commanding I Corps, was aware of the danger and at 0600 Brodie received instructions to withdraw twelve miles to Tokchon on the MSR. This was no easy order to execute while all three infantry battalions were still in contact with a courageous, aggresive and extremely determined enemy who believed that victory lay within his grasp, and it was during this period that the brigade sustained its heaviest casualties.

It was decided that the Fusiliers and the Rifles would withdraw along the track and then move eastwards into a valley leading to the MSR, where they would pass through a blocking position established by the 65th Regimental Combat Team; simultaneously, Crahay's Belgians would protect the left flank against the Chinese who were beginning to debouch from the area of the Solma-Ri defile. The rearguard would be provided by 'C' Squadron 8th Hussars, commanded by Major Henry Huth, accompanied in carriers by the Sappers of 55 Squadron Royal Engineers, who would fight as infantry. In passing it is probably fair to say that, while the Hussars had charged with the Light Brigade and served throughout the Desert War and on in to north-west Europe, giving and receiving hard knocks the while, never in their long history had they been set a more difficult task, nor one on which depended so many lives.

The withdrawal of the Fusiliers and the Rifles was to be co-ordinated by Lieutenant-Colonel Foster, to whom Huth made available his '1', '3' and '4' Troops, plus two tanks of RHQ Troop, while '2' Troop was sent to support the Belgians and SHQ Troop plus an FOO Cromwell were retained in reserve. Because of a ground mist, which undoubtedly aided the Chinese, the tanks were somewhat later breaking their laager south of the saddle than they had intended. Moving through Miller's lines, '1' Troop (Lieutenant P. Boyall) took up position covering a re-entrant in the hills to the west of the track, while '3' Troop (Lieutenant M. Radford) and '4' Troop (Lieutenant J. Hurst) continued up the road to cover a similar re-entrant to the north. Suddenly, '3' Troop came under heavy and accurate mortar fire which forced the tank commanders to slam their hatches. Closed down, a tank is almost blind, and although the Centurion was somewhat better in this respect than earlier designs, vision was further restricted by the mist and two of '3' Troop's tanks ran off the track into paddy-fields. One, having shed both tracks, had to be destroyed by gunfire, but the other was recovered about noon. In the meantime, the whole area had been infiltrated by about 200 Chinese who displayed not the slightest fear of the tanks and swarmed all over them, attempting to attach shaped-charges and pry open the hatches. The Centurions responded by hosing each other down with their Besa co-axial machine guns. Eventually, the attack broke and the enemy ran for cover, a house which provided a temporary refuge for one group being blown apart with two rounds of 20-pounder high-explosive.

As the mist cleared the tanks took up their covering positions, where they remained for the next four-and-a-half hours. By 1000 they were able to inform Foster that the track was clear, although the danger of sniper fire still existed. The Fusiliers' wounded were evacuated in carriers and soft-skinned ambulances, the latter being shot at all the way despite their clear markings, and then 'X' and 'Z' Companies marched off over the saddle. By 1100 'W' and 'Y' Companies had come down from their positions on the western slopes, leaving pickets to cover their withdrawal. As the Rifles, who had succeeded in breaking contact, began descending the eastern slopes, Foster called in the pickets and then made his way through 'B' Company's position, pausing to confer briefly with Miller.

Thus far, the Ulstermen had sustained comparatively few casualties. They reached the track at 1225 and began marching towards the saddle with 'C' Company leading. After half a mile had been covered, the Chinese, seeing their prey slipping from their grasp, reacted violently. Intense mortar and machine-gun fire from the western slopes began sweeping the track, which was all but devoid of cover. The remaining section of 3-inch mortars went into action at once, but was unable to suppress the fire. Men began to go down and progress was reduced to a series of small rushes. Most of 'C' Company managed to reach the saddle, which was itself under fire. At this moment the Chinese, estimated to number 2,000, swarmed off the western hills to cut the track south of the saddle. Major Rickcord decided that for the Rifles to continue further would be to invite a massacre, and the column swung east up the slopes of Mau San, picking up the twenty or so remaining men of 'B' Company as it went, then marched south along the ridge towards the lateral valley.

The enemy attack also caught the Fusiliers' rearguard, some members of which managed to fight their way through while others adopted the same route as the Rifles. Foster was pinned down in ditch with a fusilier and a lance-bombardier, a few yards from an abandoned jeep. The three ran to the vehicle and drove for half a mile through a hail of fire until they reached a ford in which the engine stalled. Here, Foster was killed outright by a burst of machine-gun fire; the fusilier was also hit but was helped to safety by the uninjured lance-bombardier. Lieutenant-Colonel Foster had served in the Royal Northumberland Fusiliers for 25 years, and his father for 30 years before that.

When it was clear that the Rifles were taking an alternative route, it was decided to abandon the saddle, now held by the tanks, part of 'C' Company and the sappers of 55 Squadron. The only course was to run the one-and-a-half mile gauntlet to the south and the infantry, a number of whom were wounded, piled aboard the tanks. What followed was the most horrific episode of the entire battle. Guns blazing, the Centurions forged along the rough track, their hard suspensions producing a bucking effect which threw some of their passengers to the ground. The whole area was seething with Chinese behind every bank, lining every ditch and inside every house, and they fired continuously at the unprotected infantry riding on the engine decks, some men being hit time and again. They also launched frenzied attacks against the tanks themselves, some of them being crushed under the tracks while others were cut down in swathes, but seemingly oblivious of their terrible losses. One tank of '3' Troop fell victim to a hollow-charge, and another in '4' Troop, swerving to avoid a party of tank-hunters, careered down a bank and overturned, hurling its infantry into a paddy-field. Sergeant Cadman, commanding an RHQ Troop tank, was aware of an enemy soldier hammering on his cupola hatch and swept him off by driving through a house. Beyond this, he ran over a machine-gun detachment beside the road. He was then confronted by an infantry company which rose from the bed of a stream to fire at him, but blew them apart with his last few rounds of high-explosive. Then, suddenly, they were through into the old Brigade Headquarters area, where Huth and his SHQ tanks were waiting for them. The Centurions presented a horrible sight, their decks piled with dead, dying and injured, their sides running with blood and their tracks smeared with grisly debris. Huth immediately ordered them to pass through to the MSR and obtain help for the survivors while he continued the battle with the rest of the squadron.

Elsewhere during the day the gunlines of 45 Field Regiment and '11' Battery had again come under fire, although this had not hindered their withdrawal. The Belgians, reinforced by an American infantry company, were retreating steadily but in good order, covered by '2' Troop's Centurions. Unfortunately, one of the tanks became stuck in low reverse gear, which meant that it could only move backwards at less than walking pace. Over the radio, Huth gave permission for it to be destroyed but Lieutenant-Colonel Crahay, who wished to retain its firepower as long as possible, would not permit this. This slowed the rate of retreat, although in due course the Belgians and '2' Troop reached Huth's position and the latter assumed direct control of the armour.

With the Chinese pressing hard, an attempt was made to speed up the withdrawal by towing the cripple with Lieutenant Paul's tank. As the tow chain was being shackled under fire a round detonated a phosphorus grenade in the dischargers mounted on Paul's turret, which was traversed to the side, and the burning fluid dripped through the engine louvres, starting a major conflagration. After the crews had baled out, Huth fired an armour-piercing round into both tanks, destroying them. Then, he treated the advancing enemy to three minutes' sustained Besa fire, traversing steadily across their ranks, and withdrew 100 yards where he was joined by Lieutenant J. Lidsey in an RHQ tank. Together the two acted as rearguard, imposing regular checks so that the infantry could put some distance between themselves and the enemy.

At this point the Rifles reached the escarpment overlooking the lateral valley. Some of the Chinese had pursued them up the slopes of Mau San, but had been kept at a respectful distance. Now, parched and utterly weary, the men looked out over the scene below: 'Across the valley and now nearing the MSR was a long column of infantry – Fusiliers, Belgians, a company of Americans, and a few Riflemen. In the valley floor two Centurion tanks stood in the open, their guns pointed westwards; and, in front of them, the paddy-fields swarmed with Chinese moving east in open order and rapidly closing on the tanks.' Seldom has a margin of safety been so clearly visible. Under mortar and machine-gun fire from the Chinese on Mau San, the Riflemen scrambled down the escarpment and across the intervening paddy-fields to join the column, those at the rear clambering aboard the tanks. The retreat continued as before, but the worst was now over. Two more tanks arrived to strengthen the rearguard and the enemy pressure eased. As the column reached the MSR the Centurions fired the last shots of the battle, then, having satisfied themselves that the Chinese were no longer pursuing, they withdrew. But for Huth and his handful of Hussars in their shot-battered, blood-streaked Centurions, the probability is that comparatively few infantrymen would have reached safety that afternoon.

At the MSR the column turned south through a blocking position established by the 65th Regimental Combat Team and marched the remaining four miles to Tokchon. Here the brigade occupied temporary positions until relieved at 2330 by the 15th Regimental Combat Team, a reserve formation. It then marched a further six miles towards Uijongbu before being met by trucks which carried it to Yongdongpo, on the south bank of the Han. After a breakfast of bacon and eggs produced by the Quartermasters and their staffs the men slept the sleep of utter exhaustion.

During the battle 29 Brigade Group sustained more than 1,000 casualties. Of these, the greater part were Glosters, but the Royal Ulster Rifles also suffered severely, losing ten officers and 176 men, killed, wounded or missing, the majority during the last day's fighting. 45 Field Regiment recorded having fired more than 22,000 shells in 80 hours, while '170' Battery, which was to be awarded the Honour Title of Imjin, expended 12,000 rounds during the same period. None knew better than Lieutenant-General Milburn the crucial role the brigade had performed on US I Corps' sector, and he sent his official thanks to Brigadier Brode:

'I want to commend you and your officers and men for your gallantry in action while defending the Imjin River line against greatly superior enemy forces.

Subjected to exceedingly heavy pressure you did not falter and met his attacks with a fighting will and courage beyond his, as attested by the hundreds of enemy dead in the closest proximity of your position. As you disengaged you fought and our common enemy has good cause to remember the 29th Brigade as a formidable opponent . . .

We are all proud of you.'

On 28 April the brigade, in fresh uniforms, its equipment losses made good and with reinforcement drafts filling some of the gaps in its ranks, moved into the line again on the quiet sector of the Kimpo Peninsula; only the Glosters, still too few in numbers for the moment, remained in reserve.

Yet, while Brodie's command was still a fighting formation, the same could not be said of its opponents in the recent battle, the crack Chinese 63rd Army. No accurate figures exist for its losses, but most estimates suggest that it sustained about 11,000 casualties, approximately 40 per cent of its combat strength. On 25 April, the day it came closest to encircling 29 Brigade Group, orders were issued for its withdrawal. It was sent back to China and played no further part in the war. A few of Peng's troops advanced to within five miles of Seoul, but they were quickly dealt with; in total, the April offensive cost the Chinese Red Army some 70,000 casualties. Stubbornly, Peng refused to accept defeat and on 15 May he launched a fresh offensive on the eastern sector of the front. This also failed disastrously and when Van Fleet mounted a counter-offensive along the entire line it was soon apparent that the Communists had had enough, for whereas formerly it was rare for individual Chinese soldiers to surrender voluntarily, now the survivors of platoons, companies and even battalions were coming in willingly. It was now obvious, even to Peng, that the tactics of the horde could not prevail against scientificaly applied firepower and professionalism. In June the Soviet delegate to the

United Nations proposed a ceasefire and the following month representatives of both sides met at the village of Kaesong.

By the end of May 29 Brigade Group was again occupying positions overlooking the Imjin. During the month three Glosters had returned unexpectedly from behind enemy lines. Private Lionel Essex, wounded, had been looked after by Korean villagers, at terrible risk to themselves, and was found by a Greek patrol during the UN advance. Privates Fox and Graham had been captured during the breakout from 'Gloster' Hill. Together with Captain Farrar-Hockley, the Adjutant, they had escaped from the hut in which they were being held. Some days later Farrar-Hockley was recaptured in a Buddhist monastery in which they were hiding, but managed to convince his captors he was alone. The following day Fox and Graham left the monastery and made good progress towards the south, only to be picked up by a North Korean unit during the afternoon.

The attitude of the North Koreans was very different from that of the Chinese. The prisoners were fed and allowed to rest for three days. They were then given a shave and brought before a colonel who, in the course of his interrogation, told them that their captured comrades, about 500 in number, had been marched north to Pyongyang, and that he intended releasing them as it was too much trouble for him to do likewise. They were given safe conduct passes and escorted towards the UN lines, which they reached on 12 May.

The rest of the prisoners faced two years of brutal captivity in which cruel indifference to wounds and disease was combined with hard physical labour, beatings and incessant mental pressure to provide 'confessions' and other propaganda material for the Communist cause. Many did not survive and the health of others was permanently broken. During the long months of captivity, Carne drew additional strength from his faith, carving and polishing a small stone cross which he later presented to Gloucester Cathedral.

The prisoners returned home in 1953, Carne to receive the Victoria Cross and the American Distinguished Service Cross, the Freedom of Gloucester and, in 1954, the Freedom of Falmouth, his birthplace. The media would gladly have made a celebrity of him, but that was not the wish of this quiet, courageous man.

Conclusion

The complex origins of the various actions described in the previous chapters defy simple analysis, but it is possible to assess the motivation of those involved and summarize their effect. In every case it will have been noted that first-rate leadership, especially at the junior levels, was a critical factor.

At Waterloo the veteran infantry of the Old Guard recognized instinctively that their best chance of survival lay in preserving their discipline, but clearly their *esprit de crops* was also a major factor. 'In victory,' goes a saying of the French Army, 'we are more than men; in defeat, we are less than women.' These men, the admired élite of the élite, who had spent their lives serving Napoleon and acted as the instruments of history on battlefields across Europe, had just witnessed the sudden, total and inexplicable defeat of their comrades in the Middle Guard by weary British infantry whom logic said were on the verge of collapse. The effect on the rest of the French Army, equally weary, was disastrous. It had been deliberately deceived regarding the Prussians' closing in on its right flank, and the repulse of the Middle Guard signalled the end of its attempts to defeat Wellington's Anglo-Dutch troops, in which so many lives had been lost. Beyond the control of its officers, it broke and fled in blind panic. It was a spectacle which the Grenadiers and Chasseurs of the Old Guard could only regard with contempt, as was evidenced by the short shrift they gave to those of the fugitives who tried to seek refuge in their squares. Moreover, having the personal safety of the Emperor in their charge, they would rather have died than fail in their duty. Some of their battalions were overrun, but others escorted Napoleon from the stricken field in good order. Decisive as was the defeat, the Old Guard preserved its honour, and this was something at least in which its countrymen could take comfort.

Those who defended the Alamo, on the other hand, were men of a very different stamp. They were volunteers, lacking formal military discipline, and their traditions were those of adventure on an open frontier rather than those of the battlefield. They hold a unique place in these annals, since they fought and died for their ideals. Ably led by Colonel William Travis, they fulfilled his objectives of buying time in which the army of the young Republic of Texas could be properly organized and trained, and of inflicting crippling casualties on their enemy.

The Foreign Legionnaires who formed Captain Jean Danjou's Third Campany at Camerone were professional soldiers, but they were regarded by the general public and the rest of the French Army alike as mercenary ruffians who were expendable in the dirtiest and most dangerous tasks. Such an attitude, amounting almost to ostracism, produced a self-contained *esprit de corps* in which the Legion was regarded as a man's country, home and family. This closeness and fellow-feeling engendered in the ranks, extending beyond simple comradeship, is also evident in today's highly trained and selectively recruited élite forces and, now as then, their members fight as much for each other as for any other reason. At Camerone, therefore, the men fought primarily for the Third Company and, when most of their comrades were killed or wounded, the handful of survivors charged with the bayonet in a spirit of suicidal vengeance. In the short term, the fight at Camerone saved the French siege train; in the long term, it led to the recognition that the Legion was one of the most formidable fighting forces in the world. Nor, by any means, was this the last occasion on which Legion units fought to the bitter end.

Whatever may have been the faults of Lieutenant-Colonel George Armstrong Custer, commanding the US 7th Cavalry, he succeeded in giving his regiment a distrinctive style and a pride in itself. There may indeed have been tensions among the officers, and the ranks may well have contained a high proportion of young recruits, but when the regiment was froced to fight a merciless battle for survival at the Little Big Horn it was not found wanting, as its Indian opponents testified. The very fact that Custer and five companies had been massacred and severe casualties had been sustained by the rest of the regiment, and this in the United States' Centenniel Year, provoked such a public outcry that within a comparatively short period the army's response had ended the long succession of Indian wars.

Regimental spirit is more highly developed in the British Army than in any other. Detractors can claim, with some justice, that this creates a narrow, tribal outlook, but the fact remains that it can be a source of immense strength, especially in the sort of fighting under discussion. When the ammunition supply of the 24th Regiment failed at Isandhlwana the Colours were sent to the rear but the men remained in their ranks, fighting with bayonet and butt until they were overwhelmed by the tidal-wave of the Zulu army; few can have had any illusions about their fate, and the Zulus took no prisoners. That night, at the isolated post of Rorke's Drift, a company of the regiment, under the inspired leadership of two elderly subalterns, beat off repeated attacks by the Zulu force many times their number. To some extent, the shock of the defeat at Isandhlwana was balanced by the astonishing defence of Rorke's Drift, but it taught the sharp lesson that liberties could not be taken with so formidable a warrior people as the Zulus. In fact, the casualties inflicted at Isandhlwana and Rorke's Drift tore the heart out of the Zulu nation so that while its impis continued to fight with all their old ferocity, they no longer believed that the war could be won.

It is the ancient and ingrained tradition of artillerymen in first class armies that they will fight their guns as long as it is physically possible for them to do so. This was demonstrated at Néry in 1914, where the stubborn fight put up by a single gun was a major factor in the enemy's defeat, which in itself contained far wider implications for his strategic plan. Three years later it was a single German artilleryman, whose identity has never been firmly established, who drew the sting from the great British tank attack at Cambrai. The exemplary stand made by the 5th Battery at Bois des Buttes was but one of many which blunted the great German offensives of 1918. The Germans had been promised that these would result in the decisive defeat of the Allies and when, despite all their efforts and sacrifice, they did not, their morale was affected to the point at which they no longer believed that victory was possible.

Among the armed services of the United States, the Marine Corps has always prided itself in being in a class of its own. The small Marine garrison which defended Wake Atoll, conscious of its traditions, inflicted an astounding toll of sunken warships, aircraft destroyed and heavy casualties on the Japanese before it was finally overrun, at the second attempt. In so doing, it did much to restore American self-confidence and destroyed the myth of Japanese invincibility.

The defence of Outpost 'Snipe' by 2nd Battalion The Rifle Brigade and 239 Anti-Tank Battery also provides a fine example of professionalism at work. Isolated and under constant attack. 'Snipe' was a painful thorn in the side of the Axis, inflicting a heavy tank loss which could not be made good and was therefore made a major contribution to Rommel's defeat at El Alamein. Likewise, the remarkable stand made by 5th Battalion The Hampshire Regiment and 155 Field Battery at the advance post of Sidi Nsir, Tunisia, not only wrote down the enemy's strength but also bought time in which the defences of Hunt's Gap could be consolidated, thereby defeating a potentially dangerous German counteroffensive.

During the terrible struggle for Tarawa the Japanese fought and died in a spirit of religious dedication to the Emperor. Yet, while they inflicted heavy losses on the 2nd Marine Division, their self-sacrifice had no effect whatever on the conduct of the Pacific campaign. In truth, the Japanese were somewhat the prisoners of their own philosophy, for since death in the Emperor's service was already accepted as the norm, the end of the Tarawa garrison could hardly be acclaimed as being above and beyond the call of duty.

To defend the Admin Box Brigadier G. C. Evans had only one understrength but efficient infantry battalion, plus the better part of an armoured regiment which could only offer limited support at night. The rest of his garrison were largely administrative troops who were somewhat intimidated by the reputation of the Japanese as jungle fighters. In these circumstances Evans used fear as a powerful motivation by pointing out that the only alternative to determined resistance was capture with a very limited chance of survival. With each success confidence increased until the entire garrison was fighting like veterans, while the massacre of the patients and staff at the Main Dressing Station provoked a fierce desire for revenge. The Admin Box proved to be the rock upon which the Japanese '*Ha-Go*' offensive battered itself to destruction and provided British and Indian troops with their first clear-cut victory in Burma.

Paratroopers naturally regard themselves as an élite. Those who defended the northern end of Arnhem bridge, of whom the 2nd Battalion The Parachute Regiment formed the major part, had already proved their toughness and battlecraft in Tunisia and Italy, and they regarded themselves as a match for anyone; it was a point the Waffen SS Panzergrenadiers to whom they were opposed, themselves Germany's élite, were compelled to concede. Their fight won them great honour, and while it failed to influence the outcome of the battle at Arnhem, it contributed to the spectacular Allied success at Nijmegen.

The Battle of the Imjin, in which 29 British Brigade Group fought as part of the US I Corps, was remarkable for combining many of the motivations previously mentioned, including tradition, regimental spirit, professionalism, discipline and self-sacrifice. It was thanks to 29 Brigade's stand that I Corps avoided encirclement and the Communist drive on Seoul was halted. Shortly afterwards, recognizing the futility of further offensives, the Communists indicated their willingness to negotiate a settlement.

Since the Korean War there have been few periods when armed conflicts have not been raging somewhere in the world, and these too have produced their crop of desperate stands, as the following examples show.

In Vietnam the Communist forces regularly attacked isolated posts, but this was not an end in itself, for the real object of the operation was to provoke the dispatch of a relief column which could be ambushed and destroyed at a site of their own choosing. In this way they could inflict serious losses on the government forces and, if the post fell into the bargain, so much the better. The technique was employed effectively against the French and, later, against the South Vietnamese Army (ARVN), with the result that the morale of the anti-Communist forces was steadily eroded.

Such a scheme was in the mind of Brigadier-General Chu Huy Man, commander of the North Vietnamese Army's (NVA) Western Highlands Field Front, in October 1965. Man could deploy three NVA regular regiments, the 32nd, 33rd and 66th, plus a number of local Viet Cong battalions, and his plan was to attack a small camp at Plei Mei and destroy the relief column sent to its aid as a preliminary to capturing the provincial capital of Pleiku. Much importance was attached to the operation as it was the first time that the NVA had mounted a divisional-sized operation in South Vietnam.

Plei Mei was a Civilian Irregular Defence Group (CIDG) base from which limited operations were carried out against the NVA's lines of communication. It was held by some 350 Montagnard tribesmen, organized in three companies, plus twelve Americans belonging to a Special Forces advisory team. The defences were in the shape of an equilateral triangle with a bunker at each corner and consisted of barbed wire entanglements, ditches and a minebelt; within, trenches connected the bunkers, command post, communications centre, ammunition dump, dressing-station and accommodation blocks; there was also a helicopter landing pad within the perimeter.

After dusk on 19 October one of the Montagnard companies left Plei Mei on a combat patrol and marched to a location some four miles to the north-west of the camp. Two outposts and five pickets were set outside the wire while the remainder of the garrison settled down for the night. At 2300 the camp came under heavy mortar and machine-gun fire which destroyed the communications centre, ammunition dump and dressing-station. As Man's 33rd Regiment closed in to attack, one outpost and two of the pickets were quickly overrun. At 0030 assault went in, gaps being blown in the wire with satchel-charges and Bangalore torpedoes. By 0100 recoilless rifle fire had reduced the north-western bunker to a mound of battered sandbags and the attackers gained the interior of the compound, despite the heavy casualties they had sustained. The garrison fought on, the barrels of their automatic weapons glowing red in the darkness.

The success of the assault placed the commander of the 33rd Regiment in something of a dilemma. The attack on the camp was supposed to provide the bait for the relief column, which was to be ambushed on its way from Pleiku by the 32nd Regiment. If the camp fell, there would be no need for a relief column, and the point of the operation would be lost. He therefore fed just sufficient troops into the battle for the defenders to believe that they were in serious danger of being overrun. Yet, notwithstanding this cynical abuse of their courage and the bodies of their comrades piled in and around the defences, the NVA soldiers persevered and by 0600 had eliminated the north-eastern bunker, confining the garrison to their one remaining strongpoint. By now, however, it was light enough for the US Air Force to intervene decisively, and throughout the day it punished the 33rd Regiment with bombs, napalm, rockets, cannon-fire and gunships. With the pressure reduced, it became possible to fly in medevac and supply helicopters, albeit at some risk. During the evening the third Montagnard company succeeded in working its way back into the camp and the situation was restored, although Plei Mei remained isolated and under fire.

Although the garrison of Plei Mei had been placed in a unique situation in that its continued resistance was important to both sides, its conduct had been heroic and was to produce remarkable dividends. The 32nd Regiment succeeded in ambushing the relief column, but the ARVN fought back and, with sustained air support and assistance from the US 1st Cavalry Division (Airmobile), inflicted serious loss on the attackers and broke through to the camp on 25 October. As the 33rd Regiment had also incurred heavy casualties and lost many of its heavy weapons because of continued American air attacks, Man had no alternative but to abandon the operation. He withdrew his battered division into the Ia Drang valley, near the frontier, concentrating it on and around the Chu Pong massif with a view to renewing the offensive the following month. The sheer numbers which he had employed against Plei Mei and the relief column, however, invited a major Allied response and before he could take the initiative again the 1st Cavalry Division began landing close to his concentration areas. The result was a fiercely contested battle in which the Communist regiments were torn apart by the weight of American firepower.

Following the departure of British troops from Aden in 1967, the former colony and its surrounding protectorates became known as the Marxist Republic of South Yemen. One of the objectives of the new government was to destabilize the neighbouring Sultanate of Muscat and Oman by means of a guerrilla campaign in the Dhofar mountains, lying in the remote south-western corner of the country. This began in 1970 and placed the United Kingdom in a difficult situation, for while it had treaty obligations with the Sultan, it was no longer politically acceptable for British troops to be deployed east of Suez. It was decided, therefore, in great secrecy, to commit part of the Special Air Service Regiment as advisers to the Sultan's ground forces, who were making little headway against the insurgents. The war reached its psychological turning-point on 18 July 1972 when the rebels mounted what was intended to be showpiece operation against the government post at Mirbat, a small coastal town amounting to little more than a village.

The defences of Mirbat consisted of a wire perimeter and two small mud-brick forts, the heaviest weapons available being an ancient 25-pounder emplaced near one of the forts, and a single mortar. The garrison consisted of a 10-strong SAS training team under the command of Captain Michael Kealy, 25 men of the Dhofar Gendarmerie, 30 former rebels who had changed sides, all armed with modern weapons, and 30 Omani Askaris with older bolt-action rifles.

Approximately 250 insurgents had been assembled for the operation, armed with AK-47 assault rifles, mortars, machine-guns and anti-tank missile-launchers which were effective against buildings and prepared positions. At about 0530 they dispersed an outlying picket and then launched an all-out attack on the perimeter, advancing in disciplined rushes while their mortars and machine-guns engaged the forts and the SAS quarters, which were clearly known to them. The garrison's response barely contained them at the perimeter, although the 25-pounder was firing at point-blank range, and anti-tank rounds began to knock the flimsy fortifications apart. At close quarters, the battle raged for three hours with the utmost ferocity. Kealy, however, had managed to radio for assistance and at 0900 a pair of Strikemasters of the Sultan's Air Force came in low, stafing and bombing. This took the steam out of the dissidents' attack. A second strike, delivered at 0915, coincided with the arrival of eighteen reinforcement SAS troopers, who were landed on the beach by helicopter. They immediately took the initiative and the enemy fled.

Ten wounded prisoners were taken and 30 bodies were left behind, although others were taken away. That, however, was not the end of the matter. Volatile by nature and strongly motivated by tribal feuds, the dissidents indulged in bitter recriminations which resulted in further fighting among themselves. When the dust settled less than half of the original force remained. Never again were the rebels able to mount a similar operation and, although they remained active until 1976, their support dwindled steadily in the aftermath of Mirbat. The garrison's casualties amounted to four killed, two of them SAS, and three wounded, including one SAS. Kealy was rewarded with the Distinguished Service Order.

In 1982 the token Royal Marine garrisons on the Falkland Islands and South Georgia received just sufficient warning of the Argentinian invasions to prepare their response. At Port Stanley the garrison moved out of its barracks at Moody Brook to take up positions around the town and harbour. The sheer size of the Argentinian invasion force, more than 800 men drawn from a special forces unit and a Naval Infantry battalion, supported by warships, aircraft, a squadron of LVPT-7 amtracs and heavy weapons, might be taken as a compliment, but it also meant that the fight could have only one ending. After attacking the empty barracks, the special forces unit concentrated on Government House, sending in a snatch squad to seize Governor Rex Hunt. Most were shot down in the grounds and three survivors tamely surrendered. The amtracs reached the shore safely but their column was halted by a picket which knocked out the leading vehicle with two anti-tank rounds before withdrawing. A landing craft was also seriously damaged by the same means. Gradually, however, weight of numbers pressed the Marines back on Government House, where Major Michael Norman, the detachment commander, proposed to the Governor that they should break out and continue to resist in the wild hinterland. The Governor did not regard this as a practical proposition and reluctantly ordered him to cease firing at 0925. Argentinian photographs showing the Marines' surrender did as much to arouse deep anger in the United Kingdom as the invasion itself and, from the victors' viewpoint, were counter-productive. There were no British casualties. The Argentinians said they had lost one man killed and two wounded, but according to one of Norman's men, 'there were blokes laid out all over the place'. A minimum estimate put the enemy's loss at five dead and seventeen wounded, discounting the occupants of the wrecked amtrac and landing craft; the probable total loss was in the region of 50 killed and wounded. 'Don't make yourselves too comfortable,' one Marine warned his captors as the detachment was driven to the airfield for repatriation, 'We'll be back!'

At the abandoned whaling station of Grytviken on South Georgia, Lieutenant Keith Mills and his 22 Marines had been ordered to offer a token resistance of 30 minutes and then surrender. Privately, Mills did not think much of the idea and commented forcibly that when the enemy arrived he was 'going to make their eyes water'. When the Argentinian corvette *Guerrico*, accompanied by the transport *Bahia Paraiso* with 500 Naval Infantry aboard, entered the bay at 1030 on 3 April, Mills rejected a surrender call and warned them that any attempt to land would be met with force.

The Argentinians began transferring troops to the shore, using three helicopters. The Marines shot down a Puma, from which no one emerged, disabled an Alouette, and pinned down the enemy infantry. Yet, impressive as was their performance thus far, they were merely getting into their stride. The captain of the *Guerrico* unwisely brought his vessel inshore to give support with his 40mm guns. The Marines waited until the corvette was in range, then opened up with everything they had. An 84mm anti-tank round skipped off the water to blast a hole through the ship's side and two 66mm anti-tank rounds struck near the 3.9-inch gun turret, jamming the weapon's elevation. A second 84mm round struck the Exocet missile-launchers but did not explode; had it done so, fire would have engulfed the ship and the probability is that the operation would have been cancelled. Simultaneously, more than 1,200 rounds of small-arms and automatic fire raked the superstructure. *Guerrico* sheared away for the open sea, whence she opened fire with her main armament; to the Marines' amusement, the rounds from the jammed gun sailed harmlessly over their heads.

Casualties had also been inflicted on the enemy infantry, but the Marines' ammunition supply was dwindling and their retreat was barred by cliffs. The 30-minute deadline had long passed and Mills, having satisfied himself that he had made sufficient eyes water, negotiated a surrender. Only one Marine had been wounded in the engagement. Mills received the Distinguished Service Cross and his stand further hardened British public opinion in support of the dispatch of the South Atlantic Task Force. The Argentinians were generous in their praise, but the ferocity of the defence had left them depressed about their future. When,

217

three weeks later, the leading elements of the Task Force arrived off South Georgia, their morale took a further knock when the submarine *Santa Fe* was crippled before their eyes and forced to beach herself. After an impressive display of precision naval gunfire, the 156-strong garrison meekly gave up without firing a shot.

In conclusion, therefore, it can be seen that it is clearly impossible to legislate for the sort of action described above, although had the Warsaw Pact attacked NATO, plans obviously existed for key points to be defended to the last with a view to inflicting maximum disruption on the enemy's plans. The last stand or epic fight against odds, call it what one will, remains a phenomenon. So much depends on the prevailing circumstances, on the quality of leadership, and perhaps above all on men's perception of themselves and their enemies, that detailed examination remains a largely academic exercise, albeit an important one that will repay the study of those concerned with morale and tradition. It is in the nature of history that the future will provide further examples of the phenomenon.

Bibliography

Anon. *The Royal Ulster Rifles in Korea.* William Mullan, Belfast, 1953

Carver, Michael. *El Alamein.* Batsford, 1962

Clammer, David. *The Zulu War.* David & Charles, 1973

Coleman, J. D. *Pleiku – The Dawn of Helicopter Warfare in Vietnam.* St Martin's Press, New York, 1988

Cooper, Bryan. *The Ironclads of Cambrai.* Souvenir Press, 1967

Downey, Fairfax. *Indian-Fighting Army.* Scribner's, New York, 1941

Dunstan, Simon. *Armour of the Korean War 1950–53.* Osprey, 1982

Foley, John. *The Boilerplate War.* Frederick Muller, 1963

Forbes, Archibald, et al. *Battles of the Nineteenth Century.* Cassell, 1896

Frost, Major-General John. *A Drop Too Many.* Cassell, 1980

Fuller, J. F. C. *The Decisive Battles of the Western World.* Eyre & Spottiswoode, 1954

Furneaux, Rupert. *The Zulu War – Isandhlwana and Rorke's Drift.* Weidenfeld & Nicolson, 1963

Geraghty, Tony. *Who Dares Wins – The Story of the SAS 1950–1980.* Arms & Armour Press, 1980

— *March or Die – France and the Foreign Legion.* Guild, 1986

Hammel, Eric, and Lane, John E. *76 Hours – The Invasion of Tarawa.* Pacific, California, 1985

Harding, Colonel E. D. *The Imjin Roll.* The Gloucestershire Regiment, 1981

Haythornthwaite, Philip. *The Alamo and the War of Texan Independence 1835–36.* Osprey, 1986

Howarth, David. *Waterloo – A Near Run Thing.* Collins, 1968

Hughes, Major-General B. P. *Honour Titles of the Royal Artillery.* Royal Artillery Institution

Lewis, Bruce. *Four Men Went to War.* Leo Cooper, 1987

Lloyd, Alan. *The Zulu War 1879.* Granada, 1973

Longstreet, Stephen. *War Cries on Horseback – The History of the Indian Wars.* W. H. Allen, 1970

Lucas Phillips, C. E. *Alamein.* William Heinemann, 1962

Macksey, Kenneth. *Crucible of Power – The Fight for Tunisia 1942–1943.* Hutchinson, 1969

McKee, Alexander. *The Race for the Rhine Bridges.* Souvenir Press, 1971

Marshall, S. L. A. *Crimsoned Prairie – The Indian Wars on the Great Plains.* Macdonald, 1972

Meyers, L. F. *History, Battles and Fall of the Alamo.* Published privately, San Antonio, 1896

Moore, William. *See How They Ran – The British Retreat of 1918.* Leo Cooper, 1970

Naylor, John. *Waterloo.* Batsford, 1960

O'Ballance, Edgar. *The Story of the French Foreign Legion.* Faber & Faber, 1961

O'Kane, Henry. *O'Kane's Korea.* Published privately, 1988

Pericoli, Ugo, *1815 – The Armies at Waterloo.* Seeley Service, 1973

Perrett, Bryan. *Tank Tracks to Rangoon.* Robert Hale, 1978

— *Weapons of the Falklands Conflict.* Blandford, 1982

Playfair, Major-General I.S.O. et al. *History of the Second World War: The*

Mediterranean and Middle East. vol IV, Her Majesty's Stationery Office, 1966

Rees, David, ed. *The Korean War-History and Tactics.* Orbis, 1984

Rogers, Colonel H. C. B. *Napoleon's Army.* Ian Allan, 1974

Ryan, Cornelius. *A Bridge Too Far.* Hamish Hamilton, 1974

Schultz, Duane. *Wake Island – The Heroic Gallant Fight.* St Martin's Press, New York, 1978

Scott Daniell, David. *Regimental History of the Royal Hampshire Regiment.* vol 3 1918–1954. Gale & Polden, 1955

Selby, John. *U.S. Cavalry.* Osprey, 1972

Seymour, William. *Yours to Reason Why – Decision in Battle.* St Martin's Press, New York, 1982

Shaw, Henry I. Jr. *Tarawa – A Legend is Born.* Macdonald, 1968

Sims, James. *Arnhem Spearhead.* Imperial War Museum, 1978

Terraine, John. *Mons.* Batsford, 1960

— *White Heat – The New Warfare 1914–18.* Sidgwick & Jackson, 1982

Tinkle, Lon. *The Alamo – 13 Days to Glory.* McGraw-Hill, New York, 1958

Utley, Robert M. *Bluecoats and Redskins – The United States Army and the Indian 1866–1891.* Cassell, 1975

Wilmot, Chester. *The Struggle for Europe.* Collins, 1952

Zaloga, Steven J. *Armour of the Pacific War.* Osprey, 1983

— *Amtracs: US Amphibious Assault Vehicles.* Osprey, 1987

REGIMENTAL AND OTHER JOURNALS CONSULTED

The Back Badge (1951–2), Journal of the Gloucestershire Regiment, gives some details of the 1st Battalion's epic stand on 'Gloster' Hill, and foreign press reaction.

The British Army Review. Issue No 57 of December 1977 – *The Action at Sidi Nsir* by Lieutenant-Commander G. S. Stavert, who was one of '155' Battery's officers during the battle. Issue No 85, April 1987 – *The Croix de Guerre Gunners – 5 Field Battery at Bois des Buttes, 27 May 1918,* by Captain G. Donaldson, Royal Artillery, provides an excellent summary of the background and course of the action.

Ca Ira (1948), the Journal of the West Yorkshire Regiment, contains a full account of the 2nd Battalion's exploits in the Admin Box, written by its commanding officer, Lieutenant-Colonel G. H. Cree.

The Gunner. Issues of April, June and July 1943 and February 1963 contain further details of '155' Battery's stand at Sidi Nsir.

The National Geographic Magazine, vol 170, No. 6, December 1986. Robert Paul Jordan's article *Ghosts on the Little Big Horn* describes the ballistic analysis carried out when the battlefield was stripped by a recent grass fire, the results enabling the course of Custer's last battle to be traced with greater certainty.

The Rifle Brigade Chronicle (1942) includes an account of the action at Outpost 'Snipe' as well as the personal narrative of Sergeant C. V. Calistan.

The Royal Artillery Journal vols LXXVIII No. 4 and LXXIX No. 1 describing, respectively, the parts played by 170 Independent Mortar Battery and 45 Field Regiment at the Imjin and elsewhere in Korea.

The Royal Hampshire Regiment Journal of August 1947 contains an account of the fighting at Sidi Nsir which supplements that in the regimental history.

St George's Gazette, the Journal of the Royal Northumberland Fusiliers, vol LXIX, No. 821, recounts the action of the Regiment's 1st Battalion during the Battle of the Imjin.

Index